For Mike —
Affectionately,
Dave

12.31.78

IMAGES FOR
SELF-RECOGNITION

IMAGES FOR SELF-RECOGNITION
The Christian as Player, Sufferer and Vandal

DAVID BAILY HARNED

A Crossroad Book : *The Seabury Press* : New York

1977 · *The Seabury Press · 815 Second Avenue · New York, N.Y. 10017*

Printed in the United States of America

Designed by Victoria Gomez

Library of Congress Cataloging in Publication Data

Harned, David Baily.
  Images for self recognition.

  "A crossroad book."
  Includes bibliographical references.
  1. Man (Theology) 2. Self. I. Title.
BT701.2.H28   233   76–30642
ISBN 0–8164–0334–1

The author is indebted to the editors of *The Virginia Quarterly Review* for permission to reprint, as a portion of Chapter 4, "The Deviant Self: Everyman as Vandal," from vol. 51, no. 3 (Summer 1975) of *The Virginia Quarterly Review*, pp. 329–46.

CONTENTS

PREFACE

I *mages for Self-Recognition* concludes a project that I began in India half a dozen years ago while serving as professor of Christianity at Punjabi University in Patiala. *Grace and Common Life,* which explored the relationship between faith in God and the primary instruments of socialization in the West, the family and playing with peers, was published at the end of my tenure there. A second essay, *Faith and Virtue,* was completed while I was visiting professor in the department of Christian dogmatics at the University of Edinburgh in 1972. It recorded some of the ways that the family could become a structure of destruction and it developed the meaning of playing fair. The final revision of this sequel has occupied me during another term as a visiting professor at the University of Edinburgh. It is a pleasure to record my indebtedness to this institution where I was once a student, and especially to Professor Thomas F. Torrance and Dean D. W. D. Shaw of the Faculty of Divinity. The writing of these books would have been far more difficult had it not been for the generosity of the National Endowment for the Humanities and the Center for

Advanced Study of the University of Virginia, and to them also I am very grateful.

Although my own understanding of the theological enterprise deters me from those frontal assaults of theologians upon one another that many of my colleagues relish, the paucity of my references to other theologians is certainly no fair measure of what I have learned from them. I also want to acknowledge my indebtedness to a number of good friends who read these pages in one form or another and from whose criticism and encouragement I have benefitted: James F. Childress of Georgetown University, Stanley Hauerwas of the University of Notre Dame, Dan O. Via, Jr. of the University of Virginia, Robin Gill and A.I.L. Heron of the University of Edinburgh, and particularly Rowan Greer of Yale University have offered valuable suggestions.

This essay is dedicated with love and respect
to the grandparents of our sons:
Mary Baily Harned
Estelle Molava Heydenreich
Robert A. G. Heydenreich
In memoriam
William Biechele Harned (1907–1956)

DAVID BAILY HARNED
Advent, 1976
Edinburgh

INTRODUCTION

This essay is a sequel to *Faith and Virtue* and its predecessor, *Grace and Common Life.* Like the others, it is intended to be part of a sketch of a new sort of natural theology. Because it is a single element in a larger design, there is reason to apologize to readers of the earlier works for the unavoidable repetition they will encounter here, as well as to new readers for occasional references to arguments contained in the other essays and not defended extensively again in these pages. *Faith and Virtue* argued that conduct is a function of the way persons see and that one important reason why persons act in different ways is that they do not see in the same fashion. Persons see the world differently because sight depends upon the condition of the imagination, and especially upon the various and often conflicting master images that persons have of themselves, for these are the sources of their perspective upon everything else. It is the representation of the self as a player that seems to be the most satisfactory instrument for the clarification of sight and the achievement of moral life—so *Faith and Virtue* contended—for this image can express the traditional consensus of the West concerning the cruciality of justice as fairness or fair play for the maintenance of life together. But the essay concluded with the promise of a sequel "intended to deal with the ear and with the significance of listening," for the nature of self-hood is inevitably distorted when attention is confined to the importance of a single sense. These chapters attempt to fulfill that promise as well as to move beyond it to explore the more explicitly theological issues involved in the attempt to adumbrate a Christian interpretation of the self.

As it is understood in these three essays, Christian theology has a single object, the self-disclosure of the triune God as it is confessed by faith and expressed in the stories and imagery of the Bible. The being of God has been revealed in and through the acts of God, and supremely in the incarnation. Theology emerges from a community that has been constituted by divine revelation and the faith that revelation has kindled, and theology is responsible to that community and exists for its nurture. It is, then, an historical affair, for the community encompasses many generations, and so it involves not only dialogue with the Bible but dialogue with the many centuries that have been in dialogue with the Bible. Some elements of this understanding of the theological enterprise need to be emphasized because, although they would certainly not find universal acceptance, they are important for the redefinition of natural theology that is proposed and pursued in these essays. First, theology is entirely a *confessional* affair, not an uncommitted investigation but a response to God's own initiative, and an expression of faith. The *prius* of knowledge of God is the acknowledgment that we stand in the presence of God; those who are touched by his hand must respond either in faith or in unbelief. Only if we begin with God shall we end with him: on this first principle all valid theological reflection is predicated.

Second, theology is also a *practical* endeavor. The one reality that is its object has disclosed himself in the course of revealing his will for the world that he has made and is bringing to fulfillment. This self-revelation has had as its purpose the judgment and renewal of human community, so that the community can become an instrument in the service of his sovereign will. Theology is concerned with what God has done and is doing and has promised to do, for only in these acts is his being disclosed. But in the accomplishment of this task theology becomes necessarily concerned with the renewal of selves and their societies. It is no more possible to divorce theology and ethics than it is to sever the acts of God from his being. Because it is confessional, theology can be nothing else than practical.

Third, theology is not a process of asking questions but of submitting to them; it is a *response* to an interrogation rather than an original inquiry. Its fundamental difference from all other intellectual disciplines is that persons are themselves called into question by their cognitive object instead of finding themselves free to ask of it whatever questions they devise. Because it is a confessional affair, theology does not ask when or where or whether God has revealed himself, but whether its own cognitive instruments are adequate to his self-disclosure, whether they are scientific in the sense that they are properly correlated with the distinctive nature of their object, whether they are faithful to the unique reality apart from whom they would have no reason to be. The revelation of God in Jesus Christ that continually calls into question every aspect of the life of the community certainly does not exempt theology itself from question. How could theology examine the fidelity of the witness of the community to the divine self-disclosure if it were not concerned first of all to submit its own perspectives and questions to question? The answers it finds are always reflections of the questions with which it begins, and so nothing is more important than critical scrutiny of the perspectives it employs, so that they do not interfere with the cognitive process. The aim of theological investigations, then, is finally to question human questions in the light of the questions that are addressed to the community by its own transcendent cognitive object.

Fourth, theology is concerned with the *nurture of persons* rather than with debate about issues, although the latter, of course, can never be separated entirely from the former. Its focus is upon the upbuilding of persons because the will of God is climactically disclosed through a single person, Jesus Christ, into whose likeness all other persons are intended to grow. Persons are fashioned into his image through hearing and responding by grace to the proclamation of the Gospel, and by sustenance within the community of faith through its Scriptures, prayers, liturgical life, and common social goals. So theology deals with the veracity and faithfulness of the proclamation of the Christian message: its responsibilities are oriented toward the preaching of the Gospel through word and sacrament. There is little reason, then, for theologians to engage in frontal assaults upon one another that are confined to academic precincts, and good reason to suspect that this involves a misdirection of the theological enterprise unless it occurs at the outset where methodological issues arise and where, at least from the perspective of this essay, it is necessary to insist upon the practical, confessional, communal nature of the discipline.

Finally, theology is an art as much as a science, for it deals with the life of the imagination. It is a science in the sense that it has its own particular object and must develop a method for the study of this object that is appropriate to its nature. The emphasis upon the practical and confessional character of theology must not be allowed to obscure the fact that it is bound by the canons of logic, although the logic can only be developed through dialogue with the subject of its inquiry and must not be imposed upon it from some external perspective. On the other hand, it is also busy with the life of the imagination, for our capacity to acknowledge and understand the majesty and mystery of God depends upon our command of a rich inheritance of images. No one has drawn attention more powerfully than Austin Farrer to the way the biblical witness to the revelation of God is expressed through a bewildering variety of images, some of which are particularly recurrent and seem to dominate the narrative. "Divine truth," Farrer writes, "is supranaturally communicated to man in an act of inspired thinking which falls into the shape of certain images."[1] These images and stories, which stubbornly resist translation into propositional form, are so much a part of the self-disclosure of God that we cannot retain the revelation without them. Every attempt to find functional equivalents for the preaching of the early Christian community must wrestle with the irreducibly imagistic character of the Bible and the unsubstitutable importance of some of its dominant imagery. Consequently, the only method for theological investigation that is genuinely scientific is one that recognizes the aesthetic component of a self-disclosure in which substance and form cannot be disjoined.

In the light of these comments on the theological enterprise, it seems questionable whether natural theology, at least as it has been traditionally conceived, can have any validity at all. *Faith and Virtue* expressed great skepticism of it as an independent discipline, partly because there are reasons to doubt that it has ever functioned significantly for many persons who were not already persuaded by faith, but primarily because its independence would violate the fundamental Protestant conviction of the priority of divine initiative in relation to human action. In my judgment, if natural theology is to be a valid and significant discipline, it must reflect the characteristics of the theological enterprise as a whole on which emphasis has already been placed. Consequently, in the introduction to the earlier essay I described natural theology as a discipline that accepts the truth of revelation in Jesus Christ and *then* examines the texture of our ordinary experience for its witness to the holy, without any pretense of immaculate neutrality.[2] Everything depends upon the *a priori* assumption of the givenness of the Gospel, and the exploration of experience does not have, in any traditional sense, an apologetic aim. Natural theology, as it is pursued in these pages, is a confessional affair, but it is a distinctive mode of reflection that deserves the label "natural" because its concern is not directly with the explication of God's self-disclosure but rather with the ordinary experience and self-understanding of people in the light of that revelation. It is important to stress the word "ordinary," for the focus is not upon putatively "religious" experience, a notoriously elusive if not illusory category. As *Grace and Common Life* insisted, it would be a mistake for this particular theological discipline to orient itself toward experiences that are less than fully and universally human. Then the stranger might well despair of understanding and the Christian of his own humanity.[3] The focus of natural theology, then, is not upon special experiences that involve only a privileged minority but upon experience that in one way or another is the lot of everyone—although the resources for its most discriminating and exhaustive interpretation seem, to the eyes of faith, to lie within the Christian tradition.

Natural theology is no less practical than it is confessional. *Faith and Virtue* enumerated a number of services that it can perform for Christian community and argued that the most important of these is the way that it can anchor confessional statements in the texture and density of our common life and provide some remedy for the gnosticism that perennially afflicts Christian thought, clarifying the significance of faith for the illumination of small joys and confusions and hardships, refusing to allow language about God to lose touch with the immediacies and ambiguities of our condition.[4] The task is as important as it is difficult, for otherwise the cost of discipleship is the loss of the sense of the presence of God in the places where we spend most of our time and passion and where the magnitude of our frailty and folly is most fully revealed. But if we are often incapable of seeing the hand of God where greater discernment would recognize it, not the least of our problems is our readiness to pretend to discover his presence in whatever serves our own self-interest and his absence from whatever does not. Natural theology can provide some significant resources for obedience to the biblical injunction: "And then if any man shall say to you, Lo, here is Christ; or, lo, he is there; believe him not: for false Christs and false prophets shall rise, and shall show signs and wonders, to seduce, if it were possible, even the elect. But take ye heed."[5] As each of these essays has contended, the self remains *homo religiosus* as much today as ever it has been, and its irrepressible appetite for objects of worship will find some form of expression. The substance of the Christian vision can illuminate, judge and partially exorcize the religious pretensions that inform contemporary culture and breed the small gods and daimons that haunt the human commonwealth no less now than they did two millennia ago. There is nothing from which we more urgently need to be saved than from all the varieties of our own immanent religiosity.

Natural theology, too, is not so much a questioning as it is a response to being questioned. Its primary function is not to pursue the question of the empirical verifiability of the Christian message, for then it would betray its own confessional nature and become an apologetic affair. Any serious venture in interpretation can find some small measure of legitimation in experience, while no religious scheme will ever find full and persuasive verification there. Instead, natural theology explores the adequacy of our utilization of the biblical imagery; the question of the usefulness of these images and stories has already been answered by faith, but it is always germane to ask how satisfactory is our actual usage of them. Certainly the discipline intends to show that experience is far more bewildering and mysterious than our conventional interpretations of it can admit, but it also aims at much more than this. When Christian confession finds moorings in the messiness and ambiguity of common life, the biblical imagery can disclose hitherto unperceived proportions and nuances of itself for our time, so that our patterns of interpretation gain a greater amplitude than conventional wisdom, and specifically conventional Christian wisdom, will allow. The images themselves are enriched by their renewed contact with experience, growing and expanding in relation to the imprevisible processes of life because, like persons themselves, images of the self and its world have their own potential for development and growth.

The question, then, concerns usage rather than usefulness, although the two are certainly not separable, and it can be answered satisfactorily only if we do not attempt to withhold the biblical imagery from the untidiness of daily life but insist upon examining its relevance there. The question, of course, also concerns whether we anchor it there properly or hold it in unrighteousness so that it furthers rather than unmasks our self-deceptions, caters to our self-absorption instead of judging it, and confirms habitual self-understandings instead of overturning them. To this aspect of the question there can never be a final answer, but at least we can struggle with some consistency to allow the biblical imagery to shine in new ways upon familiar experience so that we are constrained to question ourselves and our perspectives once again. Insofar as we are able and willing to allow ordinary experience to be clarified by the imagery of faith, the process can not only act reflexively upon the images themselves, illuminating unforeseen complexity and potentiality there, but it can also increase their power to resist domination by our selfishness and all our various strategies to hold them in unrighteousness.

Finally, the aim of natural theology is the upbuilding of persons, and all the more obviously because it deals with contemporary and quite ordinary human experience from the perspective of God's self-disclosure in Jesus Christ. It is primarily theological anthropology, and it becomes cosmological as well only to the extent that the self can scarcely be understood in isolation from its world. It is intended to contribute to the development of Christian character and discrimination. Indeed, as the concluding chapters argue, when natural theology is understood as a confessional and practical venture, the question of the empirical verifiability of the Christian story can finally be answered only in terms of its capacity to nurture Christian character, of which God alone is judge. Consequently, this interpretation of natural theology is radically different from definitions of it as a preface to Christian reflection rather than as an integral part of it; as cosmological exploration rather than an anthropological investigation; as allegedly uncommitted and neutral instead of a statement of faith; as metaphysical and speculative rather than practical and absorbed with the life of the imagination; and as an attempt to demonstrate the existence of God in-

stead of an admission of the circularity of all theological reflection and of the necessity to begin with faith in the reality
of God and with the givenness of the Gospel. This essay
addresses the fundamental requisite for the upbuilding of
persons, the question of images of the self. There is little
reason to hope for persons if they are unwilling or unable to
see themselves as they really are, for the self can defend itself
only from what it can see. So there is nowhere to begin the
upbuilding of persons except with a sustained attempt at self-
recognition. Sight is individualized by the particular symbolic
universe that every self devises for itself and especially by the
dominant images of the self that persons gain from their most
significant relationships. Because these master images furnish
the self with the perspectives from which it must judge and
seek to understand other selves and its world, nothing is more
important than that it should gain some perspective upon its
own perspectives. Otherwise, it will become simply a captive
of the relationships from which it has derived its images of
itself. But it is difficult to see well and there is much that we
would prefer not to see at all, including much that lies within
ourselves.

The purpose of this essay is to contribute to a Christian
perspective upon the perspectives that we derive from our
social worlds, by examining some master images of selfhood
that seem fundamentally important both in relation to the
Christian tradition and in the light of ordinary experience.
Because of its emphasis upon the cruciality of sight for the
achievement of moral life, the argument of *Faith and Virtue*
pointed beyond itself to another essay if it were to contribute
substantially to self-recognition, for persons experience
themselves as bodies whose commerce with reality is as much
oral-aural as it is visual, and the self changes its appearance
as it is interpreted from the perspectives of the different
senses. This sequel begins by exploring the oral-aural world
that the self also inhabits and drawing from it the representation of the person as sufferer as a complement to the figure
of the self as player. Because maturation is, in part, a movement away from dependence upon the senses that involve

proximity toward greater reliance upon those that do not, these two master images are sufficient to capture the primary organizations of the sensorium—in other words, the different ways that the senses of the adult can be weighted in relation to one another. But they are not sufficient to teach us as much as we need to know about the strange continent of the self, with all its peaks and valleys, inlets and bays, tangled places, quicksands, and shifting crevasses that seem too dangerous to explore. Another master image is necessary, one that can enable us to grasp whatever there is in the self that wars against every attempt at rational self-understanding, and this is the representation of the self as vandal.

These three, then, are proposed as fundamental resources if imagination is to be sufficiently provisioned, and provisioned in a Christian way, to recognize the dimensions of selfhood in our time. It would be rash to claim that we need no more than this for adequate self-recognition, for we could scarcely dispense with the welter of other imagery that is afforded by our social relationships. The argument is simply that these three master images are essential: we will never learn to see ourselves well if we are willing to settle for resources less rich and complex than all that the images of player, sufferer, and vandal contain.

It has long been a theological convention in certain quarters to contrast Hebrew and Greek ways of thinking in terms of a distinction between an oral-aural universe and a visual cosmos. One motive for this has been the ambition to vindicate the distinctiveness of the Hebrew-Christian tradition and to safeguard it from what could be construed as foreign intrusions. The convention has been a mistake, however, for neither is it entirely accurate nor, even if it were, would it be of fundamental importance for contemporary theological construction. Nevertheless, there is a certain truth in the contrast that is independent of its historical accuracy: persons do tend to imagine that their most profound commerce with reality has been either predominantly visual or primarily oral and aural. From the different ways in which the most memorable events in the history of an individual or society are imagined to have occurred, there arise different models of selfhood. The problem, of course, is to integrate the models with one another rather than simply to juxtapose them in some external fashion and to display their complementarity rather than merely their difference.

The first part of this work deals with the bodily life of the self, the contrast of Hebrew and Greek and what it discloses about the tendencies of the imagination quite apart from the historical validity of the distinction, and with the reasons why the representation of the self as sufferer is the most apposite image of the person that can be drawn from a universe that is experienced as primarily oral-aural rather than visual. The second part is concerned with the reality of evil in human affairs and especially with the need to develop an imagination for evil if we are to be able to defend ourselves not only against others but, first of all, against what we can do to ourselves. Self-recognition demands an image of the individual that can introduce us to the possibility of malevolence that has no motive whatsoever and malice that is expressed simply for the pleasure of the expression, as well as to powers in the unconscious that can interrupt and spoil the rational narrative of character despite everything that we intend. In the representation of the self as vandal, an image as familiar as the house next door or the school across the street and yet also freighted with mysterious and terrible implications when vandalism is explored more carefully than conventional wisdom will allow, there is an indispensable complement to the figures of the player and the sufferer.

The concluding chapters argue that self-understanding depends not only upon master images, however, but also upon stories with which the self learns to identify and within which the images themselves gain a specificity and concreteness that they can never achieve in isolation. Apart from stories, these images grow ambiguous and opaque. To phrase the matter differently, images can be named in a variety of ways, but until they are named in one fashion or another they will not divulge their precise significance; the function of a story, then, is to enable us to name images in a way that is consonant with

Christian faith. A story moves from a beginning to an end and, insofar as the route between them upsets our assumptions and expectations, it can serve as a medium of new disclosure: in retrospect, the events of the middle do not have the same significance that we had imputed to them. The paradigm of a religious story, from this perspective, is one that provides an end that incorporates and lies beyond all imaginable beginnings and ends, and that can satisfy the irrepressible eschatological appetite of the self, affording it a sense of an ending that can illuminate its beginnings and invest with new and different significance the time between the times in which all of us must live. The conclusion of the argument is not so much an argument as it is an analysis of the presupposition that has informed the argument: that the most important story there is for self-recognition remains the biblical tale that is fashioned into its final form in the Letter to the Romans, the narrative of two Adams—a first and a last—in whom all persons are incorporated. The claim that God's son became Adam is integral to the New Testament story of the Redeemer, and the portrayal of Jesus as the New Adam is one of its central themes. Indeed, many of the Fathers of the Church saw it as the dominant motif there and it was profoundly important for the development of the ancient Eastern liturgies.[6] As the Fathers understood the Adamic typology, there was a sense in which it included everyone, even though many were destined never to realize their inclusion. It is an instance of the circularity of theological investigations that the Adamic narrative has been presupposed in this quest for images of the self; they have not been found independently but have been chosen in response to it. On the other hand, because every story can be read in idiosyncratic and partial ways, the images are represented as instruments for its proper interpretation.

There are several emphases in this book that have been equally evident in its predecessors. One is the claim that the self remains *homo religiosus* as much today as ever, although this is scarcely reason for self-congratulation. The notion of the emergence of a secular society is one of the most dangerous of our illusions concerning ourselves, for we need to be redeemed not from our lack of religion but from our endless varieties of immanent religiosity and the daimons they create. The player, the sufferer, and the vandal are all images that disclose religious dimensions in themselves and in the persons whom they represent. A second emphasis concerns the dialectic of liberty and limitation: liberty is meaningless without the limits that render it concrete; limits themselves have a creative role to play in the actualization of our freedom. The way down is the way up: through the density and detail of the finite we come to the infinite; through limitation we learn to engage our freedom; through submission we find the resources to achieve independence. No lesson is clearer in the story of the incarnation, cross, and resurrection of Jesus Christ. This sort of *coincidentia oppositorum,* this dialectical relation of liberty and limitation, is the basis of the complementarity of the player and the sufferer and it provides the fundamental standard for the appraisal of every image of the self. Third, in both style and substance this essay is a dialectical affair, insisting that it is better to affirm "both-and" than "either-or," especially when we must deal with the profound dissimilarities between and yet the complementarity of both hearing and seeing, suffering and playing, constraint and freedom, obligation and self-expression, imagery and narrative, and beginnings and ends, as well as with the reality of both the conscious and the unconscious, self-possession and compulsion, fair play and foul. Each derives much of its significance from its relationship to the other, so that both are jeopardized whenever attention to one is allowed to obscure the importance of its companion.

Finally, despite the stress laid upon the confessional and communal nature of the theological endeavor and its concern for the upbuilding of persons, natural theology certainly does possess a negative and critical aspect. Precisely in elaborating the religious nature of the self we establish a perspective for the criticism of the immanent religiosity that continues to afflict contemporary culture; in stressing the cruciality of particular master images of the person, we are involved in the criticism of others; in rehearsing the matter of the Adamic narrative, we develop criteria for judging both the form and substance of other stories, some of which may be more familiar to our contemporaries than is the biblical tale, but all of which seem, at least to the eyes of faith, less capacious and rich; in utilizing these particular patterns for the interpretation of experience, we seek to demonstrate that it is more mysterious and complex than other schema of interpretation will admit; and in allowing the biblical imagery to shine on ordinary experience in this fashion, we hope to expose at least some of the endless ways it can be held in unrighteousness by those who are Christians as easily as by those who are not

This is an important task and someone must do it, but no one will do it well who does not recognize that it is far less than the proclamation of the Gospel, in the service of which every form of theology finds not only its final but its only reason to exist. How well the images of the player and sufferer and vandal serve to condense and crystallize the meaning of the story of Adam for self-understanding is a question that others must decide. Certainly the images are no substitute for the richness of the narrative of the triumph of grace. But they will have served significantly, indeed, to whatever extent they redirect our attention to the old story that never grows old, because through it is disclosed the power of him who is the beginning and the end and who promises to make all things new.

IMAGES FOR
SELF-RECOGNITION

Chapter One

VISUAL
AND AURAL WORLDS

W. B. Yeats once remarked that poetic failures occur when the will, impatient with the imaginative process of discovery that is the prelude to creation, attempts to do the work of the imagination. The comment pertains to many human failures and not only to those that can be charged against poets, and perhaps it brings us as close as brief diagnosis can to the abiding malady of our time: an atrophy of imagination, compounded by a disorderly will that knows no reason to acquaint itself with the contours of actuality. We seek to manipulate a world that we have not troubled to know; we grow anxious at our failure to find gratifications that careful scrutiny would show could not be found; we struggle to persuade ourselves that will is solitary and sovereign in a world malleable to all its demands—if only we will try harder —and forgiving of all its excesses. We forget how urgently the will is in need of domestication by imagination, for we have grown uncertain of the meaning of imagination and, therefore, we have exaggerated the measure of our strength and our liberty.[1]

In these pages, imagination is not understood to be a single power or faculty of the self, still less merely the source of its dreams and fantasies, but the sum of all the resources within us that we employ to form accurate images of the self and its world.[2] The imagination is concerned with the discovery of potentiality and new possibilities, with what is not yet, but only because it is oriented first of all toward actuality. Where else, indeed, could genuine possibilities be found? The images that the imagination produces are not intended to disguise or embellish reality; an image is simply a representation of the self or part of its world, either actual or possible, that has an immediacy and concreteness which conceptualizations lack. Because of their concreteness, images are more important for the exercise of human agency than are conceptual prescriptions. This essay explores several images of the self and contends that these are indispensable if will is to be tamed by imagination rather than fed upon illusions of its own devising. What it is profitable to will depends upon the identity of the self that wills. A sense of identity is the result of a process of imagining; it is simply a cluster of images that inform the consciousness of the self, bringing specificity to its volition and liberty, and counseling it to pursue something rather than everything. On the works of the imagination everything else depends, and among its works the most important are the images of the self that it offers us for interpreting our nature and possibilities and perils.

Images for Self-Recognition is the last of three works on a common theme. *Faith and Virtue,* to which these pages form a sequel, proposed some first steps toward self-recognition in the context of the claim that moral life depends upon the condition of our sight: we are free to choose and pursue some course of action only within the world that we can see. But seeing is not a simple affair: it is difficult to see in the dark or to see objects that move very rapidly, and it is even more difficult to see that someone else is real, quite independent of oneself and endowed with hopes and passions no less imperious than one's own. Among the reasons why different people act differently, then, perhaps the most fundamental is scarcely esoteric: they see differently, and in this there is no cause for surprise because it is not easy to see very well at all. *Faith and Virtue* then addressed the question of why it is that different people see as they do. Sight is individualized, shaped for better and for worse, by a whole household of images that find their residence within the self long before the eye scrutinizes a particular face or examines some new situation. The eye disengages images from the objects that it discerns, and these gain a new life, quite independent of their origin, within the consciousness of the individual.

This imagery, the harvest of our yesterdays, determines in large measure not only how but also what we shall be able to see today, for it constitutes a residue through which everything else whatsoever is filtered. It is properly called a symbolic universe, for it is not merely neutral and pictorial; ingredient in it are valuational schemes, some shards and fragments of which are more congruent with one another while others are less, and these render it an instrument for the interpretation of reality. There is no access to consciousness that can circumvent these valuational constructs: ". . . we are increasingly discovering that the message which comes through the senses is itself mediated through a value system. We do not perceive our sense data raw; they are mediated through a highly learned process of interpretation and acceptance."[3] Not only in our most elaborate attempts to unravel the complex patterns of human relationships but even in the most rudimentary appropriation of sense data, everything is mediated through a symbolic universe where "the" world is indelibly marked as "mine." Therefore, sight does not offer to everyone the same neutral realm bereft of value and untouched by the presence of the self, where row upon row of entities stand marshalled like toy soldiers awaiting our inspection. Seeing has to do not only with what passes before the eye but also with the ways that the eye has been provisioned for its interpretations of the world. Consequently, it is a mistake to operate with an inflexible distinction between "literal" and "metaphorical" usages of sight. Seeing is a distinctively human affair, and literal and metaphorical uses of the word belong to a continuum.

Faith and Virtue stressed the formative role of self-images in the development of the ways that we see. A symbolic universe includes many images of the self and many images of the world, constantly reinforcing or conflicting with one another, but sight depends primarily upon the former because they afford the self the various points of vantage from which it interprets whatever it sees—and from which, of course, there is always much that it cannot see. Everything else depends upon perspective, and perspectives are established in and through the images that the self possesses of itself, its functions, and its roles. The world is seen in relation to the unity and variety of the projects that express and confirm the ways that we imagine ourselves. A sense of identity emerges from imagination's portrayal of the self's solidarity with and distinction from what lies beyond the self: we begin to see ourselves in relation to parents, then to peers and teachers, and finally to a variety of institutions and interests and values and still other figures of authority, some of whom are represented in the internal dialogues of the self with itself even though they are now dead or have never been encountered at all except at second hand. These alliances, no matter how soiled by betrayals and the disappointment of expectations, still involve a measure of trust and loyalty, confidence in the trustworthiness of the other and the commitment to be trustworthy toward the other. These are the twin ingredients of *fiducia* which, along with *assensus,* constitutes what the Christian tradition has described as *fides* or faith. So the images that provide our sense of selfhood and shape our sight are developed from relationships that involve a tangled skein of faiths, some of which are very modest or occasional or even unrecognized. Often they conflict with one another, so that we are many selves instead of one or else a succession of quite different persons, our lives bereft of much coherence or narrative quality. Nevertheless, faith is inescapable if we would ever be persons possessed of sufficient clarity of sight to discern a realm within which it will be possible to choose and to act upon our choice.

No matter how minimal or unrecognized are our faiths, however, they contain at least an implicit religious dimension, not because we necessarily regard as "ultimate" the powers in which we trust but for the reason that the perspectives from which we view the world are enshrined in the self-images that have been gained from our relationships. These socially derived images determine where we will stand in order to evaluate the world, which interests will exclude others in our appraisals of things, and how much there is that we shall never be able to see. The problem is that the sources of our imagery tend to exempt themselves from our scrutiny; the perspectives that they afford involve no perspectives upon themselves and, still worse, no opportunity to understand ourselves except as functions of these relationships. The answers that we find depend upon the questions that we ask, of course, and our socially derived perspectives determine what questions can be asked and how many others will seem illegitimate or will remain forever beyond our comprehension. The hegemony of one perspective can be overthrown in a moment by another, but temporarily this one is not qualified or relativized but reigns exclusive and supreme. Consequently, if we are unable or unwilling constantly to question our questions, we have tacitly accepted as absolutes the other selves and communities and institutions to which we are related. Nothing is more important, but our allegiances always render the validity of the questions difficult to question. So sight leads us toward the sort of alienation in which we become nothing but members of the communities to which we belong—and it is precisely in this "nothing but" that we find our greatest solace and security. This is our misfortune: on the one hand, we are free to choose and act purposefully only within the world that we can see; on the other, the world shapes our way of seeing until we are no longer free for it except on the terms that the world itself has set.

A sense of identity is always reason for gratitude, for it is a store of imagery that a self can possess only because of what the self has received from others: values with which to identify, institutions to which to swear loyalty, a taste for the self that is derived from and sustained by the ways that it is valued by other persons. Because of the indebtedness that it involves and the difficulty of its achievement,we are often reluctant to confront the ambiguity of the results: a sense of identity is at once a victory and a defeat, not only the fulfillment but also the expropriation of the self, for it is the destiny of the self to become more fully personal only by way of yielding some of its individuality to its communities. Identity is always purchased at the cost of a measure of alienation, in the sense that our perspectives upon self and world are derived from rather than directed toward the realities with which we identify. If the self is to retrieve itself from its alienation, discovering some perspective upon its perspectives so that it can envision itself as more than a constellation of functions and roles and extensions of communities and institutions greater than itself, the remedy will be found in "master images" of selfhood that will liberate it from captivity to partial or parochial interests that eventually seem as though they were unqualified and unqualifiable. A "master image" is not one that supplants others or does such violence to them that their significance is truncated; on the contrary, its function is to reconcile lesser images with one another, to unify them, to qualify and relativize them so that the demands they levy upon the self are consonant with the meaning they provide and their contributions to identity. Its service is to render identity a less protean affair and more than a euphemism for social captivity, by liberating the individual from the grip of scattered absolutes.

In *Faith and Virtue,* the representation of the self as player was proposed as the most appropriate master image of the self in a world in which the most important prerequisite for moral life is rectitude of sight. The image counsels empathetic regard, for all persons are at least potentially players in the same game, while it also precludes every absolute and unqualified claim, for nothing in human affairs is more than a form of play. These are the most important lessons that sight must learn: empathy and the relativity of every perspective, especially one's own. Play, together with the household or family, is one of the two primary instruments of socialization in the West, tutoring persons in the meaning of justice as fairness and in its cruciality for the maintenance of commu-

nity. There are, then, more than sufficient grounds in experience for treating the figure of the player as a master image.
On the other hand, play involves an assumption of basic trust
that is scarcely justifiable in a world apparently characterized
by randomness and accidents; so *Faith and Virtue* contended
that the image is finally legitimated only by the disclosure of
God, the one reality who requires absolute seriousness but
whose revelation also means that all else is unserious by comparison.

The disclosure of the holy endows existence with a strange
mixture of seriousness and unseriousness that it did not hitherto possess, first of all because self and society are now
displaced from the center of things and the comedy of their
pretensions is exposed. Persons are liberated from the fearful
burden of belief that they alone are responsible for the
world's destiny or that there is no court of appeal beyond the
contemporary social order. Now they are free to close their
eyes for a moment, for as guests in the world they can afford
to ignore some of the cares once enforced upon them by the
illusion that they were its proprietors. By means of the image
of the player, persons can best acknowledge the disparity
between their apparent situation in the world and the subversion of all worldly claims, customs, and authorities by the
address of a power that transcends the world and calls persons to its service, thereby qualifying every finite relationship
including the relation of the self to itself. There is no more
room for the sort of deadly seriousness about the self and its
projects that conflicts irremediably with faith in God and that
populates the world with hosts of small gods and daimons.

But the image not only relativizes every function, role, and
perspective that the world affords; it also counsels the self to
act in such fashion that nothing less is granted than what
justice requires. There is no justification for the failure to play
fair. So it provides the best way for the self to grasp the
dialectic of its freedom from a world that is less than God, and
its obligation to abide always by rules of fairness, because it
too is less than God and is no more than one among many
different creatures who are all involved in the same game. The

self is neither less nor more than a player: this dialectic of liberty and responsibility means that it must step back and question its questions and perspectives so that its particular loyalties and projects do not render it blind to what fairness dictates toward all that is. No image could more strongly emphasize the importance of rules and norms if the self is to express its own potential and vitality. The player is the autonomous self, living within a world of coherent *nomoi* to which he freely obligates himself for the sake of the fulfillment of his own possibilities. The choice belongs to the player himself, but the *nomoi* are indispensable for his own self-expression and self-fulfillment, and are obligatory if he is not to be victimized by the pretensions of relative entities to have absolute authority. Autonomy means more than the capacity for self-determination and freedom from alien domination or arbitrary constraints. It designates the power of the self to bind itself to an order, to norms such as fairness, to laws that the self promulgates but that can also be construed as universally valid. This binding of the self by itself is inseparable from its fulfillment.

These explorations into the relationship between seeing and moral life, therefore, inevitably lead to the question of images for self-recognition, to the sense of identity of the self that sees, for these images structure sight and determine how expansive and discriminating it will be. Because its socially derived perspectives inhibit critical examination of the relationships that are most consequential for its sense of identity, however, the self slides toward alienation into society until it is "nothing but" its functions and rules, unless it can gain some perspective upon its perspectives and develop master images of itself that can relativize and domesticate the images provided by its relationships. The representation of the self as player, partly justified by ordinary experience and more completely vindicated by the self-disclosure of God, counseling fairness or justice not only toward others but also toward oneself, furnishes at least some of the resources that sight requires and offers a perspective upon the perspectives that the world affords, qualifying and relativizing worldly claims so that autonomy remains a real possibility for the individual Nevertheless, the image is a portrayal of ideality rather than reality, especially in the sense that the assumption of basic trust upon which playing depends means living against the appearances of a contingent world in which much is random and coarse. If we are, indeed, free to choose and deliberately pursue some course of action only within the world that we can see, then do we not need to see more of our own condition than a single master image can provide? If even the atom demands both wave and particle theories for its interpretation, there seems small chance that one image could prove satisfactory for the comprehension of a creature as elusive and elaborate as the self. One purpose of these chapters is to explore the incompleteness of the representation of the self as player as fully as earlier works surveyed its diverse and numerous strengths.

The problem of the self's alienation from itself into society is actually less intractable than it was portrayed to be in *Faith and Virtue,* for selves belong to nature as well as to the histories of their communities: we experience ourselves as bodies and are constantly involved in bodily commerce with our environment. This is, of course, the indispensable condition of all our social relatedness. From this source, too, we gain images of ourselves that are fundamental ingredients of our sense of identity. There is no real danger that the self can lose itself entirely in society, at least not without a massive effort at self-deception, because bodily experience is constantly dealienating—testifying that there are ineradicable appetites that social loyalties can never satisfy, reminding us in a thousand ways of our frailty and contingency, surprising us with unbaptized expressions of exuberance and vitality. So bodily experience itself counsels employment of the figure of the player or of some equivalent image in order to express what the body "knows"—that the self can never be identified wholly with its social functions and roles.

In Arthur Koestler's novel of the Moscow purge trials, *Darkness at Noon,* it is a toothache that enforces upon Rubashov the awareness that selves are more than functions of their communities. Formerly a high official of the Party, he is now consigned to a prison cell, and there in his ceaseless dialogues with himself as he awaits execution he christens the silent partner in his discourse "the 'grammatical fiction' with that shamefacedness about the first person singular which the Party had inculcated in its disciples."[4] He tries to understand the difference between "suffering which made sense and senseless suffering," and he reflects that:

> The sole object of revolution was the abolition of sense-less suffering. But it had turned out that the removal of this second kind of suffering was only possible at the price of a temporary enormous increase in the sum total of the first. So the question now ran: Was such an opera-tion justified? Obviously it was, if one spoke in the ab-stract of "mankind"; but, applied to "man" in the singular . . . the real human being of bone and flesh and blood and skin, the principle led to absurdity.[5]

Rubashov is besieged by images of three persons for whose deaths he was directly responsible—Richard, Little Loewy, and Arlova, who had been his mistress—and the pain of his tooth intensifies whenever he calls to mind their faces or hears their names mentioned by his interrogators. In its own way, the pain is proof "that the tenet is wrong which says that a man is the quotient of one million divided by one million"[6] and that something was amiss with the logic that regarded Richard, Little Loewy, and Arlova as replaceable units and dictated their deaths. Yet when Rubashov himself taps the prison code for the first person singular, 2–4, on the stone wall of his cell, "the wall remained mute. . . . He listened. The knocking died without resonance."[7] His experience of bodily pain brings him a measure of dealienation and it is consis-tently correlated with his uneasy remembrances of those whom he had treated as though they were no more than their functions and roles. But this is not sufficient, for Rubashov still suffers an atrophy of imagination. He can find no image that will express the aspects of selfhood which the logic of the Party ignores, that will confer shape and substance upon "the

grammatical fiction" who is his silent partner, and that can
bring resonance to his tapping the cipher for the "I" against
the confining stone.

Just as different persons see differently because of their
commitments to different self-images, so do they experience
themselves as bodies at different times in different ways, and
this additional diversity of experience can scarcely fail to find
expression in a diversity of self-images.[8] Among the possible
reasons for this, two are of particular importance: the maturation of the self and the problem of cultural differentiation.
Freudians have long understood the process of maturation, in
part, as a movement away from the senses that depend upon
proximity—touch, taste and smell—toward greater reliance
upon the "abstract" senses of sight and hearing that more
directly contribute to the cognitive enterprise. A marvelous
illustration of this, as well as of the perils it involves, is recorded in *A Portrait of the Artist as a Young Man*, as Stephen
Dedalus distances himself more and more from the rude disarray of the streets of Dublin in emulation of the winged
artificer whose name he bears. The bodily experiences of
child and adult, then, tend to differ significantly from one
another and, consequently, to support divergent self-images.
The problem of cultural differentiation is addressed by Walter Ong in *The Presence of the Word*, where he attempts to
demonstrate that there was a basis in the life of the senses for
many of the dissimilarities that existed between the Hebraic
and the classical Greek worlds of thought. Ong argues that:

> it is useful to think of cultures in terms of the organiza-
> tion of the sensorium. By the sensorium we mean here
> the entire sensory apparatus as an operational complex.
> The differences in cultures can be thought of as differ-
> ences in the sensorium, the organization of which is in
> part determined by culture while at the same time it
> makes culture. . . . Growing up, assimilating the wisdom
> of the past, is in great part learning how to organize the
> sensorium productively for intellectual purposes. Man's
> sensory perceptions are abundant and overwhelming.
> He cannot attend to them all at once. In great part a

given culture teaches him one or another way of productive specialization. It brings him to organize his sensorium by attending to some types of perception more than others, by making an issue of certain ones while relatively neglecting other ones.[9]

Ong contends that there has been some sort of correlation between the Judeo-Christian tradition and a particular organization of the sensorium, for faith has to do with things unseen. It flourishes in an oral-aural universe but is thrust into jeopardy when a culture gains a more visual orientation. It is sound rather than sight that affords access to interiority, to personal presence; thus hearing is of particular importance for a culture that believes itself to stand in the presence of transcendent personal powers. Sight, at least as Ong understands it, is inherently depersonalizing: for instance, staring at someone else reduces the other to a mere surface, a thing. If Ong were entirely correct in his observations about sight, the contention that moral life depends upon how well we are able to see would have little apparent merit, and from a Christian perspective it would seem even less persuasive if Ong were also correct in arguing that faith is at home only within an oral-aural world. Before pursuing these questions, however, and exploring further the contrast that he establishes between predominantly visual and primarily aural organizations of the sensorium and the consequences that it might have for the emergence of a sense of identity, there are reasons to suggest one semantic change in the argument that began in *Faith and Virtue:* the substitution of "vision" for "sight." One of the strengths of *The Presence of the Word* is that Ong is sensitive to the actual interdependence of the senses; the way in which he writes of divergent modes of organization of the sensorium reflects this recognition of their unity. The substitution of vision for sight renders it far easier to acknowledge this interdependence and subordinates the contrast of visual and aural to the quest for self-images, instead of either resolving its meaning too quickly or else dismissing its possible significance.

While the relationships among the various senses lie beyond the scope of this essay, no examination of their differences can afford to forget their actual interdependence. For
example, it is only as we learn to correlate the data afforded
by sight and touch that the world discloses to us its dimension
of depth. Acquaintance with depth is bound up with experiences of intentional commerce with our environment, in the
course of which we encounter resistance and learn to exercise
force. The retention of these experiences of motion and intentional effort is implicit in our present perception of depth,
even though we may be unconscious of remembering and
now entirely inactive. So Hans Jonas can write that "the possession of a body in space, itself part of the space to be
apprehended, and that body capable of self-motion in coun-
terplay with other bodies, is the precondition for a vision of
the world."[10] The excellence of sight, therefore, has nothing
to do with its independence; on the contrary, seeing is an
activity of the whole self operating in accordance with some
of its most distinctive powers—intentionality and motility and
initiative. The obverse of this is that we see with several
senses, not with the eye alone. We derive pictures from the
sounds that strike the ear. Hands can see and speak, even if
their possessors are blind or dumb, discovering the shapes of
different things, communicating to others the urgency of our
concern. The eye can speak no less well than the hand, con-
veying more in a glance than a dozen words could do. Because
there is a sense in which the ear can see or the hand can speak,
the way that Jonas distinguishes between sight and vision is
persuasive. Sight is a primary constituent of vision but less
than the whole, while vision is much more than the sum of its
physiological parts: it designates the developed capacity of
the self to deal with all the various sense data that are filtered
through its own particular symbolic universe. Jonas comments:

> There is a mental side to the highest performance of the
> tactile sense, or rather to the use which is made of its
> information, that transcends all mere sentience, and

> . . . it is the image-faculty, in classical terms: *imaginatio,*
> *phantasia,* which makes that use of the data of touch.
> . . . Blind men can "see" by means of their hands, not
> because they are devoid of eyes but because they are
> beings endowed with the general faculty of "vision" and
> only happen to be deprived of the primary organ of
> sight.[11]

Imaginatio denotes all that the self exercises in order to form
proper images of its own nature and context. Because the self
is a creature that imagines, and that imagines best when it
relies upon the full range of its resources, all its senses become, in greater or lesser measure, contributors to vision.
Because each sense has its own distinctive mode of operation
and offers its own singular impressions of things, it illuminates a different aspect of the situation of the self within the
world. So there is much we must learn to envision that is not
filtered through the eye. Imagination is the bond of the
senses, integrating the impressions they afford within a symbolic universe that humanizes and individualizes our commerce with others and with ourselves because of the
particular images of the self that award it a distinctive character.

The distinction between vision and sight, then, enables us
to acknowledge more satisfactorily the interdependence of
the senses, and it also subordinates the contrast between visual and aural so that the latter does not appear as a problem
that must be resolved before any claims can be launched
concerning the excellence of vision. On the other hand, certainly as it is conventionally understood, vision still more or
less implies the priority of sight as a paradigm of human
responsiveness to the world and suggests that the person is
best imagined as one who sees. The representation of the self
as player, too, has been elaborated with reference to sight: it
expresses the possibilities and warns of the perils that seeing
entails; it portrays the possibility of autonomy that sight appears to afford. So we return to explore the contrast between
primarily visual and predominantly aural organizations of the
sensorium with a question of fundamental importance: If vi-

sion is ever to grasp the complexity and richness of selfhood, must it not be provided with a second master image that is primarily aural rather than visual? Must not the implicit emphasis upon sight that is involved even in speaking of vision be explicitly balanced by a new master image that represents the self as one who hears? In order to answer the question satisfactorily, it is necessary first of all to develop the contrast between visual and aural as sharply as possible. Second, it is no less important to examine the several reasons, including the interdependence of the senses, why the contrast must be qualified. Then, third, it is necessary to explore what the consequences of reliance upon the predominantly visual or aural might be for the self's understanding of itself. Finally, we must ask whether Ong is correct in suggesting that there are specifically Christian reasons to prefer one orientation rather than the other. Whether or not an additional image is necessary, of course, depends upon the significance of the contrast itself.

In the visually oriented culture of the West, it scarcely has seemed necessary to defend the preeminence of the eye among the different senses. Plato and Aristotle described the highest activities of the mind in metaphors drawn from sight. Although they declared its excellence more often than they explained it, the priority of the eye became the common assumption of the philosophers who succeeded them. Common speech has reflected and confirmed what philosophers have taught, or else wise men learned their teaching from common speech: we explain a problem in mathematics time and again to a little boy until suddenly he exclaims, "I see!" Art and literature were governed during most of their history by the same assumption, just as Christopher Isherwood writes in *Goodbye to Berlin:* "I am a camera with its shutter open, quite passive, recording, not thinking. Recording the man shaving at the window opposite and the woman in the kimono washing her hair."[12] In the mute universe of Newtonian science, observation was the paradigmatic human activity. In Christian theology, too, it was believed that the end of the self was to achieve the vision of God: the fulfillment of the relationship between the divine and the human was expressed in metaphors that dealt with the eye.

Perhaps the principal reason for this traditional emphasis concerns the importance of *distance.* The realm that sight encompasses is held at bay so that it can be brought into focus: space intervenes between the self and its object and the distance between them provides a sort of refuge. The world is sterilized and made less exigent, for it voices no claims to distract our attention. The objects that present themselves to our perception, extending indefinitely toward the horizon, are ranged in an order that leads away from the self rather than toward it: we are left outside the world that we have made and at least for the moment it is powerless to levy any claims upon us. Then the image afforded by the eye can be severed from its source in the environment, disengaged from our constant welter of sensations in order that rational worlds might be carved in memory and anticipation. The life of the imagination is liberated from the less tidy life on which it must feed and we are able, at leisure and in continued safety, to retain images after potentially destructive realities have passed away. Because the eye can winnow images from the world while it holds reality at a distance, because it presents whole galaxies of particulars simultaneously to the self while demanding no commitments except attention, sight is the sense that seems to confer freedom upon us, liberating us to choose this and not that, yet never enforcing upon us the need to choose anything at all. We seem, indeed, masters of all we survey: certainly there are threats as well as lures to be glimpsed against the horizon, and against some of them our strength might not prevail; but at least for the moment there is safety in the distance that sight preserves.

The ear is unlike the eye. The eye is able to focus only because of the distance that intervenes between itself and its object, but the ear must strain to catch a rapidly receding sound. Distance enables the eye to capture a number of objects simultaneously while the ear, more dependent upon proximity, experiences the world in a sequential way. The individual has opportunities to master a world that distance allows him to bring into focus, but he is vulnerable in a world where sounds constantly violate the perimeters of selfhood. Distance means liberation from the world; proximity tends to reduce the self to a patient, constantly liable to surprise. The self is bound to its environment by sounds that intrude upon a passive subject:

> He cannot let his ears wander, as his eyes do, over a field of possible percepts, already present as a material for his attention, and focus them on the object chosen, but he has simply to wait for a sound to strike them; he has no choice in the matter. In hearing, the percipient is at the mercy of environmental action. . . . With all the initiative left to the outer world, the contingency aspect of hearing is entirely one-sided.[13]

The eye introduces us to space and stasis and simultaneity while the ear acquaints us with time and movement and sequence. Despite the historicity of human life, space and distance are initially most important for the self. There can be no seeing at all unless distance permits focus, unless separation from the world affords us a place of our own where perspective is possible. The self cannot identify with its neighbors until it has learned to distinguish between them: unless we are aware of distance there can be nothing except mutual entanglement in which we no longer know what belongs to the other and what is ours; indeed, we no longer can find a self endowed with the capacity to know anything at all. Nothing is more important than the ability to step back, to move away so that we are not victimized by the immediacies of a situation from which we cannot differentiate ourselves.

Everything depends upon distance, on separation, on the maintenance of a space between. The eye requires it and finds it and then offers it to the whole self and all else is founded upon this primordial achievement. The territorial imperative that constrains us to find a place of our own is far more than a selfish violation of what is intended to be a shared world. The self is disoriented and lost when it cannot maintain the integrity and capaciousness of its psychic space, dwindling to a protean creature given its shape of the moment by whatever noise happens to fill its emptiness, and psychic space is intimately correlated with physical distance and a place of one's own. But our ears deliver us over to all sorts of random sounds that breach the fortifications intended to preserve our distance from others: now we are vulnerable to whatever noise impinges first or most loudly upon the territory of the person. The distant world that was ordered and enlightened by our perspective is suddenly shaken by the sound of thunder: a cacophonous noise or unwarranted word slashes into consciousness and we are diverted from our purposes or conscripted for purposes that are not properly our own. The contrast between the cosmos that the eye discerns and the chaos that confounds the ear must not be too sharply drawn. After all, the eye is prone to error and distraction, while the ear can sometimes recognize in a familiar sound a reassuring presence that quickly consolidates the whole universe, transforming an alien land into a comfortable habitation where there is nothing to fear. Nevertheless, when chaos waits to trap the self its means of entrance to the citadel of the mind is through the ear, and if there is a clean, well-lighted place in which the self can dwell, it is spied out by the eye. This is the first truth that must be recognized about the ear: the distance and space that the eye discovers are essential for human life and hearing is the way by which their integrity is jeopardized.

The contrast between visual and aural cannot be phrased only in these terms, however, for it also concerns our access to interiority. For the eye, the world presents only its surfaces; sight has no way to explore whatever lies beneath or behind the exterior of things. We can observe the gestures of the old man who lives next door, but we cannot see the intentionality that brings coherence to his movements, the hope that sparks them, the determination that sustains them, the end they attempt to achieve. The depth that the eye discerns is no more than the distance between entities ordered from the forecourt of vision toward the horizon; the depth within the entities themselves remains undisclosed. The eddies and currents within ourselves of which we never become the masters, the transcendence of others that is partly revealed and partly veiled by the phenomenon of speech, the small raptures afforded by a familiar noise that we have not heard for a long time or by a smell remembered from a vacation many years ago—none of these can the eye see. Sound is our special clue to the mysteries of interiority; the eye is impatient with mystery, which it equates with the sort of obscurity that can be banished by more careful observation or a bit more light. Walter Ong writes:

> We tap a wall to discover where it is hollow inside, or we ring a silver-colored coin to discover whether it is perhaps lead inside. To discover such things by sight, we should have to open what we examine, making the inside an outside, destroying its interiority as such. Sound reveals interiors because its nature is determined by interior relationships. The sound of a violin is determined by the interior structure of its strings, of its bridge, and of the wood in its soundboard, by the shape of the interior cavity in the body of the violin, and other interior conditions. Filled with concrete or water, the violin would sound different.[14]

When we listen to the world, it discloses rich and baffling dimensions hidden beneath the externals that the eye observes and we are confronted with the presence of transcendence and the transcendence of personal presence. It is supremely the interiority of persons, of course, to which sound provides access when it appears in the form of language. Not least of all, words enable us to grasp our own interiority, for they are the instruments by which we can organize the confusion of our experience and place it at the disposal of the intellect. Because it is the expression of interiority, because the interiorities that dominate our lives belong to selves, sound is inherently socializing. Because of the proximity of the world to the defenseless ear, however, hearing also opens us to all sorts of unwelcome intrusions and to a thousand distractions so that psychic space, as we have noticed, is cluttered with unwanted furnishings we would never have chosen for ourselves. We become patients victimized by the loudest or latest noise, falling from the cliffs where nothing seemed to obscure sight into an endless sea of sound. Because of the elusiveness and ambiguity of sounds that do not carry within themselves sufficient clues to their origin, sound often tells nothing for the moment except of our contingency and of the possible perils before us. So strange sounds are threatening not simply because they are strange but also because they remind us of what has become far too familiar, our precariousness and the suddenness with which all defenses can be breached, all plans denied and hopes overthrown. The ambiguities of sound are all the more richly complicated because we must struggle to hear not only what words denote but what is intended by their speaker, not only what is said but what is merely adumbrated because convention or shame has blunted the axe of language, plumbing beneath the recalcitrance and incompleteness of words that sometimes tell too much, or sometimes a story of which their author is unaware, or sometimes far less than either speaker or hearer wants or deserves.

In the everyday world, too, words are used deliberately to manipulate or deceive: we are worn into acquiescence by the insistence of a voice that will not keep silence, forced to accountability toward others on their own terms and in ways that preclude accountability toward and for ourselves. So the ear traps the self in a welter and jumble of competing and conflicting claims, voices begging, importuning, threatening, commanding, whining, pleading, never ceasing. Because the ear relates us most intimately to other selves, it presents the danger that we will be reduced to other selves, made simply vessels and vassals of the social gods that alienate individuals from themselves. The reason why these powers approach us best by way of the ear is that the particular language we hear is not a neutral medium but is rich with valuations, reflecting and enforcing a history of communal commitments to certain expectations and conventions and, indeed, to a whole way of life. (But it is also true, of course, that words have far greater authority when they are reinforced by personal presence than when they are merely seen in their cooled and reified and derivative form in a newspaper or book.)

On the other hand, in the discrepancies between what is expressed and what seems to be intended, between the flat and stale phrasing and the curious resonances and nuances that seem to cling to the voice that utters the phrases, between the self disclosed in its linguistic usage and the presence of the self that is veiled by the words, the ear gathers something of the secrecy and strangeness of those who speak. There are apertures through which we can glimpse something of the transcendence of personal realities, something of the mysterious quality of existence with which the eye never becomes acquainted. The most curious function of the ear, therefore, lies in its witness that the world given to us by the senses is not the whole world: in hearing the spoken word that humanizes our environment, we are constrained to acknowledge that there is more to this environment and to the self itself than the dimensions to which the various senses provide access.

The difference between seeing and hearing can be phrased in various ways. The contrasts between the near and the distant and between the surfaces of the world and its interiority are reflected in other distinctions as well, but at least these will serve to establish the difference. Whether or not it holds particular significance for the development of self-images and, if so, what its specific consequences for them might be, however, are questions best postponed until the contrasts have been qualified in several ways. It is necessary to state the qualifications, if only in order to show that despite their importance they do not invalidate the fundamental distinction. First, once again there is reason to stress the actual interdependence of the senses. The distinction between seeing and hearing is not intended to suggest their independence: near and distant are terms relative to one another; surfaces disclose clues to their interiors while interiority endows surfaces with their particular shapes. The abstraction is actually twofold: of seeing and hearing from their collegiality with one another and with the other senses, and of the self as organism from its own internal richness. We see colors, for example, simply because we are sensitive to color, while acts that we claim as our own involve intentionality and will. Maurice Merleau-Ponty describes the difference in this fashion:

> If I wanted to render precisely the perceptual experience, I ought to say that *one* perceives in me, and not that I perceive. . . . Sensation can be anonymous only because it is incomplete. The person who sees and the one who touches is not exactly myself, because the visible and the tangible worlds are not the world in its entirety. . . . I am not myself wholly in these operations, they remain marginal. They occur out in front of me, for the self which sees or the self which hears is in some way a specialized self, familiar with only one sector of being.[15]

The danger of the first abstraction is that it can reinforce our tendency to imagine the senses as "a collection of adjacent organs" instead of "a synergic system, all the functions of which are exercised and linked together in the general action of being in the world."[16] Nevertheless, if the senses did not all have their own distinctive modes of operation, they could scarcely complement and assist one another as they do: their synergy presupposes their differentiation. So the contrast of eye and ear remains valid, but only so long as the senses are seen not merely as adjacent organs but as ingredients in a "synergic system." This qualification is important, and to its consequences we shall have occasion to return. It is the second abstraction, however, that is more troublesome and that requires serious qualification of the contrast.

The contrast between the mastery of the world that sight seems to promise and the bondage to it that hearing involves must be qualified for several reasons, among which the most important is that it rests upon a deficient and truncated notion of selfhood. It is true that there is a physiological basis for arguing that sight offers a great measure of freedom to the self and that the initiative of the eye differs greatly from the passivity of the ear which, as Jonas states, "is at the mercy of environmental action."[17] As Merleau-Ponty remarks:

It is not the object which obtains movements of accomo-
dation and convergence from my eyes. It has been shown
that on the contrary I would never see anything clearly,
and there would be no object for me, if I did not use my
eyes in such a way as to make a view of a single object
possible. And it is not the mind which takes the place of
the body and anticipates what we are going to see. No;
it is my glances themselves—their synergy, their exploration, and their prospecting—which bring the imminent
object into focus.[18]

But the self is more than an organism; its ways of seeing,
as we have argued, are shaped by images of itself that are the
most important ingredients of its particular symbolic universe
through which all perceptions whatsoever are filtered. These
images are socially derived: the self is taught its ways of seeing, in the sense that it derives its perspectives from its most
important relationships. If the eye does not confer upon us so
much freedom from the world as it seems to promise, however, neither does the ear render us so much its captive—and,
once again, simply because sensory experience is experience
of the whole self and occurs in the context of memories and
anticipations. It is true that hearing is fate: the banging of a
door can irremediably divert our attention. But it is also true,
as Merleau-Ponty comments, that "all perception, all action
which presupposes it, and in short every human use of the
body is already *primordial expression.* "[19] We can choose to be
inattentive to a conversation across the room and, in our
attentiveness and inattention, we stamp the aural world, too,
as distinctively our own. Our concentration is an expression
of our own loyalties, projects, and sense of identity. If the
vulnerability of the ear leaves us at the mercy of the world,
learning to listen is a victory over it, for the latter requires
discrimination and patience and the exercise of will. The sequential interpretation that listening demands involves possibilities of error that are far less common in the instance of
sight. So the self must train itself to avoid misunderstandings
and learn to interpret words in relationship to a particular
context and in the context of particular relationships. Never-

theless, the fundamental contrast remains: visual initiative and aural responsiveness, the choice of focus or unwanted diversion and interruption. The reasons for qualifying the original contrast are important but they do not serve to invalidate it.

A third qualification is necessary because of still another abstraction: the aural realm has been discussed without reference to speaking. Yet hearing is important precisely because it enables us to learn to speak and, by our words, to organize the confusion of our sensory experience and place it at the disposal of the intellect so that we can exercise our freedom and intentionality. Is this not more than sufficient reason to minimize the contrast between the agency of the self that sees and the passivity of the self that hears? Language brings us to ourselves and brings us into the world so that we can express ourselves and communicate with others. It tailors the world to the proportions of the self and constitutes, "where incoherent sensations leave off, a universe to the measure of man. Each individual who comes into the world resumes for himself that labor of the human species, essential to it from its inception."[20] Language is never a neutral affair and this is disclosed in the creative power of speech; as Georges Gusdorf writes: "the word owes its efficacy to the fact that it is not an objective notation, but an index of value."[21] Because language always expresses valuation, speaking transforms the world into a project of our own, hews it into conformity with the creatures who have made it their home. But the claims levied upon us by the voices of others remind us that the world is also their project and suggest, indeed, that it is so much theirs that it is scarcely ours at all. The suspicion is well founded, in the sense that learning a language involves socialization into a particular scheme of standards and values. There is no way to appropriate it without submission to the expectations it is continually refashioned to express. So speaking leads to our externalization and surrender to conventionality until, once again, it seems as though we are nothing but other people. Gusdorf comments:

> Language inserts itself into the self-consciousness of each man as a screen that distorts him in his own eyes. The intimate being of man is in fact confused, indistinct, and multiple. Language intervenes as a power destined to expropriate us from ourselves in order to bring us into line with those around, in order to model us to the common measure of all. . . . To the degree that we are forced to resort to language we renounce our interior life because language imposes the discipline of exteriority. . . . All language has by constitution the quality of common denominator. To speak then is to alienate oneself in order to mingle with everyone else.[22]

This problem of mingling with everyone else is exacerbated because the creative possibilities for self-expression that language affords are limited by the exigencies of communicating with others. Communication entails using words in conventional ways, with all the imprecision or else the minimal content of their everyday signification. So the speech that enables us to master the world also delivers us into its hands: the problem is that a master can command his servant only in language that the servant understands. Speaking, therefore, is not only a creative act but also an expropriation of the self, condemning us to feel and value as others do, to share their prejudices and conventions, to succumb to the improbable anxieties and trivial expectations of the realm of the everyday. The voice raised in protest can express itself only through the instrumentality of what it is protesting against.

It is important to acknowledge the tension between these equally fundamental functions of language, the expressive and the communicative. Speaking involves a remarkable combination of the power to liberate the self and the capacity to alienate the self from itself, the power to grasp and disclose our interiority and the capacity to divorce us from the interiority that is our own. The creativeness of speech is evidence that emphasis upon the passivity of the ear through which we learn to speak can be exaggerated; it does not, however, justify questioning the fundamental contrast between the senses. On the one hand, the stress upon creativity itself needs to be balanced by attention to the communicative aspect of language, which involves a sort of passivity and, in greater or lesser measure, capitulation to the crowd. On the other, the fact that it is only by hearing that we learn to speak is not reason to qualify our insistence upon the passivity of aural life. Instead, it establishes a basic criterion for appraising an image of the self derived from the aural realm: the image must express the way in which certain sorts of passivity eventuate in opportunities and enrichments for the self that the self could never achieve independently or by its own initiative. The contrast between seeing and hearing, then, retains its validity. It involves at least three abstractions, however: of the different senses from their collegiality with one another, of the self as organism from the amplitude of its internal life, and of the aural from what is actually an oral-aural universe. The acknowledgment of these abstractions affords some reason to qualify the distinction, and yet the qualifications are themselves subject to qualification and furnish no grounds for abandoning the contrast itself. It is time, therefore, to return to the principal question: what are the consequences of the contrast and why is it significant for the development of images of the self?

The polarity with which we began, between the near and the distant, is the source of many other differences for self-understanding. Sight is concerned with the solidity of things and the ear with their motion, the one with being and the other with becoming, the first with form and order and the second with events that surprise and engulf us despite ourselves. The eye discerns a world that is moribund and mute; it communicates its life to us through the ear and suddenly we are plunged into a maelstrom of sound that teaches us the transience of everything, thereby robbing us of some illusions of security. All sound is evanescent, while the world of the eye is motionless and enduring. Sight enforces the illusion of immortality, for we seem to share the permanence of the objects before our eyes. These all march away from us toward the horizon, so that we are left outside the world, unclaimed, free, independent, and blameless. But sounds rush toward us and strike us from behind, suddenly, unexpectedly. In their imprevisibility and unpredictability and suddenness, sounds are also reminders of the self's contingency: in the evanescence of our words, in the abruptness with which sounds come to menace us, in the ephemerality of our hearing and heeding promises, in the fading of a voice on the telephone, in interruptions and misunderstandings and silence after laughter, in brusque dismissals, and in the goodbyes voiced by someone moving to another town—in all of these there are reminders that we must surely die. Sight has deceived us. We are mortal, too.

The self that sees and the self that hears, then, stand in different relationships to themselves as well as to their worlds. Not only do their worlds appear different, they perceive their own possibilities and nature in diverse ways. In one world, the self as agent shapes the environment in accordance with its own perspective. In the other, the self as patient is arrested by sounds each of which testifies that there are powers abroad other than and frequently greater than its own. When a model of the self begins with the experience of hearing, then life is *passio:* we eddy in the wakes of others, unable to shut our ears as we can shut our eyes, often unable to choose the focus of our attention because a louder or more peremptory voice can deafen us to others that we would much prefer to hear. In a visual world, the self seems to be endowed with free choice and its actions display its own initiative; in the other world, it is constrained to act in response to overtures that it did not initiate. In one realm, where there are only surfaces, more careful observation can correct error and banish every puzzle; in the other, where there are different dimensions and depths, endless nuances and diverse intonations, where sounds are not only media of disclosure but also tokens that something of the world remains forever undisclosed, there are mysteries that even the most careful listening will never dissipate.

When sight counsels that we are free of the world, then, sounds remind us that we are inextricably bound to it. What is seen leaves the self untouched unless it wills to respond, but what is heard draws the self within the circle of another's need or aggression: remoteness we can conserve in one world, while intimacy is enforced upon us in the other. In the first, the self experiences itself as solitary subject; in the second, as one agent among many. For the self that sees, community is best understood as a form of voluntary association of autonomous individuals, but the illusion of independence that sight can foster is shattered by the emergence of an oral-aural universe. For the listener, community is the context in which the self comes to discover itself: the individual experiences himself from the beginning as one among many who hear and speak the same language, and the language expresses a system of shared standards, values, and expectations. Then, when another person addresses me as "thou," and I am able to hear the magnitude of this address, I am suddenly ushered into a relationship quite different from all my other involvements with the world. Hitherto unrealized powers of selfhood are liberated and crystallized by their concentration upon another "thou" who, drawing me from myself, offers me more of myself than I could ever find alone. When sound acquaints me with another who is a "thou" for me, as I in turn become a "thou" for him or her, I learn that I am not the center of the world. The other is a center, too, and why should not the perspective of this other be as valid as my own? But if both of us are centers, then no person is really the center of everything. Then neither can I rest content with an inflexible distinction between "us" and "them," for the projects and values of particular communities must all be subordinated to the impartial rule of justice or fairness. A relationship between two selves, initially quite tentative and ordinary, eventually confronts me with a norm that judges not only my own behavior but the conduct of the communities to which I belong.

So the self that lives in an oral-aural world experiences itself from the beginning as claimed and called to account for itself, deprived not only for the worse but for the better of the apparent liberty that is correlated with the neutrality of a visual cosmos. The self is claimed by the projects of its own communities, claimed by values that in their transcendence of its particular communities furnish a stronger foundation for them than they can furnish for themselves, claimed not only by the voices of others but in and through its own linguistic usage, for the naming of the world is an appraising of it and language socializes the self into particular schemes of standards and values. In a visual world, when it is forgotten how our social relationships determine our perspectives, the notions of independence and initiative and autonomy are fundamental for the description of the self. On the other hand, the sense of contingency and vulnerability, and the social involvements that hearing incorporates, mean that aural experience can serve as a metaphor for creatureliness and as justification for a command-and-obedience model of selfhood. Hearing and sight, then, are not only different as sensory encounters but also suggest different interpretations of the person, for the contrast of the near and the distant enshrines many others: passivity and activity, responsiveness and origination, bondage and liberty, sociality and independence. In a visual cosmos, the self is an agent; in an aural world, it is a patient. In the former, the individual is safe, at least for the moment; in the latter, he is always vulnerable. In one world, the self is free; in the other, it is claimed, called to account, and asked to respond to the initiatives of others. In one realm, the self is distinguished sharply from its environment; in the other, sounds bind it tightly to its social context and remind it of its contingency. One world contains only surfaces; in the other, there are many and various clues to the interiority of selves.

These observations conclude the introductory argument of the book. It began with the contention that a sense of identity is an imaginative act, a compendium of self-images that are reconciled with one another and unified by one or more master images of selfhood. The imagery is derived not only from social relationships but also from our bodily experience, which is powerfully dealienating in its persuasiveness that we are more than and other than our social relationships. Just as we are not all involved in the same relationships, however, neither do we experience ourselves as bodies in the same way, not only because the process of maturation includes a change in sensory dependence and greater reliance upon the abstract senses of sight and hearing, but also because sight and hearing are themselves very different sorts of sensory experience, and emphasis upon one of them rather than the other leads to a different understanding of the self.

The self's transactions with its world involve all of its senses, of course, but it can scarcely imagine their operations as a synergic system, and so imagination will focus upon one rather than the others as the source of its most crucial and revelatory experience, and its choice will fall upon one of the abstract senses. While it is true that we have frequently conflated more "literal" and more "metaphorical" usages of eye and ear, as well as exaggerated the differences between them because of the several abstractions that interpretation required, our concern is not primarily with the actual life of the senses but rather with the different ways that this life can be imagined in reminiscences of one's most important commerce with reality, with the different valuations that imagination awards to aural and visual impressions. This imaginative activity is inevitable and, whether or not faithful to actuality, is profoundly consequential for self-understanding. In a developed culture it will be expressed in and preserved by a legacy of stories and legends that prove to be predominantly visual or oral-aural. The claim that vision is the determinant of moral life, however, suggests that sight alone can be regarded as a paradigm of the self's commerce with its environment, and the implication of the primacy of sight is reflected in the interpretation of the self as player. Therefore, if the argument is correct that vision is structured by images of the self, and that stress upon visual or aural eventuates in diverse self-images, then a master image of the self as hearer is indispensable if vision itself is not to be distorted and partial. Vision will be defective if it is not equipped with imagery drawn from both sources and if the representation of the self as player is not companioned by another master image that enables us to grasp our passivity rather than our agency and our vulnerability as well as our liberty. On the one hand, it must be as different as are the two forms of sensory experience. On the other, it must be as complementary as are the different senses to one another in their synergic unity.

Because eye and ear serve not only as names of senses but also as metaphors for two apparently different sorts of relationship, one of which accents accountability and the disclosure of transcendence while the other emphasizes individual freedom and mastery over the world, it is tempting to conclude that there are particular affinities between the Christian vision and a universe that is predominantly oral-aural rather than visually oriented. Walter Ong is one among many who correlate a particular organization of the sensorium with the Judeo-Christian tradition. After all, in the world of the Bible, God discloses himself by speaking, just as by speaking he bestowed existence upon the world. Heaven and earth are created by the Word and the renewal of persons is accomplished by the Word made flesh, whose presence and power are mediated through speaking and hearing the Gospel. Despite the very considerable amount of visual imagery in the Bible, the prophets of the Old Testament frequently appear as iconoclasts who protest against every attempt to describe the relationship between the holy and the human in visual metaphors. The self is a hearer, a creature whose whole health is contingent upon the penitent and obedient ear, and the human reality to which hearing brings the self is a fabric of promises, for its sovereign power is the God of the Covenant, whose mercy is evident in promises offered and whose power is disclosed in promises kept. Consequently, especially on Protestant soil, it has often been argued that self-images which emphasize the oral-aural aspects of experience are superior to all others because they furnish a command-and-obedience model of existence before God. Martin Luther admonishes: "Even if you do not see you shall see by hearing. . . . He who will not take hold with his ears but wants to look with his eyes is lost. . . . Stick your eyes in your ears."[23]

The contrast between Greek and Hebraic cultures that has been a commonplace in much recent Christian theology has been elaborated to serve this sort of admonition. It is said that one tradition was concerned primarily with contemplation and the other with action: Greek reflection turned toward the unchanging and eternal and was static in comparison with the dynamism of Hebraic concentration upon history and becoming. The distinction between static and dynamic can be rephrased in terms of the opposition of abstract and concrete: Greek thought is analytic, replete with careful distinctions, while Hebrew thought is wholistic, replete with images of high specificity. The contrast is reflected in different interpretations of the self. For the Greeks, the individual consists of body and soul, the latter immortal and only accidentally and temporarily related to the former; for the Hebrews, however, there is no immortal aspect of the self and soul and flesh are inseparable. Finally, for Greek thought, human community is a collection of individuals: there can arise irresolvable conflicts between individual fulfillment and social obligations. The Hebraic tradition, on the other hand, envisions the self as relational, fulfilling itself in and through its involvements with others: the idea of the individual is an abstraction from the historical reality of social relationships. The writers who have emphasized these alleged differences have argued that the reason for them can be found in the life of the senses, in the dominance of either a visual or an aural orientation. So Thorlief Boman writes:

> When Socrates was seized by a problem, he remained immobile for an interminable period of time in deep thought; when Holy Scripture is read aloud in the synagogue, the Orthodox Jew moves his whole body ceaselessly in deep devotion and adoration . . . for the Hebrew the most important of his senses for the experience of truth was his hearing (as well as various kinds of feeling), but for the Greek it had to be his sight; or perhaps inversely, because the Greeks were organized in a predominantly visual way and the Hebrews in a predominantly auditory way, each people's conception of truth was formed in increasingly different ways.[24]

More recently, however, the contrast has been subjected to devastating criticism.[25] What has been disputed is not whether there are differences between the cultures but whether it is necessary to identify Christian commitment with an orientation that is primarily aural. That equation is a mistake, for cultural differentiation is a contingent historical fact and not a theological first principle. What Christian faith involves is *obedient vision.* Vision is the author of our conduct and it is so much the fundamental human capacity that, because of their incorporation in it, all the different senses in greater or lesser measure are able to see and hear.[26] The qualifier implies that the self is also a hearer and understands itself as such and that what it must envision is an oral-aural as well as a visual world. Together, the words counsel that it is wrong to identify faith with a particular organization of the sensorium; instead, they suggest a world where there is neither Jew nor Greek.

The immediate tasks are two: specification of some criteria for judging the adequacy of a second master image, and the discovery of an image that fulfills them. In the course of our quest for a representation of the self as listener, we shall learn that there is more to selfhood than can ever be captured by reliance upon the abstract senses of sight and hearing as clues to the nature of the self's commerce with its world. Some of what more there is, buried far below the surfaces that the eye discerns, is not only indisputably ours but also seems set to destroy everything else that is ours—at least if we cannot bring it to the forecourt of vision. So the search for a new image will end with a new beginning. Our first responsibility, however, is not to chart such strange terrain but only to answer the question: How can we best imagine a person who believes that he lives within a predominantly oral-aural universe, who believes that these impressions are more significant than all others, who experiences himself as a hearer before all else?

Chapter Two

THE IMAGE OF THE SELF
AS SUFFERER

O ur search is for a master image of the human that will complement the representation of the self as player. Our problem is to integrate these divergent understandings of the self derived from predominantly visual or primarily aural experience, despite the powerful tendencies of the imagination to tear them apart, just as eye and ear operate not merely as adjacent organs but as a functional unity in our actual commerce with the world. From the more literal to the more metaphorical usages of eye and ear in the continuum of our explorations, the visual and the aural have exhibited their inseparability. The words that we hear are interpreted by the eye that notices the countenance of the speaker or catches a familiar gesture, or else the ear recognizes a threatening intonation that belies the smile that charmed the eye. Unless sight preserves the distance between ourselves and our world, we cannot become intentionally involved with it; but if the world does not press itself upon us through the ear, we shall have no motivation to struggle to break out of the prison of our selfishness. If the transcendence of other selves is not disclosed to us in their speaking, we shall have few reasons to explore and cherish the depths that lie within ourselves—for it is not easy for us to see ourselves when we are alone. Unless we obey the voices that tutor us in the meaning of fairness or justice, we shall find no paths toward the autonomy that sight promises we can attain. Unless we acknowledge what aural experience teaches about our vulnerability, contingency, and passivity, we shall see too little of ourselves ever to become our own masters, and so neither shall we be able to see the world well. We begin, then, with the self as agent, endowed with independence and initiative, and with the self as patient, too, dependent upon others and acting primarily in response to their initiatives. We must learn to imagine them together: a new image must exhibit its *complementariness* with the figure of the player.

In *Hebrew Thought Compared with Greek,* Boman comments upon a complementarity between the two cultures like that between wave and particle theories of the atom: each expresses what the other does not recognize, so that they mutually supply one another's lack. But his usage of the idea of complementarity reduces it to little more than a synonym for juxtaposition and, consequently, seems to imply that visual and aural experiences are simply the products of organs that happen to live in the same neighborhood. In contrast, complementariness is employed in this essay to include two inseparable assertions rather than only one. First, it means that the different images must agree in their testimony concerning what is most fundamental about the situation of the self, for were this not true they would be related to one another merely in an arbitrary and external way. Second, it also means that each image must disclose something of fundamental significance that the other does not express. The way in which they mutually supply one another's lack is important, however, precisely because of their identical witness to what is most essential, for otherwise the attempt to imagine the complexity of the self would have no unifying and integrative power.

There are at least three criteria that a second master image must satisfy if it is to be an appropriate companion to the figure of the player. First, it must exhibit complementariness, in the sense of identity and difference at the same time, in what it affirms concerning the relationship of limits and liberty in creaturely life. Second, it must also reflect complementariness in what it expresses concerning the relationship of dependence and fulfillment. Finally, there is a theological criterion: visual and aural experiences would scarcely be imagined as complementary if the images derived from them portrayed the self in such disparate ways that from one perspective its nature appeared religious while from the other it seemed entirely secular.

First, then, the representation of the self as player affirms a dialectical relationship between liberty and limits, vitality and form, expression and order, Dionysius and Apollo. Playing is the school that best tutors selves to understand a discipline or code not as arbitrary and external authority but as intrinsic to self-expression and indispensable for self-development. Limits, rules, boundaries, and possibilities of penalty do not confront the self as its fate. Instead, they are actively embraced, becoming a world of coherent *nomoi* to which the autonomous self, as we have said, freely obligates itself for the sake of the fulfillment of the self's own possibilities. The choice is one's own, an act of freedom, but at the same time the further expression of freedom presupposes the choice. So grammar and syntax are affirmed, for example, in order to express the self, communicate with others, and grasp all the rich consequences of communication. Order is not affirmed simply for its own sake, but rather because of its integral relationship to the bodying forth of all the wildness and wilderness of human passion and vitality. Freedom is vertiginous, sterile, and abstract until it is endowed with structure and concreteness by the acknowledgment of limits; only then does it become *creaturely* freedom, latent with real possibilities, instead of the spurious freedom to do everything that is in fact identical with no freedom at all. What is important is that the representation of the self as player not only acknowledges limits as inherent in our creaturely situation but insists that these limits are themselves indispensable for the expression of creaturely liberty, spontaneity, and inventiveness. Nowhere is this more evident than in the artist's venture. The choice of a particular medium involves the sort of specification of freedom that is integral to creativity and the medium itself seems actively to collaborate with the artist, permitting one thing and opposing another. Few statements have ever held more truth than Igor Stravinsky's dictum, "Whatever diminishes constraint diminishes strength."[1]

So this is the first requisite: the expression by a new image of a dialectic of liberty and limits that is identical with the one affirmed in play. Together with the identity, however, there must also be difference. In play, the limits are freely affirmed for the sake of freedom itself. In aural experience, the limits are imposed, and the problem is to show that they are liberating and not merely restrictive, that they enrich persons in different ways and in greater measure than persons could ever achieve if they were simply left to themselves. A paradigmatic resolution of the problem can be found in the biblical narrative of God's ways with his creatures. In the cross of Christ forgiveness is offered to the wayward self and there is nothing more liberating than the word of forgiveness. But forgiveness is inseparable from judgment, from the acknowledgment of limits and the recognition that they cannot be violated with impunity. When persons are reconciled with God, limits are honored anew and understood as integral to self-realization.

Second, there is a similar dialectic between dependence and fulfillment, passivity and achievement, that is expressed by the figure of the player. The image offers the hope of autonomy, which is a condition that individuals must always achieve for themselves; it cannot be inherited or deeded or purchased from someone else. In the end, however, nothing about its attainment is more obvious than the ancient axiom that there is little we have that we have not received from others. A sense of the worth of the self and of the worthwhileness of its strivings is the *prius* of all its achievements, but this taste for one's own individuality depends upon the treatment that one has initially received from others: it is a reflection of their caring and encouragement. Nowhere is this more evident than in the presupposition that playing entails, the assumption of basic trust that, although it cannot ever be wholly justified, can scarcely be entertained at all unless other selves have counseled us by their deeds as well as their words that "everything is alright." The self cannot freely offer itself to others or bind itself to principles and rules unless it has first learned to possess itself; the lesson, however, can only be taught by others, communicated through their expressions of trust and confidence in the self struggling to master itself. The sense of identity that an individual develops is a gift from others, derived from a complex of relationships, the most consequential of which the individual certainly did not initiate for himself. So the bonds are indissoluble between the achievements of the self and the gifts it has received from others.

This is the second requisite: the affirmation through the new image of a dialectic of dependence and fulfillment that is identical with the one that is expressed by the figure of the player. Together with the identity, once again there must also be difference. The achievements of the player could not have been realized were it not for gifts from others. In aural experience, the focus lies upon the passivity of the self and the claims imposed upon it. *Claims no less than gifts afford new opportunities for self-realization.* The voices that call the self to account and threaten to alienate it from its own purposes also offer it a measure of potential enrichment that it could never discover by its own initiative. Nowhere is this more evident than in learning to speak: we are claimed by a certain structure of standards and values, but at the same time we are enabled through it to grasp and express our own singularity. The problem, then, is to show that our vulnerability is essential to our self-fulfillment and that passivity is not entirely a condition to be overcome, but itself leads to opportunities that agency could never find. The development from infancy to maturity, therefore, is seriously misconstrued if it is understood primarily as a progress from dependence and passivity to independence and agency. Again, a paradigmatic resolution of the problem can be found in the biblical narrative. It is the self's acknowledgment of dependence upon God that frees it from bondage to the powers of this world, and the delegated lordship of the creature over the creation is preserved only as long as the self acknowledges the priority of divine initiative and affirms its dependence as the legitimation of its rule.

Third, there is a theological criterion that constrains us to return briefly to the quality of visual experience: the two master images must agree in their representation of selves as *homines religiosi*, irrepressibly religious creatures whose thirst for the divine can manifest itself in many and strange ways but can never be wholly eradicated. It is sometimes alleged, however, that the visual realm is without religious significance, while the aural furnishes all that faith requires. In *The Presence of the Word*, for example, Ong appears to correlate with the polarity of religious and secular the distinction between a sensorium that is primarily oral-aural and one that is predominantly visual. The same implication is evident in Kierkegaard's portrait of Don Juan, the aesthetic man who is innocent of religious entanglements—except, perhaps, for whatever theological resonances are cradled within the anxieties that sometimes shadow his pursuit of the things that catch his eye. But Hans Jonas is much closer to the truth in *The Phenomenon of Life*, where he alludes to the religious elements in a visual cosmos in the course of tracing the excellence of sight to three sources: it is able to present many things simultaneously, it neutralizes causality, and it preserves a space between the self and the world. Each of these characteristics, he argues, provides

> the ground for some basic concept of philosophy. *Simultaneity of presentation* furnishes the idea of enduring present, the contrast between change and the unchanging, between time and eternity. *Dynamic neutralization* furnishes form as distinct from matter, essence as distinct from existence, and the difference between theory and practice. *Distance* furnishes the idea of infinity. Thus the mind has gone where vision pointed.[2]

The eye refuses to allow us to remain in an aesthetic world but leads us on to the precincts of religion. But this theology, with its focus upon the *totum simul* of eternity, with its stretching toward the infinite and boundless, and with its emphasis upon the contemplative ideal in the form of the detached knower, is alien to the biblical universe. In itself the eye is an angelic sense, looking beyond the rude constraints of the earth, impatient with the slow march of temporality, knowing and wishing to know nothing but boundless freedom: sight is the biological justification for the perennial Gnostic dream of another world far away from ours and different as light is from the dark, and the foundation for the Gnostic suspicion of the intimacy of touch and the exigence of sound. It is a mistake to regard the visual realm as secular, therefore, not only because it becomes stubbornly theological when we fall into the absolutisms involved in our failures to question the perspectives that we gain from communities and powers greater than ourselves, and not only because everything that the senses tell us is filtered through a symbolic universe that is warped and stained by our selfishness, but also because the mind goes where sight points, and sight points toward a religious world.

Consequently, the image of the self as player properly has a theological dimension. First, it is at least *formally* religious, in the sense that it expresses the only appropriate human stance within a world where nothing must be regarded with ultimate seriousness except the one power that is truly ultimate, while on the other hand insisting that nothing must be granted less than fair play. Because the assumption of basic trust that playing presupposes cannot be entirely justified in a contingent world characterized by randomness and accidents, the image cannot finally be legitimated except on religious grounds. Second, the image is also intended to serve specifically Christian purposes, for its insistence upon the dialectical relationship of limits and liberty means judgment upon the religious universe that sight suggests. Belief in a transcendent lord strips the world of its divinity and demands the qualification of every finite relationship, and so it is through this image that we can gain some new perspective upon our previous perspectives, finding that our own questions are now called into question. A complementary master image must also display the religious nature of the self, of course, but with the difference that it must be *materially* religious, representing the self in its responsiveness to the sovereign initiative of God rather than primarily as a subject or free agent. While the principle of fair play is no less applicable within an aural world than it is in a visual universe, the new image must express the ways that even this norm must sometimes be qualified and surpassed by the dictates of obedience to God.

In the light of these criteria, how shall we represent the self that emerges from an aural universe where life is first of all *passio* and we are at once the beneficiaries and the victims of the initiatives of others? What is the most apposite master image? In *The Laws,* Plato provides an option that seems singularly apt as a complement to the figure of the player. The Athenian Stranger declares:

> As the shipwright first lays down the lines of the keel, and thus, as it were, draws the ship in outline, so do I seek to distinguish the patterns of life, and lay down their keels according to the nature of different men's souls; seeking truly to consider by what means, and in what ways, we may go through the voyage of life best. Now human affairs are hardly worth considering in earnest, and yet we must be earnest about them—a sad necessity constrains us. . . . I say that about serious matters a man should be serious, and about a matter which is not serious he should not be serious; and that God is the natural and worthy object of our most serious and blessed endeavors, for man, as I said before, is made to be the plaything of God, and this, truly considered, is the best of him; wherefore also every man and woman should walk seriously, and pass life in the noblest of pastimes, and be of another mind from what they are at present.[3]

What the image of the self as plaything of God is intended to mean is somewhat obscure, especially because in another context the Athenian Stranger treats it as synonymous with

puppet. It is certainly intended to qualify the self's seriousness about itself and its ventures, to rescue it from the false
consciousness in which relative and absolute duties are confused with one another, and to affirm that persons cannot find
fulfillment in the social order alone. But it is less certain what
measure of agency the image attributes to the individual,
although if it is the best of the self to be the plaything of God,
then the image would scarcely allow selves to understand
themselves merely as the victims of powers greater than their
own. Perhaps the figure of the plaything does suggest some
integral relation between the chastening of the lord and the
achievement of strength, or between discipline and fulfillment, but this is little more than implicit. A more important
problem is that, between the relationship of the self to God
and its relationships to its historical communities, there appears to be only a negative tension: the former qualifies the
seriousness with which the individual should approach the
latter, but the latter does not seem to afford opportunities for
the enrichment and further development of the former.

It would be difficult, therefore, to argue that the image
could be interpreted in a fashion that would satisfy the criteria
already established, for it seems to express no integral connection between the claims that other selves impose upon the
individual and the individual's own fulfillment. But the greatest inadequacy of this representation of the self is neither its
ambiguity concerning individual agency nor its perhaps un-
duly minimal assessment of the opportunities that human
community affords. The problem, in a sense, is its unfortu-
nate contemporaneity. In an essay on images of the self that
reign in contemporary culture, Julian N. Hartt cites three as
the most pervasive and influential: the victim who is trapped
inextricably within a system, the stranger who has evaded the
"sad necessity" to be earnest about human affairs, and the
plastic self that assumes whatever shape or posture it pleases
or that is most pleasing to its peers and valued in the market-
place.[4] The image of the plaything can easily be understood
as a synonym for any or all of these, reinforcing the self's
sense of impotence before powers greater than its own and

persuading it that, for one reason or another, the creative possibilities inherent in its social relationships have suffered massive erosion. It can easily represent the individual as nothing more than a puppet, the victim of whatever voice has sounded most recently and loudly within the ear, summoned from nothing for a moment by the speech of others. So the self is as others desire it to be and, because any life seems better than none, at least this assures it of some precarious hold upon existence until the moment when design or accident or disinterest causes other people to turn away. Or perhaps the self will do whatever others desire it to do, feeding its agency wholly from their initiatives and thereby exempting itself from judgment by any persons or standards outside these relationships, believing that it is better to measure selfhood in terms of functions and performances than to have no gauge of it at all. Despite its antiquity and original theological connotations, then, the image of the plaything can too easily suggest or reinforce some of the most destructive assumptions from which many in the modern world try to fashion a similitude of identity. It is certainly arguable that much truth must be acknowledged in this portrait of the human condition, but the problem is that whatever truth it holds must be acknowledged in a way that will provide us with imaginative resources to resist it rather than simply to surrender.

Consequently, this essay proposes as an alternative a master image that is perhaps the oldest and richest description of our situation: *the self as sufferer,* a sufferer who also understands himself as a player because his suffering has taught him that he can do no better than this and who must understand himself as committed to playing fair because the suffering of others has taught him that he cannot do less than this. No one is free of suffering; the question is not how it can be evaded but how it can be borne, and what possibilities it holds for the enrichment of the self. Suffering must not be identified with pain, however. Pain is a physical sensation that all animals sometimes endure, but suffering is a distinctively human experience because in one way or another it is a function of meaning. Pain can be a cause of or an ingredient in suffering, of course, but frequently it is entirely absent, and especially from the more complex sorts of suffering that are the consequences of betrayals of oneself or of others. But neither is suffering synonymous with sorrow or anguish. The distinction is particularly important in this context, where suffering is intended first of all as a reflection of a particular organization of the sensorium and as a representation of the situation of a self whose agency is shaped, for the better as well as for the worse, by the initiatives, gifts, claims, lying, loving, and various different attitudes and actions of other people. Suffering, then, is reason for gratitude as often as it is cause for anguish. It is important to begin with the recognition that the figure of the sufferer suggests both the restriction of possibilities and their enrichment, the exploitation of the self but equally its fulfillment, childish dependence and impotence but also its responsiveness to the needs of others. The image is initially passive and empty: vulnerable and as yet undefined, the self it represents awaits the shape that will be given to it by the claims and appeals, assurances and warnings, and the words of liberation that echo in the ear.

The task that must now be addressed is a demonstration of the complementarity of the sufferer and the player. The various dimensions of the new image must all offer their own testimony to the integral connection between the claims that others impose or the limits that the world enforces and the enrichment and liberation of the self. Nothing could be more obvious than the relationship between self-fulfillment and other persons who provide assurance, offer encouragement, affirm promises, and swear loyalty. But the connection is less evident between fulfillment and all the voices that arrest us to serve their purposes and answer their needs, enforcing upon us obligations that seem irremediably to block the paths we would have chosen for ourselves. To answer the question of complementarity, we must explore the relationship of the sufferer to its God, to its own body, and to its neighbors and communities.

The self and its God. Although the image of the sufferer begins as a neutral portrayal of the self, simply a concrete expression of what emerges from an imagining of selfhood that stresses the experience of hearing, from a Christian perspective no other image can claim more fundamental or comprehensive significance. In the biblical narrative, selves are offered dominion over the whole creation, but the condition of it is the acknowledgment of the priority of divine initiative and of human creatureliness and limitation. After the fall, selves confront the judgment of God, who visits suffering upon his people in order that they might return to him and escape the loneliness into which their sin has brought them. Suffering is a motif that informs all of the New Testament, and one of the reasons for its importance there is that the Hebrew tradition finally had no way to interpret the self to itself except as a sufferer, for the tradition understood selves as creatures summoned to existence by a Word spoken to them and claimed in existence by the presence that dwelt within the sovereign Word. The image was important, then, if the Christ were to be represented as man at all. On the other hand, if this man were to be represented as the Christ, the anointed one of God come to minister to enemies and strangers and the ungodly, and if it were to be claimed that in him alone had the full proportions of humanity been disclosed, then it was also necessary for the image to be transformed in the light of divine revelation in order to divest it of a multitude of ambiguities so that the sufferer could be seen as agent and the servant as lord, obedient to a voice that other ears would not hear. In Jesus, humanity is revealed as suffering: it means being for and being with, in obedience to the Father. The obedient one suffered perfectly the initiative of God and he was enabled to obey because God himself was in Christ, reconciling the world to himself through his suffering. Being for the creature, Jesus lived with the creature: his work was shaped by the exigencies of the fallen human situation and his liberty was made perfect in his acceptance of the creature's suffering beneath the judgment of God. Between his *kenosis* and his *plerosis,* his self-emptying and his self-fulfillment, the relationship is internal or dialectical: the lordship of the servant is not a reward for his suffering, something merited but external. The servant role of the Lord is not a stepping away from lordship but the revelation of what lordship means. In the great kenotic passage of Philippians, it is said that the movement downward, the suffering, is causally generative of the movement upward: it is only by his penetration of all the constraints and limits of the finite and definite that the Christ —as well as everyone else—comes to infinite illumination, fulfillment, the Father. The *kenosis* and the *plerosis* constitute a unity and are not two disparate movements: the way down *is* the way up. The author counsels us: "Let this mind be in you, which was also in Christ Jesus: Who, being in the form of God . . . took upon him the form of a servant."[5] This is the essential Christian warrant for insistence upon the dialectic between limits and liberty that the images of player and sufferer can express equally well. In the achievement of selfhood, there is no fulfillment but by way of suffering, for the downward is causally generative of the upward, as in the instance of the Christ.

Suffering has frequently become a synonym for the totality of the Christian life. Calvin expresses its centrality through the phrase, "bearing the cross," which means neither stoic acceptance of the misfortunes of life nor masochistic attraction to punishment, but participation in Christ's own suffering at the hands of men and the suffering of the Father's initiative, whereby freedom is found through obedience. In his fine study of Calvin's interpretation of discipleship, R. S. Wallace writes:

> God wills that our whole life should be conformed to the death of Christ. This means that we must become conformed to Christ in outward circumstances as well as in inward attitude . . . those who are destined to be thus conformed to Christ are called to bear in addition to the ordinary afflictions which are the common lot of mankind also a special chastisement from the hand of God which they must suffer as the representatives of His son on earth. To be a member of the Church means, for Calvin, to enter a sphere in which *because we are devoted to God we are devoted also to suffering.*[6]

The theme is even more dominant in the works of Kierkegaard, who argues that: "Aesthetically viewed, suffering stands in an accidental relation to existence, it may indeed be there but it may also cease, while viewed religiously the cessation of suffering is also the cessation of the religious life."[7] First, suffering is the distinguishing mark of faith because the believer not only has a relationship to God but is also separated from God, and were the separation not to induce a profound sort of suffering the believer would be less than serious about God. Second, the self also suffers because there is no appropriate way whatsoever for it to express the seriousness of its commitment:

> Herein lies the profound suffering of true religiosity, the deepest thinkable, namely, to stand related to God in an absolutely decisive manner, and to be unable to find any decisive external expression for this (for a happy love between human beings expresses itself externally in the union of the lovers). This inability is rooted in the necessary relativity of the most decisive external expression, in its being both too much and too little; it is too much because it involves a certain presumptuousness over against other men, and it is too little because it is after all a worldly expression.[8]

The individual suffers because he must "die away from immediacy." There is no way in the world for him to give direct expression to his faith. He is unable ever to express the infinite resignation in which everything is offered up for the sake of the absolute and everything is received again in faith, even as Abraham received again his child Isaac, for it would scarcely involve infinite resignation to surrender all things in the confidence that they would be returned. Suffering and our love of God are inseparable; indeed, for Kierkegaard the extent of our suffering is the gauge of our love of God, and this is our greatest and most creative enrichment.

The self and its body. Among all the visitors to the household of the self, none is less welcome than the sensation of pain, which is often a significant element in our experience of suffering. Pain is thoroughly untrustworthy as a symptom of disease, however, partly because there is no correlation between its severity and the seriousness of the illness, partly because it frequently does not attack us until the disease has done its work and our situation is beyond remedy. Pain simply renders much worse what was already more than bad enough. But disease is not the ordinary human condition and it is a mistake, although a common one, to approach the problem of pain from this perspective. For healthy persons pain is an indispensable sensation, teaching them many things that it is necessary to learn if they are to adapt to their environment, and enabling them to develop habits that will contribute to their self-preservation. We live in a world in which it is painful to fall from a height, approach too closely to a fire, or collide with large and solid objects; unless we listen to the lessons that pain has to teach, we shall not live long in such a world. In the end, there is no other satisfactory teacher, for we will not learn all the necessary lessons at second hand.

Physical suffering, then, contributes indispensably to the task of learning to exercise our agency in ways appropriate to the world in which we live. But pain is significant not only for adaptation to the environment but also for the development of moral selfhood. There would be nothing wrong with inflicting pain if no one could ever feel it. There would be no reason for all sorts of acts of self-sacrifice if the young and the aged were not vulnerable to painful accidents and contingencies. If there were no possibility of physical suffering, the necessary extent of our caring for others would be radically diminished. Courage and patience and unselfishness would rarely be evoked in an environment in which there were no real dangers; we would be deprived of all our opportunities to develop strength and endurance. Our own vulnerability to pain teaches us how terrible it can be to inflict pain upon others, reminding us of our shared frailty and counseling the importance of compassion and gentleness. Often the lesson is not learned, of course, but at least the opportunity to learn it remains.

In *Evil and the God of Love,* John Hick comments wisely upon the relationship between pain and community. It is true that the world is replete with instances of excessive and gratuitous pain that allow their victims to learn nothing and that in no way display the presence of the hand of God. But, he writes, it is equally true that

> men and women often act in true compassion and massive generosity and self-giving in the face of unmerited suffering, especially when it comes in such dramatic forms as an earthquake or a mining disaster. It seems, then, that in a world that is to be the scene of compassionate love and self-giving for others, suffering must fall upon mankind with something of the haphazardness and inequity that we now experience. It must be apparently unmerited, pointless, and incapable of being morally rationalized. For it is precisely this feature of our common human lot that creates sympathy between man and man and evokes the unselfish kindness and goodwill which are among the highest values of personal life. No undeserved need would mean no uncalculating outpouring to meet that need.[9]

The undeserved and pointless suffering that is visited upon others, then, can turn us away from ourselves, pierce the armor of our selfishness, and shatter our carefulness and calculations, and in such instances of unreserved responsiveness to the needs of others we find ourselves enriched and strangely liberated, more fully actualized than when we are alone or when nothing shadows the pleasures of the day. In different ways, the vulnerability to pain that we share with everyone else is a condition of our self-realization, testifying that our limitations and our common human frailty are creative determinants of the fashion in which our agency is expressed. The removal from the world that technological society has achieved for the worse as well as for the better, the illusions of security rooted in failures to plumb the imprevisibility and suddenness of life, the reluctance to admit the magnitude of our frailties and to accept the inevitability of death, the understanding of ourselves as commodities the value of which depends upon the images that we project, the dependence upon cosmetics and anodynes that enable us to disguise ourselves from ourselves as well as from others, the identification of ourselves with the roles and functions that we fulfill and with the services we command, the assumption that we can equate what we can manipulate with the whole of reality—all of these are challenged and undermined by the pains that remind us of our bodily life and expose the disparities between the way we would like to see ourselves and the way we really are. Pain can be a burden so great that it causes the self to become obsessed with itself until it is oblivious to everything else. But equally often it can initiate imaginative identification with others, generating compassion and strengthening the bonds of life together. In any event, our vulnerability to pain is not only a condition of physical survival but also a requisite for the development of moral selfhood. The dialectical relationships that complementarity involves are clearly expressed in this aspect of the representation of the self as sufferer.

The self and its communities. The distinction between the bodily and the social life of the individual can be a misleading abstraction, of course, for the self has no way to live except as a body and in community. The primordial form of community is the household or family or, more precisely, the relationship between a parent and a child. If its significance is to be understood, however, it must be explored first of all with particular attention to bodily life. The human infant differs from the young of all other animals because of its complete helplessness. Even birds are able to break out of their shells, but a newborn human can do nothing at all. It possesses no power of locomotion, no coordination, no capacity to respond to any external stimuli in a way that would defend it against danger or serve to prolong its existence. Everything that it does is done at random. Not only is this helplessness of long duration, but the infant's first steps to alter its situation do little except to expose it to even greater perils, so that its need for supervision is also greater. This, too, distinguishes it from the young of all other animals. One way to phrase this fundamental difference between the self and the other creatures that populate the world is to say that the

infant has no instincts. Instinct designates an ability to adapt
to the environment that need not be learned; it is not a "general" ability but is specific in the sense that it is "sufficiently
definite to fulfil its biological function."[10] John MacMurray
employs this distinction between instinctive and learned patterns of behavior in order to differentiate the self from all
other creatures, commenting with regard to instincts that "it
is clear that we are born with none. All purposive human
behavior has to be learned. To begin with, our responses to
stimulus are, without exception, biologically random."[11]

MacMurray's point is of great importance for the elaboration of images of selfhood. If we could specify capacities for
adaptation that required no learning, if our responses to the
environment were not initially random, if we could understand an infant satisfactorily by analogy to other animals, as
though it, too, were a little animal that progressively exercised the instincts with which it was born, then possibly one
might argue that the figure of the self as sufferer does not
possess the absolutely fundamental significance that it holds.
But in the primordial and paradigmatic form of human community the infant appears as a creature that is not endowed
with capacities to contribute to its own survival, react to danger, manage its environment, and provide for its own development. Instead, its situation is one of total helplessness,
absolute dependence, pure and unqualified suffering of the
initiative and concern of others. To cite MacMurray again:

> The baby must be fitted by nature at birth to the condi-
> tions into which he is born; for otherwise he could not
> survive. He is, in fact, "adapted," to speak paradoxically,
> to being unadapted, "adapted" to a complete depen-
> dence upon an adult human being. He is made to be
> cared for. . . . He cannot think for himself, yet he cannot
> do without thinking; so someone else must think for him.
> He cannot foresee his own needs and provide for them;
> so he must be provided for by another's foresight.[12]

An infant can live only in relation to other persons and
upon the attentions of the parent depends its ability to de-

velop a taste for itself, gain confidence in its own powers and faith in the dependability of the world. Only by suffering the agency of others will the self ever be enabled to find itself, gain all that it needs to adapt to its situation and acquire a sense of its own identity. We have already noted the difference between the sensation of pain, to which all animals are vulnerable, and the experience of suffering, which is peculiarly human because it is a function of meaning. Now, however, suffering will serve in a further sense to distinguish the self from all other creatures, for there is simply no way to imagine it in the primordial form of human community except as a sufferer whose complete helplessness differentiates it from other animals because they are capable of specific adaptations to their environment that they need not learn. Both the self's entrance into the world and its exit from it are best described as instances of suffering: this is the essential image.

Suffering serves not only to represent the beginning and end of affairs, however. The infantile helplessness that deepens as well as demands the ties of community indicates that selfhood is always a relational venture. The adult as well as the child is enriched and fulfilled by the relationship. So MacMurray is correct in concluding "that the unit of personal existence is not the individual, but two persons in personal relation; and that we are persons not by individual right, but in virtue of our relation to one another. The personal is constituted by personal relatedness. The unit of the personal is not the 'I', but the 'You and I'."[13] The original form of community, then, remains always the form of community, and the suffering that it involves continues to be essential to self-realization. In the course of its career, the self hears an "ought" less frequently and a "may" more often and then a conjunction of "ought" and "may" as, with maturity, the "ought" returns, more insistent and complex, richer because it asks for free assent rather than mere submission. Now the claims and appeals that the ear transmits concern not only our own selfhood and its development but also the projects and various needs of others, and we are hedged, fenced, limited, confined, interrupted, and diverted by suffering their demands or idle chatter or suggestions of things it would be fun to do. *Yet we need the need that others have for us and we become fully personal only in our responsiveness to these needs.* Just as we cannot offer ourselves unless we have learned to possess and master ourselves, which we cannot achieve except by way of the initiatives of others, so do we come to possess more of ourselves because of the occasions for the offering of the self that the presence of someone else provides—first of all for the simple reason that the offering affirms and strengthens the relationality that is the form of the personal. The offering is a free acknowledgment of the fundamental characteristic of human life, an expression of what selfhood is intended to be. Milton Mayeroff develops a fine metaphor for the involution of suffering and fulfillment, offering and enrichment, when he writes of the ways that the self is given its indispensable "place" in the world by the voices of others who need it:

> Place is not something I have, as if it were a possession. Rather, I am in-place because of the way I relate to others. And place must be continually renewed and reaffirmed; it is not assured once and for all, for it is our response to the need of others to grow which gives us a place. . . . For caring to be sufficiently inclusive, a man must care for himself, because the man who is unresponsive to his own needs to grow can never be in-place. And, as we have seen, caring for myself means at least to be responsive to my fundamental need to care for others apart from myself.[14]

There are many reasons why the experience of being placed by others means an expansion of our own possibilities. One of the most important is that if we do not care for other selves we will never develop the sort of perspective upon our own perspectives that will enable us to become more than we have been. Being placed contributes to vision. Caring involves an imaginative identification with others that renders it possible to see our own selves differently and more expansively than hitherto, to accept the relativity of our own needs and standards and perspectives, and to recognize that we can be called to account from points of vantage other than our own. The affirmation of others and their needs in all their difference from ourselves and our own projects enforces some of the humility without which moral selfhood is impossible, for it means *con*-scientia, the self not only thinking with itself but also thinking its way with others through some of the threads of the web of its selfishness. Being placed is as much a gift as a responsibility insofar as it liberates us from our egocentricity and awakens us to the diversity and richness of the social world. Mayeroff comments: "There is a *selflessness* in caring that is very different from the loss of self in panic or through certain kinds of conformity. It is like the selflessness that goes with being absorbed in something I find genuinely interesting, that goes with being 'more myself.' Such selflessness includes heightened awareness, greater responsiveness to both the other and myself, and the fuller use of my distinctive powers."[15]

If we care only for persons whom we have freely chosen, our perspectives can still be enhanced by theirs. But the rewards can be greater when we are the subjects of appeals and criticisms and judgments that are suffered from unexpected quarters and expressed by persons who entertain expectations and assumptions quite foreign to our own. When we are placed by the request that we care for a stranger, or by a voice that demands nothing but that is so familiar it reminds us anew how much there is we owe to others, we are forced to confront our ingratitude, our guilt, the reasons for a sense of shame or incompletion, our deviousness not only with others but also with ourselves. Being placed can bring us the gift of judgment from a perspective foreign to our own, and this is precisely what we can never offer to ourselves: judgments that afford opportunities for repentance, transformation, growth, and the reconciliations that establish a new and richer dimension in human relationships.

Christian theologians have frequently distinguished between *chronos* and *kairos,* two words for time with dissimilar meanings. *Chronos* denotes time quantified, measured by clocks, unmemorable: the distinctive mode of human existence is objectified. *Kairos* designates time filled with the presence of God, time measured and punctuated by the rhythms of the human heart, moments that are crucial for self-understanding and self-fulfillment, times of crisis. When the unvarying march of *chronos* is interrupted by *kairoi*, the self is enriched and its powers are increased. Because the self lives in space as well as in time, however, it is important to express this distinction also in terms of a spatial metaphor. On the one hand, there is space as a possession, something that can be bought and sold, traded for a different place, selected on the advice of a realtor or rented only for brief occupancy. Like other possessions, this sort of place leaves the interiority of the self untouched.

On the other hand, there is space as placement, responsibility, accountability and liability to judgment, place as an expression of the relational or dialogical form of personal life. The externality of our relationship to space that possession suggests is altered and we are no longer adrift and anchorless: other selves have given us placement, not as a possession but as a concrete determination of our capacities for responsiveness, so that we who know at least something of what we should do now know *where* it should be done. Placement draws the self beyond itself once again into the mutuality of suffering the need and dependence and initiative and availability of one another that is congruent with the original situation of the self in which it was provided with all its first resources for development and the achievement of identity. There it learns that it cannot care for itself if it does not care for others, and that it cannot care for others if it does not respect their otherness and initiative, acknowledging their right to join in setting the terms of the encounter. We need to suffer the needs of others in order to gain a focus for the exercise of powers that hitherto were disunited and diffused. If the eye did not preserve a distance between the world and ourselves, we could not act as moral agents, but neither could we serve as moral agents if other selves did not award us placement within the world. We need times made right by the initiative of God because we cannot make them right by ourselves, but also we need a place that must be conferred upon us by others because we cannot find it for ourselves.

Every self has its own projects, many and various, but these are not sufficient by themselves to place it in the world. The projects that we can choose depend upon the ways that other selves limit our freedom. It is their determination of our freedom that frees us: we are set at liberty when our liberty is limited by other agents. Freedom must not be confused with the absence of constraints; it is unimaginable, as we have said, except in relation to limits that bring it focus and specificity, endowing it with the concreteness that is appropriate to finite agency. The more concrete our liberty, the more at liberty we are. Furthermore, the projects that we choose must be selected in the light of what we can actually hope for, and what we can hope for depends upon whether others stand ready to assist in our ventures and whether our projects are consistent with the ones that other persons have already initiated. Finally, we learn to hope not only in others but *with* them, in the sense that when bafflement or boredom causes us to abandon our projects as hopeless, we can put on the imagination of other selves, clothe our own poverty in their richness, and discover new grounds for hope that recall us to our original ventures and new perspectives that unearth forgotten possibilities. For their particular shape as much as for their fulfillment, and even for the envisagement of resolutions to the problems that we encounter, our projects depend upon other selves and our placement is conferred upon us by what our neighbors do. To cite John MacMurray again:

> That my end should be good and my chosen means effective are then conditions of my freedom in action. But they are not sufficient conditions. For I am not alone in the world; there are other agents, and if they will not allow me to do what I desire to do I cannot do it. Moreover, there are few things which I can desire to do, and none that are of personal significance, which do not depend upon the active cooperation of others. We need one another to be ourselves. This complete and unlimited dependence of each of us upon the others is the

central and crucial fact of personal existence. . . . This
mutuality provides the primary condition of our freedom. Freedom is the capacity to determine the future by
action. We are agents; but this capacity to act is itself
problematical. It has to be realized through the resolution of the problems it presents, and the resolution of
these rests upon the development of our knowledge. The
fundamental condition for the resolution of the problem
of freedom is our knowledge of one another.[16]

There is no personal agency apart from the agency of others.
There is no life except life together. There is no freedom
apart from suffering. Without suffering, freedom remains
terra incognita, a wasteland that will continue to resist the art
of the cartographer. Suffering and passivity and dependence
are not only the conditions of childhood; in every life, from
birth to death, they are integral to human fulfillment, for the
fundamental unit of human existence is "you and I" and
never the self alone.

This sketch of the relations of the self to its God, its body
and its communities is not intended even to suggest the proportions of a systematic exploration, but only to show that the
representation of the self as sufferer includes numerous and
rich dimensions, that all of them exhibit the same dialectical
relationships evident in the image of the player, and that the
two images are truly complementary. First, there is the richness of the image. Suffering incorporates the problem of pain
but is a distinctively human experience because it concerns
meaning; it also differentiates the self from other creatures
that are endowed with instincts that prepare them for survival.
It expresses the situation of the infant in its primordial community of mother and child, and it also describes the way that
the self gains identity and develops its agency through its
relationships with other selves, communities, and institutions.
It stresses the dialogical form of personal life that is nowhere
more evident than in the way that the self is placed by the
strengths and needs of other people, and it represents the self
as subject to duties and obligations and commandments,
called to obedience. On the other hand, it also captures the

possibility of the alienation of the self from itself, its expropriation by powers greater than itself and for purposes other than its own. Yet the voices that we hear in the world are challenging as much as threatening: the caring that others sometimes display and sometimes demand provides occasions for offering the self that persons could never find for themselves but that contribute richly to their own fulfillment.

The caring that other voices express to us justifies, at least in some small measure, the assumption of basic trust on which our playing depends. The interruptions of other voices can sometimes create the encounters that finally legitimate caring —moments when the "I" becomes a "thou" for others, or one of them becomes a "thou" for the "I," expanding across the whole field of vision and transfiguring the "I" that suddenly glimpses the depths that our common humanity enshrines. Sometimes, too, the interruptions can remind us of the terrible fragility of the orders that we create, of the ways that our expectations concerning the trustworthiness of things can be smashed as easily as a cut glass bowl, of how long are the valleys in which we play and how dark are the shadows that lie upon them. But still the figure of the sufferer promises possibilities of self-fulfillment that are at once different from and greater than the ones that the image of the player suggests. Finally, suffering is a specifically religious category that is not merely correlated with the misfortunes that happen to fall upon us; instead, it expresses the way of the Christ and the secret of his lordship, while also capturing our separation from him in whom we are at the same time and forever incorporated.

Second, there is its testimony to the integral relationship between freedom and limitation and between dependence and fulfillment. We have argued that this must be the principal criterion of the adequacy of a master image that is complementary to the representation of the self as player. The player subjects himself to limits by his own choice, but he must choose limits if ever he is to realize his possibilities. The sufferer is subjected to limits by the initiatives of others, but discovers in his subjection a determination of his liberty and a measure of fulfillment that he could never achieve alone. We are victims of pain, and yet without the sensation of pain we could not learn to survive. We endure physical suffering, but it can teach us not to inflict suffering upon others, so that we progress toward moral selfhood. We are vulnerable to all the noises of the world, and yet by listening we learn the language that enables us to organize and master our environment. It is by way of suffering that we receive the gift of speech. Language enforces upon us a certain expropriation and yet, although it is neither our first nor our only means of expression, it is also our most perfect instrument for expressing our own individuality. We suffer claims and appeals from other selves that restrict our freedom, placing us here rather than there even though our luggage was already packed for travel, and yet such determination is essential to our fulfillment. Our relationships with other selves and communities depend upon initiatives that are not our own and upon situations that we cannot control, but from them we derive the sense of personal identity that can eventually afford us some critical perspective upon the relationships themselves. At every juncture, we learn more insistently that limitation and determination constitute not only our fate but also opportunities for enrichment and the attainment of new freedom—and so it must be if the self is made for God and if the fundamental form of the personal is dialogical and not solitary, as it is disclosed in the relationship of mother and child.

Passivity is not always an index of human failure, then, but a recurrent and indispensable moment in the life of dialogue, a humbling of the willfulness of the self, an acknowledgment of the otherness of reality, a recognition that the self is not the center of everything—and little needs to be stressed more often than this in a culture that places too great a premium upon agency, offers "independence" too soon, and averts its eyes from the frail and aged and dying. Not least important, the representation of the self as sufferer returns us to our true situation from the monstrous illusion that the whole of reality can be equated with what we can mold and manipulate. Nothing is more subversive of a Christian understanding of the human enterprise than the assumption that everything exists in order to be controlled by our technological expertise, even ourselves, and that it is nothing but a failure of inventiveness if we need suffer reality on its own terms rather than on ours. The image of the sufferer counsels the need for patience, insisting that there are not only right times but also times for waiting, and that the latter contribute in their own way to the development of the self—and, again, little needs to be emphasized more strongly in a culture in which too many persons believe that the moment is all and that temporality is nothing more than an agglomeration of discrete moments without consequences for their successors.

Third, the representations of the self as player and as sufferer exhibit their actual complementariness in many ways: if we are to be faithful either to the diversity and interdependence of the senses or to the richness of our social life in its ordinariness as well as in its ideal possibilities, each requires the other. The first image best expresses the standard by which moral selfhood can be appraised, but it is the second that best portrays the actual situation in which selves exist, where they live among other agents from whom they derive their own possibilities of inventiveness and agency. The image of the sufferer not only captures a different organization of the sensorium than does the player, it also expresses the contingency of human life, emphasizing all the ills to which flesh is heir, the pervasiveness of accident and pain and violence and disease. So it further illuminates the element of risk involved in the player's assumption of basic trust. The other side of the coin, however, is that basic trust itself entails the affirmation that even the sufferings of the self can contribute to its enrichment and to the clarification of its moral vision. So basic trust offers its own confidence in support of what the image of the sufferer attests. The vulnerability of the ear is an image that expresses the whole range of frailties and vulnerabilities in those who hear, inspiring new vigilance even in the midst of our games, and telling the player what he did not know but must acknowledge. The self is a sufferer who must imagine himself as a player if he is ever to organize his situation in the world. The self is a player whose suffering has disclosed dangers, debts, and opportunities that hitherto went unrecognized.

The image of the sufferer involves a command-and-obedience model of selfhood. The biblical tradition itself, however, suggests that obedience to persons and powers beyond the self does not represent the highest possibilities of moral life, for Jeremiah envisions a day when God will make a new covenant with the houses of Judah and Israel. Then, "I will put my law within them, and I will write it upon their hearts. . . . And no longer shall each man teach his neighbor and each his brother, saying, 'Know the Lord,' for they shall all know me, from the least of them to the greatest, says the Lord."[17] The idea of obedience is not entirely congruent with a theological universe in which the self is freed to live gratefully and where, so to speak, present imperatives are not honored in the hope of future indicatives, not obeyed for the sake of a reward. Instead, indicatives that remain in the future, but that are no less real because of their futurity, call for some grateful expression in the present of what they signify. The self is liberated to act as though tomorrow were now, as though the age to come were already present. The representation of the self as player, then, can complement the idea of obedience as well as expose its ambiguity, an ambiguity that is all the greater because of the readiness with which we rely upon it in order to excuse whatever coarseness or cruelty our careers involve. The image of the sufferer cannot itself express the perils of obedience to worldly authorities or the limits beyond which obedience is never justified. It does not prepare us to decide which claims should receive priority when we are assailed by many cries, or which appeals should be rejected, or where the distinction lies between just and inordinate demands, or how in a particular instance moral responsiveness must judge and reform the original request. But the resources that it cannot offer to the self are found in the wisdom that playing cultivates: all worldly claims have their limits, for they must neither violate whatever is involved in fairness toward one's own self nor exaggerate what fairness toward others entails.

As the exigencies of fair play are specified by temperance and courage and justice, it becomes evident that fairness toward the self and fairness toward others are correlative: neither can be achieved without the other. Faithful listening involves faithfulness to one's own self first of all, for of what value is listening if there is no real "I" who hears or if a clamor of voices manages to rob the "I" of itself? The image of the player is demanded by the figure of the sufferer, then, if we are neither to employ the latter in a way that is finally a disservice to our neighbors nor to understand ourselves through it in a way that cripples ourselves. On the other hand, the image of the self as sufferer insists that our relationships and obligations are different and deeper than simply the consequences of the initiative and freedom of the autonomous individual. Our accountability often extends far beyond the limits to which we would prefer to confine it. As beneficiaries of the agency of many other selves, as recipients of gifts from many quarters, we are always debtors who must live in a fashion that expresses gratitude for much that we neither expected nor deserved. The expression of gratitude involves new relationships that the self would scarcely choose for itself if everything that it possessed were its own unaided achievement. As one among a multitude of creatures, all of whose lives are willed by God, the self discovers itself in the midst of a solidarity and mutuality of suffering in which the ground bass of the music and cacophony of human relationships is not human choice and freedom but the priority of the initiative of God.

Never separately, only together, these two master images express what is involved in the actualities and responsibilities and possibilities of selfhood, at least when selfhood is more than an episodic affair and constitutes a more or less coherent and rational narrative. Perhaps the imagery can best be expressed in its complementariness by the assertion that *authentic existence means playing by ear.* The image of the player retains its primacy, affirming the agency and freedom of the self, insisting upon its obligation to fairness, offering a remedy for the bondage to which its socially derived perspectives can lead. But the qualification insists that the notion of autonomy is subject to limitations, intimates the reality of obligations that surpass everything that fairness might counsel, unites the normative and ideal with the descriptive and typical, and stresses the importance of the initiative of others for the achievement of our own highest endeavors. Playing by ear is an acknowledgment of the responsiveness that life involves, insisting upon the extent to which our own agency and creativeness are liberated only through suffering what others do. The phrase contends that play is finally liable to correction or interruption, or even suspension, by standards that differ from our own preferences, by events that we have not anticipated, or by the voices of persons who are not participants in our own particular venture. In the end, we are not masters of all we survey, not safely enclosed within the small worlds that we have created for ourselves, and it is precisely for this reason that there is hope for us. It is also true, however, that if we are to hear the voices of others above the sounds of our games, we must remember the dictates of fairness and we must be able to imagine all persons as at least potentially involved in a common endeavor. The justification for imagining them as such is their shared creatureliness, their dependence upon God. Playing by ear can express the way of life of persons who believe they inhabit a world that God has made and into which God comes again to comfort the fallen, heal the sick, reclaim the disobedient. But it is not easy to play by ear. It requires patience and practice and care.

It must be emphasized again, however, that like all other images the figure of the sufferer can be held in unrighteousness. Sometimes intentionally, sometimes without recognizing what they do, persons can employ the image in order to misrepresent their situation either to others or to themselves. A sense of shame or memories of appointments missed can counsel that the best way to avoid encounters with one's own self is to accede to its definition by the claims or needs of someone else. Then the self that is nothing but the victim and plaything of a world it never made can try to salvage a sense of its own worth by understanding its career in terms of suffering. More important, though, are the ways that the image can be used in the service of our own will to power. On the one hand, encouraging others to depend upon us can deprive them of their own opportunities for freedom and maturity until their destinies are consigned irretrievably into our hands: our service enchains others in servitude to us. In the figure of the Grand Inquisitor, Dostoyevski powerfully expresses this perennial danger in the relationship of parent and child. On the other hand, there is no more certain or dangerous remedy for doubts concerning the worth or identity of the self than total identification with communities and causes that are greater than itself. This captivity that the self embraces because of its own inadequacies can sanction acts of violence and fanaticism that could never be legitimated without reference to values that transcend self-interest. The sufferer needs the player as its complement, then, so that self-understanding in terms of suffering does not become one more expression of the self's will to power or merely a disclosure of its frailty and alienation from itself. Images for self-recognition can be used to prevent encounters with ourselves as we really are. Instead of serving as instruments of discovery, they can become vessels of a lie. Yet the images themselves do not adequately express the possibility of their corruption. So they do not equip vision with all that vision requires. Because they can be used to hide or disguise rather than combat some of the corruption that has already penetrated the citadel of the self, they need a complement that can introduce vision to the darkness in creatures who prefer not to recognize themselves. There is more terrain within the self to map, then, and access to it can be found through the exploration of still another sort of suffering.

The self against itself. So much are we the creatures of society that we lose the taste and talent for being in touch with our own selves. We can communicate with the other side of the world in an instant but there is no technology that will perfect the dialogue of the self with itself. Our suffering of ourselves is often no more than a suffering of other people: even the dictates of conscience are socially formed, relating us less to divine law than to conventional expectations. Our intemperate pursuit of status and the services of others, and our inordinate ambitions, provide ways for the self to become still more isolated from itself and from its elemental hungers. Finally, we can employ the imagery developed to represent us to ourselves in order to distort what we have actually been or done, and when the strategy is successful we deceive ourselves to an extent that renders us insensitive to the deception and even further removed from ourselves.

But there is another side to the matter, too, and it affords even greater reason for disquiet. In its suffering of itself, the self encounters much that eludes its comprehension: anxieties that seem to have neither name nor source, a strange exhilaration at the sufferings and tragedies that other people encounter, times of baseless dissatisfaction and unwarranted boredom, a readiness to court disaster for no reason at all, a passion for visiting the scenes of accidents, a relish for hurting others, weird and malignant dreams, and a taste of ashes. There seems to be a maelstrom in the self somewhere, luring, tugging, insatiable. Unless there is an image that can capture the strange tides within us that threaten to erode all the foundations of moral life, all of us are in great jeopardy, for we cannot defend ourselves against whatever we cannot see.

In joining the sufferer with the player, we have achieved a twofold advance. On the one hand, we have found a representation of ourselves as bodily creatures who inhabit an oral-aural as well as a visual world and whose initiative is formed and limited by the initiatives of others. On the other, we have represented the self as at least a potential accomplice in evil and not only as a victim of the evils that befall it from other sources. When it understands itself as a sufferer in relation to causes and powers greater than itself, it can act in cruel and callous ways that no appeals to self-interest could ever justify. In another sense, however, we have not advanced at all, for some of the darkness has its origin within ourselves. Sometimes we cannot master all of the territories and powers within the self. Sometimes what we do is done despite ourselves, even though not only are we ourselves the ones who have done it but, in a strange moment of fever, we may have partly intended to do what we did. The image of the sufferer will serve no better than the figure of the player to bring these problems within the range of our vision. So the pursuit of master images is far from its conclusion. In William Golding's wise and beautiful novel, *The Spire*, the tortured dean of the cathedral, Jocelin, exclaims to an aunt:

> "What is it when one's mind turns to one thing only, and that not the lawful, the ordained thing; but to the unlawful? To brood, and remember half in pleasure, half in a kind of subtle torment—"
> "What thing?"
> "And when they die; for they die, they die; to re-create scenes that never happened to her—"
> "Her?"
> "To see her in every detail outlined against the air of the uncountry—indeed, to be able to see nothing else—"[18]

What is it when one's mind turns? When it turns to one thing only, the unlawful, and half in pleasure? What sort of self is it that is pleased? What sort of self is it that does not attend to the displeased half of the mind? Why does the self prefer illusion to reality? What is there about the truth that renders it too burdensome to bear? Why do we choose to hold in unrighteousness the instruments for its discovery? Part of the answer, at least, lies in the development of an image that will enable us to chart the details of the uncountry, the land in the cellars of the mind.

Chapter Three

EVIL, JUDGMENT AND BEYOND

A child cries in the night and a parent switches on a lamp. The darkness recedes and where the night creatures prowled there is nothing that is not cherished and familiar. The child sleeps again, reassured by the comforting voice and the light and the knowledge that the windows are locked against intruders. But the lamp cannot illuminate the depths of the small self from which the strange creatures of the dark have risen and the paths by which the invaders have entered the room. Someday the child will learn that the world cannot be controlled by a switch and that parental reassurances that there is nothing to fear contain far less than the truth. These lessons no one can evade. It is more difficult, however, to learn about the threats to us that no lamp can ever illuminate, because their habitation is within ourselves. They remain invisible, and it is therefore tempting to believe parental reassurances that they are not there at all. But we must be vigilant, for we can be hurt by what we cannot see, struck down without a chance to defend ourselves or a moment to steel ourselves against the pain. C. G. Jung has frequently attacked contemporary expressions of the Christian tradition. The consistent refrain of his criticism has been that Christian faith often minimizes the strength of all the night creatures abroad in the self and set on its subversion. In *The Undiscovered Self*, for example, he argues that

> Since it is universally believed that man *is* merely what his consciousness knows of itself, he regards himself as harmless and so adds stupidity to iniquity. He does not deny that terrible things have happened and still go on happening, but it is always "the others" who do them. . . . [But] whether the crime lies many generations back or happens today, it remains the symptom of a disposition that is always and everywhere present—and one would therefore do well to possess some "imagination in evil," for only the fool can permanently neglect the conditions of his own nature. In fact, this negligence is the best means of making him an instrument of evil. Harmlessness and naïvete are as little helpful as it would be for a cholera patient and those in his vicinity to remain unconscious of the contagiousness of the disease. On the contrary, they lead to projection of the unrecognized evil into the "other." This strengthens the opponent's position in the most effective way, because the projection carries the *fear* which we involuntarily and secretly feel for our own evil over to the other side and considerably increases the formidableness of his threat. What is even worse, our lack of insight deprives us of *the capacity to deal with evil.* [1]

If Jung misjudges the resources of the Christian vision, he is nonetheless correct to insist that our capacity to deal with the self and its world depends upon the condition of the imagination. We cannot master the invisible; we cannot be vigilant against enemies whom we have not been prepared to recognize. There is no virtue in innocence if it means nothing more than our own failure to acquaint ourselves with our lack of innocence. A remarkable illustration of the power of the invisible occurs in Ralph Ellison's novel, *Invisible Man*, the title of which refers to the situation of a black person in a white world. His plight is not merely that people fail to notice him or pay no attention when they do, but that in some sense he is actually invisible. He does not count as a man because every image of selfhood in the world is white; the eyes that see him do not see him, for they are not prepared to recognize possibilities of humanness that their familiar and colorless images of the self do not include. The first pages of the book tell of an incident that occurs one night when, as the protagonist later recalls it:

> I accidentally bumped into a man, and perhaps because of the near darkness he saw me and called me an insulting name. I sprang at him, seized his coat lapels and demanded that he apologize. He was a tall blond man, and as my face came close to his he looked insolently out of his blue eyes and cursed me, his breath hot in my face as he struggled. I pulled his chin down sharp upon the crown of my head, butting him as I had seen the West Indians do, and I felt his flesh tear and the blood gush out, and I yelled, "Apologize! Apologize!" But he continued to curse and struggle, and I butted him again and again until he went down heavily, on his knees, profusely bleeding. I kicked him repeatedly, in a frenzy because he still uttered insults through his lips that were frothy with blood . . . when it occurred to me that the man had not seen me, actually; that he as far as he knew, was in the midst of a walking nightmare! And I stopped the blade slicing the air as I pushed him away. . . . He lay there, moaning on the asphalt; a man almost killed by a phantom. It unnerved me. Something in this man's thick head had sprung out and beaten him within an inch of his life.[2]

The incident concerns two strangers who meet on a city street, but it is also a representation of the strangeness that lurks within everyone. This is conduct that is "driven" or compulsive, for the assailant is quite "beside himself" in the grip of a "frenzy," caught as much as his victim in "the midst of a walking nightmare." Perhaps if there had been more expansive images of the self, or if they had not all been white, there might have been an end to the insults or an expression

of apology before a man was "almost killed by a phantom."
In any event, the tale can serve as a parable of what occurs
when we fail to cultivate an imagination for evil. If we have
only white images of ourselves, if we therefore possess no
instrument that can render visible the invisible man who hides
within us, we are defenseless against whatever there is in the
thick heads of persons that can spring out and beat them
within an inch of their lives. The poverty of our imagination
will betray us sooner or later: we will be the victims of others
and they, too, may end "moaning on the asphalt" because
something that we did not learn to see in ourselves until it was
too late sprung out and assailed them.

Ellison's use of language is remarkably apt: his references
to nightmares and frenzies and phantoms and the invisible
warn us that, just as it is difficult to see in the dark, it is difficult
to see the darkness in ourselves. It seems strange to refer to
evil as a desideratum of the eye, especially when we are as-
saulted from every quarter by pictures of a violent people and
a violent land. But these are images that remain external to
us: it is always "the others" who are responsible. Some of the
reasons for our blindness have been discussed earlier. First,
the eye presents us with the surfaces of the world but it offers
us few clues to what interiority holds: we see acts but not
motives, consequences but not intentions, and so the eye
cannot easily distinguish between accident and design. Second, there can be no focus unless we are separated from what
we see. The objects that present themselves to our perception
are ranged in an order that leads away from the self, not
toward it: we are left outside the world that we have made,
blameless. Our distance from it means that for the moment
the world is powerless to call us to account. We are free to
involve ourselves if we choose, but the choice is ours: we are
not responsible, merely watching, momentarily interested in
what will happen. Third, it is difficult to see whatever moves
rapidly. We can see the ravages that time enforces upon a
garden that no one tends, of course, or watch the ways of the
years with the little webs of lines that mark the throat of
someone we love. But the eye is not at home with motion; as

it follows shifts and changes it loses contact with what surrounds them, and so their significance is hidden. We have no
context, then, in which to assess how savagely the rhythms of
someone's life are snapped, or how shocking is the suddenness with which evil appears in the form of a random shot or
a slap that begins a surge of anguish too great to be assuaged
by tears. Causal relationships are concealed, and so the eye
cannot fully discern the awful imprevisibility of things or recognize an entirely gratuitous act. Whatever is there is simply
there, and the irrationality and suddenness that can be epiphanies of evil, these are not seen. It is scarcely cause for
surprise, therefore, that when sight becomes a metaphor for
or a paradigm of the self's most important commerce with its
environment, evil tends to go unrecognized, vision must
finally surrender to a nightmare, and the streets of the city
belong to the invisible man.

The problem is all the more complicated because evil is
itself a changeling, protean, insubstantial as mercury, loathe
to announce its presence, thriving on confusion and deceit,
expert at a thousand disguises. Like intimations of the reality
of God in our common life, signs of the presence of evil are
not easy to read; unlike the former, however, they are difficult
to decipher because the principal strategy of evil is to pretend
to be other than it is. It is clothed in lies that represent it as
good or at least necessary, and nowhere are its presence and
power more evident than in our deprivation of categories that
might enable us to recognize it for what it is. Martin Buber has
written that "The lie is the specific evil which man has introduced into nature. All our deeds of violence and our misdeeds
are only as it were a highly-bred development of what this and
that creature of nature is able to achieve in its own way. But
the lie is our very own invention, different in kind from every
deceit that the animals can produce."[3]

The misdeeds that persons commit are many and various,
but each seems to have its own particular aim or goal. The lie
is more primitive, however, for it will serve either any aim or
else no aim at all. When it does the latter, it shows that it does
not love reality, not even in some warped and twisted way, but

seeks simply to damage it, to hurl it back into a vortex of nothingness and reverse the process of creation. Overturning our expectations by its imprevisibility, bewildering conscience by its rationalizations, confounding love and trust by its baselessness, lying is the primordial violation of community. It is not only wrong but a paradigm of evil, for it strikes directly against the context within which right and wrong are significant terms. But if others lie to us, then it is clear that we also have the capacity to lie to others. If some of their lies seem to serve no end at all, then perhaps some of our own are equally purposeless. Surely if we can lie to others, we can lie as others do, sometimes with an end in view but sometimes for no reason at all, only for fun, simply to see what the consequences will be. But what sort of fun is this, and what sort of strange creature is the self that finds its fun in such a way? Moreover, if we can lie to others, it is equally possible that we can lie to ourselves and, insofar as we succeed with some consistency, truth and illusion become so tightly interwoven that we cannot untangle them even when we most desperately need to winnow the kernels of fact from the fictions we have invented. Sometimes, too, it seems that we lie despite our resolve to speak the truth, that the lie has power greater than our own and can reduce us all to a common bondage, that it springs from depths of the person that we cannot ever bring before the light of reason. Not all of the dark has its source in the self's intentionality. So we encounter a problem that eats like acid into all our ventures at rational self-understanding: some small part of what we do, although it is no less significant for being only a minor part, is done either for reasons that elude our comprehension or, perhaps, for no reasons at all. We need to familiarize ourselves with the uncountry and explore all the cellarage there may be beneath the mind, for there is a strange "despite ourselves" sometimes at work dismantling the worlds that we are trying to build. The enemy lies within.

What most of all inhibits the development of an imagination for evil, then, is neither that it is so much a desideratum of the eye nor that it can disguise itself in innumerable ways, but that it takes up its lodging within our vision so that we cannot recognize as such the evils that we do. The crux of the problem is neither the evil visited upon us nor the crimes that we commit, but what lies behind the crimes, the way that evil taints and corrupts our interpretations of our own actions and sufferings. Evil is difficult to see because, long before we have begun our vigilance against it, it has made itself at home in the last place where we would expect to encounter its presence. First, there is the burden of our egocentricity, the assumption that the self is the measure of all things. We are tempted to identify evil with whatever threatens to frustrate the hopes and desires of the individual, forgetting that it appears not in what manages to curb inordinate ambitions and aggressiveness but rather in the self that expresses itself in this fashion. Evil cannot be equated with every intimation of contingency or experience of pain or sign of enervation; nor is it synonymous with the indifference and ingratitude of others or with the frustrations and judgments that we suffer.

Second, there is the problem of our identification with our communities, the assumption that the self writ large is the measure of the world. We see in the same way that the others whom we love have learned to see, each reinforcing for everyone else a shared perspective that becomes ever less amenable to challenge and correction from a different point of vantage. Because our perspectives are socially derived, they afford us very little perspective upon their own sources; so we cannot see with sufficient discrimination to recognize the evils committed by the groups to which we belong or to acknowledge the extent of our own complicity. But every attempt to gain some perspective upon our own perspectives is invariably a hazardous venture, reluctantly begun, for it calls into question all the fundamental relationships from which we have garnered the different images of ourselves that contribute to our sense of personal identity.

Still a third difficulty concerns the phenomenon of projection to which Jung alludes, the assumption that all others are guilty of what the self will not or cannot accept in itself. Frequently the self is unable to deal with its inordinate appetites or unconventional desires, its relish for the misfortunes of others or the pleasure that it derives from some deviant form of behavior. These realities cannot be banished from the world before they have even been faced and addressed, of course, but they can be unconsciously projected upon others, to whom we impute all sorts of exaggerated desires or malicious motives, envy they have never felt or hatreds they have never entertained. The others have their revenge, however, for they become as fearsome to us as whatever it was that we could not confront in ourselves: we transform them into phantoms that terrify us and either paralyze our agency or else elicit from us an exaggerated defensiveness or aggressiveness that it would never be possible to justify if we saw these other people without distortion. In our common evasions of what we are not forced to confront, in our pretending that we did not see what in fact we saw, in our flights from what we do not or do not want to comprehend—in this there is nothing remarkable. But if it is the self with which we refuse to come to terms, it will project its shadow all across the landscape, and then out of the darkness that surrounds us will come daimons and phantoms and other creatures of the night. Jung properly stresses the way in which our views of self and world are correlative: what we cannot acknowledge in the one we transfer to the other, and thereby double the distortions involved in our relationships with actuality.

Finally, there is a warping of our vision that differs significantly from projection because its source is most frequently our sincerity, our sense of integrity, our determination to be found worthy servants of the standards and values that render life worthwhile: self-deception. Our deceptions of ourselves are successful, of course, only insofar as we remain truly ignorant of what we have done. We can maintain our ignorance because we have identified ourselves so firmly and unqualifiedly with a particular narrative or portrait of selfhood that incongruous thoughts or behavior must be rejected as not our own or else drastically reinterpreted. Our self-understanding is not placed in jeopardy by what we actually think or feel or do, because the latter is never regarded except from the perspective of this self-understanding. The maintenance of the self-deception is necessitated by the firmness with which we have identified ourselves with this particular narrative or portrait. A challenge to the self-understanding would prove too grievous and lacerating a burden to bear. The self yields to a lie, then, because there is no other way for it to save itself. Nor does it have the resources ever to recognize what it has done: its actual career is literally unimaginable, for the self is fully persuaded that it would not be itself if it had harbored these feelings or acted in those ways. Stanley Hauerwas comments:

> All men must establish some sense of identity and unity in order to give coherence to the multifariousness of our activities. Identity is the power to spell out and avow a particular aspect of our history as uniquely ours and as constitutive of the self. Our self-deception is a correlate of our need for such unity; we purposefully delude ourselves in order to preserve the central story that insures our identity. We cannot spell out certain engagements for such spelling out would be far too destructive for the kind of avowals we make and believe about who we are. ... What the self-deceiver lacks is not integrity or sincerity but the courage and skill to confront the reality of his situation without self-destruction. Self-deception is therefore a correlate of our trying to exist in this life without a sufficiently substantive and rich story to sustain us in the unavoidable challenges that confront the self.[4]

Evil arises from what is best in us as well as from what is worst, from our capacity to commit ourselves to ends and values beyond the self and our determination to honor our commitments, from our ambition to prove ourselves reliable and consistent and decent. Integrity and sincerity become the accomplices rather than the opponents of lies; evil infects our perspectives precisely because of the strength of our determination to be honorable and useful citizens. Just because of the self's sincere conviction of the integrity of the self that it believes itself to be, it has no way to confront the self that it is despite its beliefs. So evil sometimes captures us through our strengths even more easily than through our frailties. The lies against which we are defenseless are spoken as often by ourselves as by others, and were we not to continue to speak them we would be forced to confront the possibility of what would appear to be irremediable alienation from ourselves.

The first requisite of an imagination for evil, therefore, is recognition of the evil that informs our own perspectives because of our individual selfishness and communal self-interest, our processes of projection and various self-deceptions. All of these, together with the inherent incapacity of the eye and the lies in which evil clothes itself, render the task of discrimination not only more difficult but also far more urgent. If evil has infiltrated our perspectives, then it will certainly express itself in our feelings and actions. So it is necessary to recognize that the self is not innocent, not only the victim of others; it is the origin and inventor of evils of its own. Some of its crimes are intentional and calculated, some may go unremarked because they are related to projections and essays in self-deception, and perhaps some are best described as instances of driven or compulsive behavior. The image of the self as sufferer can express the various ways in which persons enter into complicity with the darkness in consequence of their social relationships and the perspectives that these establish, but it serves no better than the figure of the player to represent the self as the initiator of new evils. Hauerwas writes that "the stories that produce true lives are those that provide the skills to step back and survey the limits of our engagements."5 The problem is twofold: imagination must not only enable us to step back and survey whatever there is that can threaten the self from within, it must also enable us to see in such a fashion that the encounter will not be irremediably destructive of our sense of selfhood. In other words, we will have no option *except* to lie to ourselves if the poverty of our imagination dictates terms of admission for some potential or actual truths about ourselves that preclude the incorporation of these threatening possibilities into greater patterns of experience that are positively, even though not perfectly, good. It will not suffice, therefore, to find an adequate image of the invisible man. We shall not cure the diseases that afflict the self until we acknowledge their presence, certainly, but the acknowledgment itself furnishes no sufficient remedy. In the end, of what use is it to recognize the evils of the self and its liability to judgment unless we also know more than this and can see to the far side of judgment?

Neither the figure of the player nor the image of the sufferer can express the bondage of the self to its own selfishness and to the daimons that its projections have unleashed, or the extent of a self-deception that is a correlate of the intensity of its ambitions to be a moral self, or the certain relish with which it hears of the illnesses and accidents that others encounter. So these images can always be held in unrighteousness, sustaining and reinforcing the self's deceptions of itself, and the problem is all the greater because the images themselves do not point toward this possibility or warn the self to be vigilant against it. There is a sense in which the image of the player counsels us to regard the world as though it were a rational cosmos, and in the light of the eye's incapacity to deal with evil this is scarcely reason for surprise. The counsel must not be confused with the assumption of basic trust, on which not only play but also all other significant human endeavors depend. Basic trust involves neither great optimism nor a reluctance to face the ambiguities and perplexities of life. It simply expresses the taste for the self and the world that the exercise of human agency presupposes, and the recognition that days of darkness and trial can foster as much creativeness and strength as days of ease. Consequently, basic trust encourages familiarity with the untrustworthiness of the self, for even if such encounters are not entirely therapeutic, the knowledge they afford is better preparation for the future than innocence would be.

On the other hand, the figure of the player can appear to represent the world as a rational cosmos in the sense that it does not portray the individual as someone who spoils his play because he is not in command of himself, resists the penalties on which the continuation of the game depends, and refuses to accept rules and limits even when he understands their relation to his own fulfillment. The image can fail to challenge the self to explore the shadowed lands within itself and, because it does not prompt new voyages of discovery into the uncountry, it can inhibit acknowledgments of disorder that hold possibilities for bringing comprehension to a new level. Lack of acquaintance with apparent disorder can consign us to operate with superficial notions of coherence and to remain ignorant of the magnitude of the abyss between some aspects of life and our formalization of self and world under the rubric of play. More importantly, it can deprive us of opportunities actually to experience the way in which instances of disorder can be incorporated into greater complexes of experience that are finally constructive for selfhood, even though the immediate consequences of the disorderliness or evil cannot be expunged. Even disorder argues for order, in the sense that it challenges the individual to bring his interpretations of experience to richer and more discriminating intelligibility.

The admonition to play fair, everywhere and always, will have little effect upon human affairs if there is in the self something that does not will to be fair and that marches to the cadence of a very different drummer. Whatever effect it will have depends upon the extent to which the imagination can grasp the self's taste for deviance and place it concretely before the light of consciousness so that the self can be watchful of itself. The representation of the self as player, at least by implication, can appear to resolve too quickly the question of whether or not there is in human nature an impulse to violate order not for the sake of any particular end but simply for the pleasure of the violation, for no purpose except that it is exhilarating to wound and maim and destroy. It affords no resources to comprehend subterranean currents within the self that run counter to its conscious choices, that divert it from what it intended to do, that court death instead of affirming life, and that encourage risks that threaten ruin for the self or its companions. Persons are sufferers and players, but part of the domains of selfhood belongs to the uncountry that resists every essay in rational self-understanding; so these

images require a complement that does not rely upon a particular sense as a paradigm of human action but that can probe
the subconscious dimensions of selfhood and emphasize with
as much clarity as possible that neither do we live in a rational
cosmos nor can we ever afford to act toward ourselves as
though we were rational creatures and nothing else. Again,
we encounter a twofold problem: we need imagery that can
represent the intentionality of a self that is drawn toward evil
as well as toward good, and at the same time the imagery must
open to the individual whatever dimensions of selfhood there
are that intentionality never marshals.

But what do we mean when we speak of evil? The course
of the argument can now be clarified by some rough distinctions that it will be necessary to refine at a later juncture. Evil
is usually regarded as divisible into natural and moral evil.
The former includes retardation and illness and senility,
acute hunger and thirst, droughts and earthquakes, and a
variety of other phenomena that occur independently of persons' agency. Moral evil refers to what we originate; it applies
to human intentions and actions that are cruel or unjust, and
it is restricted to the realm in which it is possible to speak of
right and wrong. Although the distinction between what persons do and what is done to them by powers other than their
own is important, it cannot be inflexibly maintained: often
human failures contribute to the magnitude of some natural
disaster, while it is also true that acute discomfort or illness
is a factor in, even if not a sufficient explanation of, much
wrong or deviant behavior. Together, the two forms of evil
can be described as everything that inhibits the fulfillment of
human nature.

From a Christian perspective, on the other hand, this definition is not entirely adequate; theologically construed, evil is
synonymous with whatever tends to oppose God's purposes
in and for his world. Consequently, while wrong intentions
and actions are instances of moral evil, there is reason not to
restrict the latter to the former. One of the characters in
Graham Greene's novel, *Brighton Rock,* is a self-appointed
representative of right and wrong whose name is Ada Arnold.

In the course of her eventually successful attempt to avenge a murder that has been committed by a squalid boy named Pinkie, she tries to convince Pinkie's mistress, Rose, that the girl should betray her lover in order to save herself:

> "I know one thing you don't. I know the difference between Right and Wrong. They didn't teach you *that* at school."
> Rose didn't answer; the woman was quite right; the two words meant nothing to her. Their taste was extinguished by stronger foods—Good and Evil. The woman could tell her nothing that she didn't know about these —she knew by tests as clear as mathematics that Pinkie was evil—what did it matter in that case whether he was right or wrong?[6]

It matters very much, of course, but it is not everything that matters. The Christian tradition argues that all persons are sinners: all have made themselves the centers of their own lives rather than finding the center and focus of life in God. While this claim is not intended to minimize the importance of the distinction between right and wrong, it does emphasize that sin and evil encompass something more and something different than simply opposition to the dictates of morality. So Kierkegaard, for example, writes of the "teleological suspension of the ethical" in his interpretation of the story of Abraham and Isaac, intending to show that right intentions and actions are not necessarily the whole sum of fidelity to the purposes of God.[7] In the same way, a Christian perspective demands a revision of our understanding of natural evils, for the biblical narrative often claims to find the hand of God present in all sorts of natural disasters, the purpose of which is to recall the chosen people to righteousness and love in order that they might find eventual fulfillment in relation to God. The suffering proves redemptive, and so it is not accurate to represent the affair simply as an instance of natural evil. Furthermore, Christian faith is an eschatological vision, anticipating a consummation of the historical process that lies far beyond the modest fulfillments that are all the world as we know it can provide, and this perspective illuminates new aspects of our present careers. Experiences that are entirely unwelcome might yet prove good insofar as we manage to respond to them in ways that finally contribute to the realization of the kingdom of God.

It is equally true, of course, that experiences we welcome, rewards we deserve, and recognitions we merit can all prove thoroughly ambiguous goods if they divert our attention from its focus upon God's ultimate design. Wrong actions remain always wrong and their immediate consequences remain inexpugnable, but insofar as they occasion penitence or reform, or elicit judgments that have redemptive consequences, they can be incorporated into more inclusive patterns that are good and that contribute to the realization of God's purposes for the created world. An adequate imagination for evil, therefore, is not one that isolates it from the familiar detail or messiness of our life together, creating pictures that can obsess and terrify us because they are nominalist particulars unrelated to anything else at all, but a capacity to recognize it both in its contravention of and potential ingredience in the purposes of God.

The figure of the sufferer satisfactorily represents the self as subject to natural evils in all of their bewildering variety and as an accomplice in the commission of certain moral evils. Our present concern, however, is with the self as the initiator of evil and as the author of some specific forms of evil that are particularly difficult to understand. First, some of the evil that we do is committed intentionally and some of it is not. Intention denotes a choice or determination to act in a certain way: to cross a street or visit a friend or discipline an unruly child. Intentional action is not synonymous with purposive behavior: animals of all sorts can be said to have purposes but, because the concept of intention involves reflection and choice, it is applicable only to self-conscious creatures who are able to characterize their own activities. Furthermore, intentional action is not always purposive in the sense that it is oriented toward an end or goal; walking, for example, is an intentional act that frequently has no end or aim outside the action itself. Sometimes, then, it is our intention to deal unfairly with other people, but sometimes we are unjust simply because we cannot escape the habit of our selfishness or are lacking in foresight or are more than usually insensitive to what others require. In both cases, of course, the conduct is wrong. Our ability to label some actions right and others wrong does not depend upon our knowledge of the intentions of the agent. Evil can be committed unintentionally as well as intentionally, but it is the latter, of course, that raises the greater problems for self-understanding.

Second, some intentional action is motivated and some is without a motive. In this context, we shall restrict the idea of motivation to designate the reason, in the sense of aim or goal, for the choice or determination to act in a certain way.[8] As we have mentioned, not all of our intentional action can be described as purposive, as though there were an end that it sought to achieve. Consequently, sometimes when we are asked to account for our behavior we find ourselves quite unable to respond. Perhaps we find our actual motive too shameful to acknowledge or perhaps we have simply grown unreflective about our conduct. Often, however, the question seems entirely inappropriate, and it is best answered by insistence that we had no reason in mind or end in view. It would be puzzling, for example, if someone were to inquire about our motive for acting with kindness toward a small child. Sometimes we respond to questions about motivation by claiming that we behaved as we did simply for fun, just because we derived some pleasure from the act. It is doubtful whether a reference to fun or pleasure is actually a specification of motive, but in any event it sometimes raises more profound questions than it can ever answer: why is it that the self derives pleasure from acts of moral evil? What sort of creature is the self if it finds its fun in acts of deviance? We confront the possibility, then, that there can be acts of moral evil for which there are motives and similar acts for which we can specify no motives at all. The latter constitute one of the two foci of these explorations: evil that is the effect of unmotivated intentionality, that is committed deliberately and simply for fun.

Third, it is possible to distinguish between some unintentional conduct that can properly be termed accidental and other actions that, while not intentional, can scarcely be characterized as accidents: they are better understood as instances of compulsive behavior. If I stumble and, in attempting to regain my balance, knock someone else to the ground, it is appropriate to state that I am sorry but the incident was an accident: I am not culpable, at least not as I would be if I had intended what happened. To claim that I acted compulsively, however, implies something very different: I was gripped by an irresistible impulse, driven to some course of action that was out of character, irrational, against my better judgment, and done despite myself. I and yet not I: it was I who acted but I was not in command of myself. So hatred runs like fever through the veins of a crowd and persons are carried away with the mob, all of them in the grip of something stronger than themselves. In the confession that I do not know what came over me, I imply that in some sense I was not entirely responsible and yet I acknowledge a greater degree of responsibility than in the instance of behavior that I insist was merely accidental. So the shoplifter, for example, can claim that he had no reason to steal and did not in fact intend to steal but was overwhelmed by an impulse that he could not resist. It would not be appropriate to impute intentionality in this instance, perhaps, but neither could the conduct ever be characterized as an accident. Nor would it be possible satisfactorily to describe the behavior as atavistic, as though kleptomania were something that persons share with certain birds and animals but which can be remedied by more adequate socialization.

This is the second of our foci, then: acts of moral evil that the perpetrator may well deplore, that cannot readily be characterized as intentional behavior, and that persons do despite themselves—evil as the effect of drivenness or compulsion rather than of choice, as the apparent consequence of living with an invisible man who remains a stranger to oneself. The reason for particular attention to intentional actions for which no motives can be found and to instances of apparently driven or compulsive behavior is that in such conduct the narrative of selfhood loses its rationality and falls to pieces. It matters very little whether certain behavior is actually compulsive or whether we merely believe that it is, for if the belief is serious it has all the force of a compulsion, and so in either case the rational narrative of selfhood is disturbed—so great is the power that our self-deceptions hold over us. There are few mysteries in moral evil for which motives can be specified or in the evil consequences of accidental happenings. But it is different if there is a relish for destruction within the self that demands no motive for its expression, or if the self finds its household is built on treacherous ground that will not hold firm because of subterranean currents that begin to erode foundations as soon as they are laid. Further attention needs to be given to the meanings of motive and intention and compulsion, but for the moment these rough distinctions point us in the direction we must go. Self-recognition will be partial and distorted if the imagination cannot provide us with a master image that represents the self as "a dreadful eruption from an unknown world"[9] and as the origin of evil not for the sake of selfish ends but simply for the pleasure of the act.

But the initial problem remains: the night watch upon the self will finally succumb to inanition unless people can hope for more than the sort of clarity of sight that leads only to a shared conviction of "the melancholy of the common condition and the despair of not being able to escape it."[10] Familiarity with evil wearies and eventually anesthetizes the self, eroding its sensitivity, blunting its powers of discrimination, persuading it of its inability to ameliorate its situation. Unless we have images that tell of the triumph of good over evil and show ways in which instances of evil can be incorporated constructively into larger complexes of experience, persons will never be able to confront themselves without flinching when the world seems in its evening and shadows fall across once familiar lands within themselves that assume strange and monstrous shapes in the twilight. We must have images of the guilty self as forgiven as well as judged. Forgiveness is far removed from the willingness to condone anything at all;

indeed, it is meaningless except in the context of the judgment that it must invariably presuppose. There is no reason to forgive if nothing is judged wrong. But judgment holds no creative possibilities for the self if it brings the conviction of guilt without offering hope of release from it. Judgment can teach me not to repeat whatever I have done, but in itself it condemns me to remain guilty forever. Punishment does nothing to wipe away guilt. Judgment can inspire remorse or anguish for an act and its inevitable consequences, and these can contribute to self-recognition, but the bite of remorse has to do with the foreclosure of possibilities. I am locked in my past, a prisoner of irreversibility; the future is gone. Hannah Arendt wisely comments: "Without being forgiven, released from the consequences of what we have done, our capacity to act would, as it were, be confined to one single deed from which we could never recover; we would remain the victims of its consequences forever, not unlike the sorcerer's apprentice who lacked the magic formula to break the spell."[11] Repentance is unlike remorse, however, for it is a denial of irreversibility and a determination to effect something new, a hope for reconciliations that will add a richer dimension to ruptured relationships. But we can do nothing more than dream of the possibility of repentance unless imagination leads us beyond the present tangle of guilt, judgment, and punishment.

What happens when acquaintance with evil transforms it into a nominalist particular, unrelated to anything else, that fattens until it occupies the whole field of vision, is an insistent refrain in the studies of justice that inform each of Albert Camus' three novels. In *The Plague*, Tarrou tells of an occasion when he accompanied his father to court and listened to him, the prosecuting attorney, argue that the prisoner in the dock, who "looked like a yellow owl scared blind by too much light,"[12] should be condemned to die. Henceforth, he knows the extent to which the structures of his society are structures of destruction and the ways that conventional notions of justice become the accomplices of crime. So, Tarrou continues, "My real interest in life was the death penalty; I wanted to square accounts with that poor blind owl in the dock. So I became an agitator, as they say. I didn't want to be pestiferous, that's all. To my mind the social order around me was based on the death sentence, and by fighting the established order I'd be fighting against murder. That was my view."[13]

Later, however, he recognizes his own involvement with murder, for his political activities eventuate in many new deaths: the death penalty employs even the struggle against itself for its own ends. Tarrou comes to understand that the problem lies not in a particular social structure but in the nature that all persons share, and the destructive potentialities of that nature will appear in whatever structures people contrive for their own governance. Tarrou has seen the visage of evil in human affairs and he is unmanned precisely by the sincerity and integrity with which he intends to live in accordance with what he has recognized. He is a man of conscience and compassion, but he suffers from an impoverishment or defect of imagination that inhibits his participation in the ambiguous mix of good and evil that constitutes the human situation. He cannot see beyond the evil, and so what recourse can he find except to retreat from every structure and order, because all of them are infected by their authors' common taint? The evil that expresses itself in the death penalty has deprived him of the ability to discriminate between different sorts of death or to weigh lesser against greater evils. So he tells his friend, Rieux, that:

> I resolved to have no truck with anything which, directly or indirectly, for good reasons or for bad, brings death to anyone or justifies others putting him to death. That, too, is why this epidemic has taught me nothing new . . . it's a wearying business, being plague-stricken. But it's still more wearying to refuse to be it. That's why everybody in the world today looks so tired; everyone is more or less sick of plague. But that is also why some of us, those who want to get the plague out of their systems, feel such desperate weariness, a weariness from which nothing remains to set us free except death. Pending that release, I know I have no place in the world of today; once I'd definitely refused to kill, I doomed myself to an exile that can never end.[14]

Tarrou confesses to Rieux that his ambition is to become a saint in a world without God, a world where combat against evil is not only most often futile but where even commitment to the struggle irremediably taints the self with the character of its adversary. Imagination is too weary to see evil in perspective. So there is nothing to hope for and, for Tarrou, nothing but exile.

In Camus' last novel, *The Fall*, Jean-Baptiste Clamence wants to play god in a world without saints. Like Tarrou, he acknowledges his own and everyone's involvement with evil, but he does so in a way that allows him to escape the guilt and judgment that Tarrou accepts. In a cupboard in his squalid room, Clamence has a panel titled "The Just Judges" that has been stolen from the van Eyck altarpiece of the cathedral at Ghent. The painting portrays judges on horseback journeying to worship the new-born Jesus. Its importance for Clamence has nothing to do with its value, but simply with the fact that it languishes in a tenement in Amsterdam while its companion panels remain in Ghent. Consequently, "everything is in harmony. Justice being definitively separated from innocence—the latter on the cross and the former in the cupboard—I have the way clear to work according to my convictions. With a clear conscience I can practice the difficult profession of judge-penitent."[15] Tarrou knew as much as Clamence about all the realities that are "definitively separated from innocence." The latter, however, who was a very eminent lawyer before his enlightenment, uses his knowledge for different ends. The vocation of judge-penitent is really not as difficult as Clamence suggests. It consists of nothing but a recital of the various crimes and vanities for which the self is accountable, an endless confession of the ways that the self has postured and pretended, and once even believed sincerely all the lies that it told itself about itself. Yet in this narrative there is no trace of penitence and perhaps not even of remorse. There is only a terrible caricature of the penitent, as Clamence announces:

> Inasmuch as every judge some day ends up as a penitent, one had to travel the road in the opposite direction and

practice the profession of penitent to be able to end up
as a judge. You follow me? . . . . I adapt my words to my
listener and lead him to go me one better. I mingle what
concerns me and what concerns others. I choose the
features we have in common. . . . Then imperceptibly I
pass from the "I" to the "we." When I get to "This is
what we are," the trick has been played and I can tell
them off. I am like them, to be sure; we are in the soup
together. However, I have a superiority in that I know it
and this gives me the right to speak. You see the advan-
tage.[16]

Clamence exposes himself as culpable and liable to judgment in order to escape judgment: he confesses his coarse
and vicious ways precisely so that he need never change them.
He is a sort of voyeur who watches with obscene relish as
others are tutored to recognize themselves in him. In his own
fashion finally an invisible man, Clamence acknowledges no
need for the forgiveness of which he must despair in any
event, because of the strategy that he has devised to exempt
himself from judgment upon the evil that he has done. But the
price of his posture as a small god is that Clamence must
always bear the burden of "the melancholy of the common
condition and the despair of not being able to escape it." Like
Tarrou, he lives on the far side of innocence, and that is good.
But for both of them the vision of evil has enforced a measure
of paralysis and exile because they could not see beyond it.
    The career of Jean-Baptiste Clamence is a fine illustration
of the fact that acquaintance with the truth about the self is
not necessarily therapeutic, and that imagery for self-recognition can be used for quite different purposes. Like the representation of the self as sufferer, an image that expresses the
invisible man can be held in unrighteousness, so that it
becomes a legitimation of new evils. Because I can see the
deviance in myself, I am persuaded to live as though it were
the whole story about myself. The acknowledgment of the
justice of the judgments rendered against me can itself become my ultimate defense against submission to them, for it
can strengthen my resolve to defy authority. The problem,

therefore, concerns more than the discovery of an image that can clarify our vision, for the image itself can still be employed in ways that deprive the self of a genuine future. How is it possible to avoid an infinite regress, then, in which every image of selfhood requires still another because of the ways in which each can be used in the service of the darkness that lies within the self? There is no answer to the question unless forgiveness is possible. If it is not, judgment teaches no lesson except that there are grounds for cynicism about the self and everyone else; the situation is irreversible and it is best for the self to cling to its self-deceptions, for there is no way for the imagination to find the resources to sustain persons in the time of their loss of illusions about themselves. The question of whether forgiveness is possible, whether we can find the courage to accept it if others have the grace to offer it, is the crux of the problem of self-deception. If we can hope for it, then guilt and judgment are never, or at least not necessarily, the last words, although they are no less serious because of that. Now judgment is qualified by a context in which it appears as potentially a means of access to new possibilities and not merely as a cancellation of the old.

It is dangerous, of course, to argue that the consequences of evil can be incorporated into a greater complex of experience that is positively though never entirely good. The contention can breed all sorts of insensitivity toward one's own actions, or to the depths of the anguish of someone else, or to the decisive significance of what is done in this moment for how a child will understand himself in the future. Nothing must be allowed to obscure the unrepeatable importance of time present, or the fact that the effects of evil cannot be annulled or revoked, or the complete irrelevance of the idea of future compensation in relation to a present time of agony or fear. On the other hand, sudden deprivation can cleanse a swollen and clotted self and hone again the blunted edge of its responsiveness. Some instances of evil can be interpreted as deserved judgment, and the acknowledgment can have redemptive consequences. When reconciliation bridges a chasm that ugliness or betrayal has opened, the new relationship has richer dimensions than it previously possessed. So not only can evil be made to serve ends other than its own; human relationships can be all the more rewarding because they have managed to include and transcend the darkness that threatened to rupture them beyond repair. But these and endless other possibilities exist only when self-deceptions do not preclude the admission of guilt—because we trust there is hope for forgiveness—and when judgments do not deprive the self of futurity—because they incorporate the possibility of forgiveness.

From a Christian perspective, the relationship between God and his creatures is essentially one of judgment and forgiveness, and it is by way of the latter that evils are included in larger and finally redemptive designs. Because forgiveness is often discussed in a theological context, however, it is sometimes forgotten that it is the precondition of all recurrent interaction among persons, simply indispensable if life is to go on at all. Hannah Arendt correctly comments that "trespassing is an everyday occurrence which is in the very nature of action's constant establishment of new relationships within a web of relations, and it needs forgiving, dismissing, in order to make it possible for life to go on by constantly releasing men from what they have done unknowingly. Only through this constant mutual release from what they do can men remain free agents."[17] Evils must be incorporated into greater patterns that are good because, in the end, there is nothing else to do; we must forgive and be forgiven because otherwise we have neither freedom nor future. We cannot do less and preserve life in community.

But there is no forgiveness in the different lands of the spirit that Tarrou and Clamence inhabit; as the latter says, "I deny the good intention, the respectable mistake, the indiscretion, the extenuating circumstance. With me there is no giving of absolution."[18] But at least they know the taste of guilt and the reality of judgment, even though Clamence spends his days trying to circumvent it, and without this acquaintance there is no hope whatsoever for understanding what forgiveness means. Forgiveness has nothing to do with the determination to ignore or forget an offense. On the contrary, it demands intense awareness of what has been done, awareness what has happened constitutes a real violation of things, and therefore a recognition that it is necessary to speak of responsibility, guilt, and fault. Consequently, it has no particular relationship to the remission or cessation of punishment; often love constrains parents to punish a child to whom forgiveness is quickly offered, in order that the small person might understand the meaning of responsibility and learn that this is not a world without consequences.

The greatest cruelty of permissiveness is its failure to teach the involution of judgment and forgiveness, thereby offering no wisdom to those who need it most, while diminishing responsibility to the routine of condoning anything at all, an attitude that is scarcely distinguishable from either cynicism or indifference. It is not easy either to accept or to offer forgiveness, for each calls for an imaginative reenactment of the original situation that becomes more arduous in proportion to the magnitude and gratuitousness of the offense: the wound must be opened again to stop the abscess. Now, long after the passion fueled and the excuse provided by the moment, after we have been forced to lay aside the rationalizations and lies that we used to cloak the deed, perhaps after we have been constrained to see how self-deceived we were about ourselves, after anger and relish have congealed into a cold little thread of shame—now is the worst possible time for remembering, for living it all again. Nor is there necessarily less anguish for the other self, this more innocent or righteous child or parent or friend, all unprepared for the ugliness in us and now forced to reenact it in imagination, and to do this not for the savor of resentment but for our own sake. Both the forgiver and the forgiven must look backward, although not backward only, if they are to understand the significance of what is now offered and accepted. The price of forgiveness, then, seems to demand that the victim must suffer two times instead of once, and so, for those who recognize their guilt and accountability, it is far more difficult to be pardoned than merely judged—and that is part of the judgment, too. Frequently an offender cannot recognize the magnitude of what he has done until he sees how great the cost of forgiveness has been.

It is difficult to see the self except in its functions and roles and sometimes it is difficult to believe that it is more than these; but when I accept the justice of the judgment against me that the offer of forgiveness presupposes, the judgment anchors me in a particular time and place and in a particular complex of relationships that cannot be reduced entirely to performing functions and playing roles. In the acknowledgment that I am culpable, at fault, guilty, I establish once again contact with the "I" that has proven so elusive and, because the judgment is bound up with forgiveness, I have good reason to labor at the transformation of the self. The offer of pardon teaches me to live gratefully and to display gratitude, for it comes as a surprise that I have no right to expect and do not deserve. It teaches me that my perspective is partial and flawed, because sometimes I have been offered forgiveness when I saw no need for it, and sometimes when I believed there was no hope of it. The judgment that it enshrines teaches me anew the most difficult lesson there is to understand, that someone else is real, that I can properly be assessed from perspectives other and more ample than my own, that I confront real otherness in the world and not merely endless reflections of myself.[19]

Most important, forgiveness teaches that others care for me, and so it enables me to care again or more deeply for myself. Now I can confront my own flawed character, not with complacency but at least resolved that the burden of it will not prove insupportable, for there is security in the knowledge that others have seen what I now see and have not turned away from me forever. The caring of others provides a motive for striving once more to be faithful to the self-images that I suddenly betrayed, so that I am no longer tempted by a negative choice of identity—as in the instance of Clamence, who repudiates the attempt to acquit the innocent in order to assert that innocence is a lie, abandoning the attempt to find redress for victims in order to victimize everyone who falls into his hands.

The experience of pardon is the apogee of what the self can suffer: there is no more liberating word in all the world than the "you may" that forgiveness contains. The self finds a new measure of courage to accept risks and to participate in the ambiguities of life, for there is no longer reason to despair of understanding and empathetic regard by associates or friends. So the self can identify itself with images that represent fidelity to the most exigent values and rigorous standards, confident that the firmness of such identification carries no danger that admissions of failure will prove too lacerating to be endured. The experience of pardon recalls the self to the precincts of fair play from which it had believed itself self-exiled, renewing its agency and rekindling its sense of accountability, so that the judgment contained in forgiveness becomes a specification of new possibilities rather than a destructive and terminal event.

The act of forgiveness is an unconditional *Yes*. It affirms the self as self, as player when it is unfair, as sufferer when it is disobedient, as free when it believes itself bound, as a whole even when it must wrestle with the uncountry of the cellarage of the mind. First, forgiveness cannot be qualified without losing its essential character. It does not say "just this once," or "if you never do it again," or "if you say that you are sorry," or "if you will buy me another." It affirms the self *absolutely,* with no reservations. Second, it affirms the *self* absolutely; its ultimate reference is not to the deed but to the person, the *who* rather than the *what.* It does not minimize or ignore what has occurred, else there would be no need for a word of forgiveness at all: it insists that the self is accountable and that its actions were real violations of the order that life together requires. But it also affirms that the worth of the self is not a function of its achievements or services. Because the self *is,* the self is valuable: its worthiness is the function of its existence. Forgiveness reaches beneath the roles that people play and the services that they perform to affirm the source of all they think and do, the "I" that is partly expressed and partly concealed in playing and suffering and in all the varieties of deviance.

Third, the gesture of forgiveness brings its author farther than can anything else from the confines of selfishness. Unconditional affirmations of others through pardoning them are significant because the other is affirmed in his distinctness from one's own self; it is not the relationship between us that provides a sufficient reason for the act. On the contrary, it is all the more difficult to grant forgiveness when we are intimately related to the one who stands in need of it. Precisely because we have so much cherished and depended upon the relationship, because it has been so much the focus of our existence, because our sense of identity has been so richly bound up with it, we find it painful almost beyond endurance to forgive this yesterday beloved self who has betrayed and violated the bond. The demand that we do so elicits a degree of selflessness far greater than can any commerce with strangers, promotes greater anguish than transactions with less familiar persons can breed, and requires greater liberation from our egocentricity if we are to accomplish it.

Fourth, as the most profound affirmation of other selves that it is possible to express, forgiveness is the foundation for the most significant creativity that persons can ever achieve, creativity that is not technological or aesthetic but directed toward human relationships: the work of reconciliation.[20] While love can find a way through barriers that persons are ready to surrender, the process of reconciliation can conquer even the barricades that persons are ready to defend. There is a sense in which reconciliation reaps even a richer harvest than love can gather, for it means that what has fallen apart is brought together again, so that persons who were each divested of individual possibilities by the rupture, as well as deprived of additional possibilities that the relationship itself afforded, now gain much more than they originally possessed. Reconciliation restores their old options but it offers new ones, too, for the relationship has gained an additional dimension precisely because of its restoration: nowhere else is there so fully manifest the meaning of the incorporation of evil into greater designs that eventually contribute to the enrichment of the world. Love can actualize possibilities that lovelessness will never see, but reconciliation can plant completely new possibilities in fields that had been wasteland and bring them to maturity. Forgiveness is the beginning of reconciliation, and nowhere do we more fully escape the clutches of our own selfishness than in instances where the estranged relationship was one of particular intimacy, so that its disruption threatened to undermine the self's sense of its own identity. Finally, it is certainly not accidental that in the unconditional affirmation of persons by a word of pardon, we see once again that the fundamental form of the personal is "you and I" and not the self alone: there is no life except life together. Forgiveness depends

> on plurality, on the presence and acting of others, for no one can forgive himself and no one can feel bound by a promise made only to himself; forgiving and promising enacted in solitude or isolation remain without reality and can signify no more than a role played before one's self . . . here, as in action and speech generally, we are dependent upon others, to whom we appear in a distinctness which we ourselves are unable to perceive. Closed within ourselves, we would never be able to forgive ourselves any failing or transgression because we would lack the experience of the person for the sake of whom one can forgive.[21]

In the beginning, the unit is the mother and child. Later, it is the self and its neighbor. Then, perhaps, selves learn that they have no means of access to God if they turn away from the fellow creatures who stand at their side. In times of crisis, when persons thirst for forgiveness and release from the burden of the past, they must appeal to others because they cannot forgive themselves. The physical, moral, and spiritual dimensions of life all testify that the primordial unit of personal existence is not the individual but "you and I": life is suffering, mutuality, responsiveness.

We reach a conclusion, then, that initially seems cause for

surprise: it is submission to judgment—as judgment is presupposed in offering and receiving forgiveness—that is an
essential element in the highest expressions of human creativeness. Yet this should not be surprising, for it is simply a
further illustration of the dialectic of liberty and limits that is
expressed by the images of the player and the sufferer. Rules
and orders and penalties for their violation are essential to
creativity because they render our freedom specific and concrete. It is the judgment rendered against the self that invests
with meaning the final and unconditional affirmation of the
self in the free word of forgiveness. It is by acceptance of the
judgment that forgiveness involves that the self can acknowledge the otherness of other people and emerge from the
shadows that its selfishness has cast across the landscape.
Submission to judgment and acceptance of forgiveness provide reasons for penitence and the attempt to transform the
self into more than it has ever been before. The acceptance
of judgment is the cornerstone of the building of reconciliation; the flight from judgment deprives the self of a range of
possibilities to which it has no other means of access. Forgiveness looks retrospectively toward judgment and prospectively
toward reconciliation, and this is the dynamic of the most
significant human creativity. Judgment cannot be understood
as humanly significant apart from forgiveness, while forgiveness is meaningless apart from judgment. The evil that hides
within the self demands the latter, but it cannot be overcome
without the former—indeed, life cannot go on at all.

The original definition of the quest for imagery for self-
recognition now seems to have proven unsatisfactory. The
search for an image of the culpable self—origin of evil as well
as its accomplice, liable to radical judgment because of the
possibility that it is the author of intentional but unmotivated
evil, and all the more dangerous if it is the source of unintentional evil that is compulsive or driven—seems to point
toward still another search. On the one hand, as in the instance
of Clamence, an image of the culpable self can be held in
unrighteousness and used in ways that strike at the heart of
human community instead of contributing to its health. On

the other, if evil is seen in isolation from good, or if judgment is divorced from forgiveness so that it becomes a terminal event, then guilt and judgment and punishment themselves become nominalist particulars that can preoccupy and terrify people until they are deprived of all power and hope and are left with nothing except a sense of the irremediable melancholy of their condition. The need for judgment raises the question of the possibility of pardon: if the image of the self as origin of evil is to be used as an instrument of humanization rather than as a warning of the irrevocable foreclosure of the human, then, as we have seen, it is necessary to speak of more than judgment. The quest for master images of the self, therefore, now appears to demand two images to complement the figures of the player and the sufferer instead of one: the first of the culpable self and the second of the self as forgiven and once again unconditionally affirmed, one image that represents the evil in the self and another that captures the possibility of the inclusion of the evil within a greater good.

Actually, however, this is not what we need at all. Forgiveness is always more than one can expect and, of course, more than one's actions deserve; it is a small miracle, giving birth to something new because it is a reaction that is not only a reaction but also an interruption of the constant process of reactions in human affairs. In the passage from judgment through forgiveness and the transformation of the self and reconciliation there is no necessary and ineluctable logic; instead, there are drama and imprevisibility, incongruence and asymmetry between the beginning and the end. The complexity of this process and the human freedom that it discloses can scarcely be grasped by way of the juxtaposition of images that do not in themselves express the drama and irony of our temporality. We need more than we shall find in an image that represents the invisible man, certainly, but what is necessary cannot be found within the domain of images at all. The player, the sufferer, and the figure for which we are searching must eventually be furnished lodging within a narrative or story. Stories as well as images are necessary for self-recognition and, because of their form and not only because of their content, they can express the unconditional affirmation of the self that forgiveness involves as well as afford new perspectives upon evils that once threatened to occupy all our field of vision. But the search for a story must await the discovery of a third master image that is as familiar as the children who live next door and yet adequate to expose our relish for destruction.

Chapter Four

THE IMAGE OF THE SELF AS VANDAL

In *Lord of the Flies,* William Golding charts the uncountry of a Pacific island inhabited by a pack of marooned boys and a pack of wild pigs. Some of the children, led by Ralph and Piggy, tend the fire that is meant to serve as a beacon for a rescue ship; the others, dominated by Jack, are hunters. Ralph and Piggy represent the voice of reason, busying themselves with the elaboration of rules and democratic procedures: theirs is a good island and in this small Eden there is no reason to believe a boy with a strange raspberry birthmark who insists that after dark "a beastie, a snake-thing"[1] stalks the children. The hunters fail to kill their first piglet, held back by a shared vision of "the enormity of the knife descending and cutting the living flesh; because of the unbearable blood."[2] On the next occasion, however, their inhibitions vanish. A beast does appear on the island, though it emerges from neither the jungle nor the sea; a parachute carries the dead body of a pilot to the rocky escarpment that looms over the rest of the island. Then an antic wind positions the corpse in a way that terrifies the boys who behold it. At this juncture, the children have combined their pursuit of the beast with their search for meat; fun and excitement are found in the hunt, and so they desert Ralph and Piggy and refuse any longer to tend the fire. One day, in the course of reenacting an encounter with a dangerous boar, their playing suddenly changes into a sort of practical joke, the fun of which lies not in their pretending but in the hurt that they can inflict upon a friend:

> "He was coming along the path. I threw, like this—"
> Robert snarled at him. Ralph entered into the play and everybody laughed. Presently they were all jabbing at Robert who made mock rushes. . . . The circle moved in and round. Robert squealed in mock terror, then in real pain.
> "Ow! Stop it! You're hurting! . . ."
> "Kill him! Kill him!"
> All at once, Robert was screaming and struggling with the strength of frenzy. Jack had him by the hair and was brandishing his knife. Behind him was Roger, fighting to get close. The chant rose ritually, as at the last moment of a dance. . . .
> "Kill the pig! Cut his throat! Kill the pig! Bash him in!"
> Ralph too was fighting to get near, to get a handful of that brown, vulnerable flesh. The desire to squeeze and hurt was over-mastering.[3]

Soon after, they wound a great sow and pursue her through a hot afternoon until her faltering strength renders her easy prey. She falls in a clearing where bright flowers grow and butterflies dance in the sun, and there the hunters hurl themselves upon her:

> This dreadful eruption from an unknown world made her frantic. . . . Jack was on top of the sow, stabbing downward with his knife. Roger found a lodgment for his point and began to push till he was leaning with his whole weight. . . . Then Jack found the throat and the hot blood spouted over his hands. The sow collapsed under them and they were heavy and fulfilled upon her. Jack stood

up, holding out ... his reeking palms. Then Jack grabbed
Maurice and rubbed the stuff over his cheeks.[4]

Now the "unbearable blood" has become the material of a
sacrament, the sign of a rite of passage that ushers the children not into adulthood and the exigencies of disciplined life
but into a lust for destruction and an enjoyment of butchery:
a sort of sexual fulfillment is achieved not in an act of life but
in a dance of death. Clay dyes have now rendered familiars
strange to one another, and with the creation of strangers
where once there were intimates anything becomes possible,
even what hitherto was beyond imagining, for pretended ano-
nymity loosens all constraints and frees from any taint of
blame or shame.

The boys skewer the dripping sow's head on a stick that is
jammed into a cleft in the rock, offering it to the malign
presence that may be on the mountain above them, for the
possibility of "a beastie, a snake-thing" has not been entirely
forgotten. Watching the ceremony is a boy named Simon,
hidden in a leafy cavern made by the trees and vines that press
upon the small clearing. As he stares at the grinning sow's
head, at the Lord of the Flies, her "half-shut eyes ... assured
Simon that everything was a bad business."[5] The feverish
child learns from Beelzebub what Ralph and Piggy cannot yet
admit to their own rational universe, although they will find
themselves constrained to do so long before the end.

> "Fancy thinking the Beast was something you could hunt
> and kill!" said the head. For a moment or two the forest
> and all the other dimly appreciated places echoed with
> the parody of laughter. "You knew, didn't you? I'm part
> of you? Close, close, close! I'm the reason why it's no go?
> Why things are what they are?".... The Lord of the Flies
> was expanding like a balloon.... Simon found he was
> looking into a vast mouth. There was blackness within, a
> blackness that spread.[6]

Between hallucination and unconsciousness, Simon is seized
by an intimation of his own death. But he manages to climb
to the top of the mountain and to discover the real nature of

the beast that the boys had believed they had sighted there. When he tries to bring his good news to the other children on the beach, they are once again reenacting a hunt in the form of a dance. A storm is approaching and now it is dark, so their excitement is tinged with fear. Then they see Simon: "A thing was crawling out of the forest. It came darkly, uncertainly. The shrill screaming that rose before the beast was like a pain. The beast stumbled into the horseshoe. . . . Simon was crying out something about a dead man on a hill. 'Kill the beast! Cut his throat! Spill his blood! Do him in!' The sticks fell. . . ."[7] Simon had intended to say that the beast on the mountain, though horrible, was harmless. But the beast from the clearing, the Lord of the Flies, had come to the beach before him, and it could kill.

If fear was the context for the murder, the act itself had some different genesis: it was not the storm threatening the island but some storm generated on the island itself that accounts for what the boys have done. The dance that celebrates the triumph of man over beast seems, instead, a disclosure of the victory of beast over man—and yet that is not precisely what it is. As R. G. Collingwood has commented, dance is the mother of language and our primal tongue.[8] The dance of the children exhibits the difference between themselves and the animals they hunt, not only because it is a symbolic act but because it discloses an appetite for darkness and destruction that no other animals share. What they have done is not bestial or atavistic. Although, in the end, even the primal language is gone and "there were no more words, and no movements but the tearing of teeth and claws,"[9] the action is human action, all the more terrible because it is distinctively so. The next morning, when Ralph and Piggy reluctantly remember their own roles at the dance, Piggy, rational man to the end, attempts to blunt the force of Ralph's allegation of murder: "We was scared!" But Ralph, his voice "low and stricken," responds: "I wasn't scared. . . . I was—I don't know what I was."[10] So it ends, beyond rationality, beyond the calculation of motives or fears or the pressures of peers, beyond mistakes, beyond bestiality or atavism, beyond even their powers of imagination: "I don't know what I was."

In the last encounter between Ralph and Piggy and the "painted savages"[11] that the older boys have become, Ralph shouts, "Which is better, law and rescue, or hunting and breaking things up?" In response, a "storm of sound beat at them, an incantation of hatred."[12] Then, high above the pair, one of the pack dislodges a great rock "with a sense of delirious abandonment"[13] and it strikes Piggy a glancing blow that carries him forty feet down to the sea, where his red brains dye the wet rocks for a moment until the water carries the body of the fat boy away from the island and its terror forever. The morning after Piggy's death, the boys hunt again: this time they have only one quarry, Ralph. As he eludes his pursuers, they set the island afire behind him, and this time the smoke serves to guide a British cruiser to their rescue. When an officer from the ship surveys the circle of little boys on the beach, sticks in their hands and clay smeared across their faces, he exclaims, "fun and games!"[14] But, "in the middle of them, with filthy body, matted hair, and unwiped nose, Ralph wept for the end of innocence, the darkness of man's heart, and the fall through the air of the true, wise friend called Piggy."[15] The dance of the hunters is finished on this burning island, though not yet finished for those aboard the ship, who must continue their own pursuit of an unknown enemy abroad in a still burning world.

By the morning of the final hunt, no pretenses remain: Ralph poses no danger to those who intend to kill him; in no way, either, is their chase undertaken "for fun." From it there can come no pride of accomplishment, no fulfillment of a challenge, no testing of skills. It expresses only a sort of drivenness and drudgery and compulsion, as though the ritual of hunter and hunted had assumed a certain life of its own to which the lives of all the others were now in thrall: motiveless, playless, joyless, finally perhaps even passionless, it satisfies no rational desire and contributes nothing to the project of selfhood. In their reenactments of the hunt, all the bounds of play are broken and every rule transgressed: if Robert plays the boar, then he shall be treated as though he were. The practical joke moves ineluctably toward murder and, when Simon runs out of the trees in the dark, the dance becomes a dance of death. The hunt, which begins as a rational and disciplined affair, gains a liturgical and ritual aspect and becomes a dreadful rite of initiation—an incantation of destruction for no purpose except destruction, binding the children to destruction even when destruction has lost its savor and become a compulsion riding them all just as Jack and his band, that "dreadful eruption from an unknown world," had ridden the dead sow whose grinning head had promised that the Lord of the Flies would live within them, and in each and every one of them. A good thing is spoiled somehow: the impulse to play that is written into human nature is now disordered, corrupted, and ranged against itself and against the nature that entertains it—ours and yet not ours, our act and yet not our own, indeed, beyond our imagining unless we are provisioned with new images of ourselves that we do not want to face and cannot ever face without shuddering at ourselves and suffering at least a moment of despair.

Lord of the Flies describes the emergence of evil in Eden, on an isolated island where there seemed to be nothing except youth and innocence, and the story emphasizes the motifs that have already been specified as indispensable for an adequate representation of the self as the origin of evil. First, there is the presence of the lie, the element of self-deception apparent in Piggy's excuse, "We was scared!" Second, the sort of projection of which Jung writes is a constant refrain, from the first intimation of a mysterious "beastie" to the discovery of the dead pilot on the escarpment and most explicitly when the dancers on the beach see Simon emerge from the trees. Third, in this tangle of evil there is the intention to destroy without any apparent motive, muted in Ralph's own passion "to get a handful of that brown, vulnerable flesh," more obtrusive when he has himself become the game that his peers pursue. Most of all, there is Simon's death, scarcely an accident and yet certainly not the consequence of a communal intentional act, and perhaps the same is true of Piggy's fall to the sea.

These events are the results of a storm, a frenzy, a compulsion, or a sort of madness that seemed to come from nowhere and infect each of the castaways before anyone recognized the danger. Few of us, however, have visited uninhabited islands such as this; whatever knowledge we possess has been gathered from an atlas or the chronicle of a voyage finished long ago. So the story can seem stubbornly alien to our own experience; it is tempting and surely plausible to believe that we become involved in it simply because of the novelist's art rather than because we are ourselves capable of recognizing that the island is not *terra incognita* but a familiar land. Consequently, our problem is not only to discover a master image that can crystallize the meaning of the story for self-recognition, but to discover an image that convinces us because it emerges with its own inevitability from our commonplace experience, that persuades precisely because of its familiarity and yet also constrains the self to acknowledge dimensions of itself that everyday consciousness refuses to encompass—the land of the Lord of the Flies. There is at least one image that is readily available, so often mentioned by television or newspapers that at first it seems too commonplace and banal to be more than a poor instrument for representing the self to itself as the source of motiveless malevolence. But it will suffice. It points toward mysteries that television commentators do not mention and that newspapers fail to report.

Perhaps the figure who bears the image will appear tomorrow or perhaps he has already made his visit. Sooner or later, he will come. There are traces of his presence in schools and parks, in libraries and playgrounds, in theaters and vacant houses. He devotes his attention with fine equality to the rich and to the poor, divides his time between cars and trains, bicycles and shrubbery. Nothing in the whole realm of objects is too insignificant for his concern, for he is a vandal. No impulse thrusts its roots more deeply into the human frame than the inclination to play, and when it turns sour, vandalism is one of its most pervasive and familiar forms of expression. If "playing by ear" captures the meaning of authentic existence, it seems to describe equally well the ways in which peers incite one another to the sudden acts of vandalism that are a characteristic form of deviant behavior. Those who have written of it are close to unanimity in their emphasis upon its origins in play:[16] "stealing, the leading predatory activity of the adolescent gang, is as much a result of the sport motive as of a desire for revenue." "The juvenile property offender's thefts, at least at the start, are usually 'for fun' and not for gain." More broadly, "in its early stages, delinquency is clearly a form of play." One writer comments that "delinquency and crime are, and have been regarded as, purposeful behavior. But wanton and vicious destruction of property both public and private by teen-age hoodlums reveals no purpose, no rhyme, no reason." So another characterizes vandalism as "non-utilitarian, malicious, and negativistic" in order to distinguish it not only from other varieties of children's play but also from other types of crime.

One might well be skeptical of the claim that vandalism has neither reason nor purpose, however, at least until those who commit it have had a chance to speak for themselves. An anonymous member of a Chicago gang offers a comment that is typical of a thousand others: "We did all kinds of dirty tricks for fun. We'd see a sign, 'Please keep the streets clean,' but we'd tear it down and say, 'We don't feel like keeping it clean.' . . . We would always tear things down. That would make us laugh and feel good, to have so many jokes."[17] "For fun," "for a joke," "because we were bored"—as though it were a litany, these refrains inform accounts that vandals offer of their own activities, even though the third of them is no more than implicit in this citation. If the boy from Chicago were asked to explain his behavior, it is unlikely that he would answer that it was done without reason or purpose. More probably he would respond that it was done "for fun." The reason for it, or the ostensible motive, is "fun."

There are different sorts of reasons why persons behave as they do, many different ends toward which their actions are directed, and many different standards to which actions are meant to conform because of commitments to different ends. "Motive" is not a word that includes all reasons why we decide to act in particular ways; it refers only to a specific sort of reason. Consequently, as we have seen, there are many circumstances in which it would be gratuitous to ask about motivation, as in the instance of the customary generosity and consideration of a friend. On the other hand, were the friend to do something entirely uncharacteristic and devious that betrayed and threatened to rupture the relationship, then it would be not only appropriate but necessary to ask what his motive could possibly have been. The question of motive, therefore, ordinarily arises only in contexts where conventional expectations are confounded or where someone who is familiar to us behaves in an unfamiliar way. In these circumstances, as R. S. Peters[18] notes, we ask for the motive that has shaped a certain course of action because we want not only an explanation for it but an opportunity to evaluate and pass judgment upon what has happened. So it is important that we not only hear the reason that someone offers for his conduct but also discover the *real* reason for it. It would be rash to assume that the two coincide, particularly in cases of deviant behavior.

Motives, to recur to Peters, are "reasons of the directed sort."[19] They refer to the ends or goals that explain an action and so they can be distinguished from either causes or intentions. They differ from the former because motives cause nothing: the "causes" are persons who act in accordance with certain motives and who, in their choice of one among various possibilities, disclose something of their own character. The distinction between motive and intention, as it was suggested earlier, is that intention concerns the pursuit of a particular course of action while motive designates the goal or reason why we have exercised our choice in this way. Frequently we do not intend the actual consequences of our intention. In other words, we may rip down traffic signs "for fun" but we have not intended "for fun" the maimed bodies of the children who were involved in the crash that resulted because of the missing signs. Perhaps we were indifferent to the consequences of our intentionality; perhaps our imaginations were too impoverished to grasp many of the possible ramifications of our acts; perhaps too affluent familial situations had persuaded us that actions do not have real consequences because permissiveness will condone or money will offset every eventuality; or perhaps experience counsels that the universe is absurd, that events have no causes and that intelligibility is an illusion in the random whirl where accident is king.

For the moment, at least, it must be recognized that, when a vandal states that he acted as he did "for fun," he is acknowledging an intention and he may believe that he is specifying his motive, but he is certainly not admitting that he intended all of the consequences of his conduct. The destruction of the property was fun but the death of the child who was hurt as a consequence is altogether something else. There is no reason to portray the vandal as though he were a special monster, nicely calculating all the effects of his work, especially because one factor involved in such a portrait might well be a desire to separate him from the company of ordinary people until we are no longer constrained to acknowledge his kinship with ourselves.

In fact, however, to claim that someone enjoys something or can find fun in it does not really provide us with an explanation of why he has done it. There are many courses of action that might be fun for us but which we resolutely refuse to pursue for a variety of reasons. There are other courses of action that are fun but which we may undertake for reasons that have nothing to do with this sort of gratification. Lengthy walks may be fun, for example, but perhaps we include them in a daily regimen specifically for medical reasons. So the vandal's appeal to "fun" does not resolve the mystery of his behavior; instead, it simply directs attention to the question of why it is that people find fun where they claim to find it or claim to find it where they do. What sort of creature is the self, if its enjoyments are found in these ways? What sort of person is the vandal, if intentional destructiveness proves such fun for him that perhaps he even grows indifferent to the possible ramifications of his conduct? The reason that the vandal cites, then, is not *the* reason for his conduct, in the sense that it does not furnish an adequate principle of explanation. Why? "For fun." Why was it fun? "I don't know." It is possible that he has no clear conception of what he is doing. It is possible that he is attempting to deceive us about it. It is possible that with greater or lesser success he has managed to deceive himself about himself. The last option deserves further exploration.

In *Delinquent Boys*, Arthur Cohen devotes much attention to the phenomenon of "reaction formation," in an attempt to account for the extraordinary violence of some vandalism and the excessive energy that is expended in destructive acts that require no such savagery. One of the reasons for the incongruity, he argues, is that when a child thrusts aside the conventional morality of his community, the norms that once were effectively internalized continue to provoke anxiety. To a certain extent they can be repressed, but still they maintain a sort of ghostly life within the consciousness of the self, faintly intimating that it has not yet ended its war with itself. In order to combat the anxiety that these norms continue to provoke, then, the individual develops "an 'exaggerated,' 'disproportionate,' 'abnormal' intensity of response, 'inappropriate' to the stimulus which seems to elicit it. The unintelligibility of the response, the 'over-reaction,' becomes intelligible when we see that it has the function of reassuring the actor against an *inner* threat to his defenses as well as the function of meeting an external situation on its own terms."[20] The element of incongruity in the vandal's behavior is most readily explicable if his conduct is really shaped by the exigencies of responding to an internal division that he is unprepared to acknowledge. In other words, self-deception is not merely one element in a complex pattern; instead, the whole pattern expresses and maintains a self-deception. The violence of the act is intended to reassure the self that it has freed itself from the standards and mores of society to a greater extent than is true. Vandalism can be interpreted, therefore, as a particularly important instance of the ways that persons not infrequently lie to themselves and succeed in persuading even themselves that they are quite different than they are.

"For fun" suggests another possibility, however: perhaps the reason why it seems difficult to specify a motive is that sometimes there is no motive at all. There are many sorts of intentional acts, as we have seen, that are innocent of motives because they are dictated by convention, habit, or character. If the games that children play afford one of the most familiar instances of intentional but unmotivated behavior, it would certainly not be surprising to find motivation absent in the warping of the play impulse that expresses itself in vandalism. If "for fun" is understood as a euphemism for the unmotivated character of violent and destructive acts rather than as an expression of pleasure, if its real meaning is "for no reason at all," only then is it possible to acknowledge the indisputable truth that much vandalism is joyless and dreary and mindless, a protest against boredom that fails entirely to escape the clutches of boredom. So the vandal often confesses quite properly that he does not know what "came over him" or "possessed" or "caused" or "compelled" him to do whatever he did. "Fun" fails as a principle of explanation, then, not only because it does not provide us with a reason why persons do what they enjoy doing but even more because of its irrelevance for understanding why people do what they derive no real pleasure from doing. So we return to a new form of the question with which we began: What sort of creature is the self if it pursues violence and destruction for no reason at all?

The equation of motive with the aim or goal of a course of action has been challenged by certain writers who attempt to distinguish between "forward-looking" and "backward-looking" motive statements, and to argue that they are logically different.[21] So it might be said that a person acts as he does toward a friend because he has reason to feel indebtedness or gratitude. But the latter can frequently be rephrased as instances of the former; for example, it could be said that someone acts as he does for the reason that he wishes to repay his indebtedness or express his gratitude with unmistakable clarity. In any event, "for fun" strongly suggests that looking backward will prove no more fruitful than looking forward, if in fact the two sorts of motive statements are logically different, precisely because acts of vandalism are typically committed against the property of unknown persons who as often as not belong to the same caste or class. So there is no history of a relationship, either between persons or perhaps even between classes, that can justify looking backward *for a motive.* There are, however, other reasons for looking backward. When it seems impossible to specify the goal or motive of some action, it is appropriate to turn from the question of ends to the problem of origins in the sense of *causal explanations.* When we cannot discover the *point* of or the reason for someone's behavior, it becomes relevant to examine the conditions from which it emerges.

There have been many different attempts to account for vandalism and its pervasiveness. Talcott Parsons has stressed its connection with the struggle of a boy to assert his masculinity after an early identification with his mother: the child resists the norms of conduct that have been associated with her and that have therefore been invested with feminine significance. Other writers have also associated it in one way or another with a history of inadequate socialization within the family: vandalism can be a function of hostility toward parents, or an expression of anxiety concerning the magnitude and consistency of parental love, or a disclosure of feelings of guilt and shame that are related in some fashion to the familial situation and that inspire antisocial behavior in the expectation of apprehension and punishment that the child believes he merits for other reasons. No other form of community can match the potential of the nuclear family to become a structure of destruction. Margaret Mead, among others, relates vandalism to a particular sort of shame, rooted in a child's knowledge that his parents have not been successful, at least as the world measures success, so that the young person is consigned and fated to live in "a class below others."[22] Just as the unqualified identification of the self with its familial roles breeds one sort of alienation, so does its unqualified identification with the social and economic status of the family foster another. Arthur Cohen anchors vandalism in a quest for prestige that for one reason or another can find no legitimate realization, and so it expresses itself in forms of destructiveness that are applauded by the child's peers. Still others content themselves with a theory of "spontaneous combustion": vandalism simply happens when certain peers encounter one another in certain situations! Recently there have also been numerous attempts to interpret it as a political event, a deliberate provocation that will expose the true condition of society by arousing a violent response from an "establishment" that hypocritically pretends that it need not invoke violence in order to remain in power.

The attempt to provide causal explanations, of course, involves a shift of focus from ends or goals to origins, a move from considering the reasons entertained by an agent to exploring the conditions that have made him what he is. It is important not to confuse "necessary conditions" with a sufficient explanation: in other words, there are no grounds for the assumption that once we have specified elements of inadequate socialization we have answered all relevant questions concerning why vandals do whatever they do. Such an assumption would deny the presence of individual agency and mean that there is no longer any serious sense in which we can claim that an action is "yours" or "mine." Peters correctly insists that "if we are in fact confronted with a case of genuine action (i.e. an act of doing something as opposed to suffering something), then causal explanations are *ipso facto* inappropriate" as sufficient explanations.[23] So we are forced again to return to a form of the original question: why is it that the self responds to certain conditions in a violent and destructive way? What must be said about a self that responds to circumstances in a deviant fashion? If someone is incited to vandalism by another person, what accounts for the vulnerability of the first or the maliciousness of the second? If we attempt to answer in terms of "inadequate socialization," the question is still there: why is socialization "inadequate" in this case when similar circumstances had no such effect on someone else? If parental hostility is a factor in one instance, what must be said of its absence in the next case? If deprivation or shame or the status of an outsider seems to afford a necessary condition on one occasion, what must be said where there is affluence, status, and an especially strong sense of family pride?

There is no reason to demand a single causal explanation —indeed, the complexity of human affairs counsels very great skepticism concerning such a grand theory—but there is every reason to insist not only upon the difference between contributory conditions and sufficient explanations but also upon the phenomenological inadequacy of all the various theories. None is germane in more than a severely limited number of instances and, more important, few attempt to come to terms with the reasons, or alleged reasons, that are offered by the vandals themselves—"for fun," "for a joke," "because we were bored." If answers prove elusive, at least vandalism is not simply the strategy of a minority that has suffered social or familial deprivation. On the one hand, it tells that our taste for pleasure is more capacious and per-verse than we would like either others, or especially ourselves, to recognize. On the other, persons often act destructively and violently, without either motive or sufficient cause, long after the acts themselves or even their taste in memory have lost the capacity to excite or please. So these patterns of behavior seem to conflict with every rational attempt at self-understanding.

The image of the self as vandal can introduce to conscious-ness much that we need to know, not only for our own sake but also because, "if we see, clearly and with conviction, that every human baby born bears the potential resources of the arsonist, the vandal, the murderer, then we shall raise our children differently."[24] First, there is its completely "non-utilitarian, malicious, and negativistic" quality, particularly insofar as there is no reason or motive or sufficient condition for it. The vandal is intent upon destruction for no reason at all. Second, the project of self-deception figures in it in vari-ous ways, and not only in the phenomenon of "reaction for-mation." One example of this is the child whose unassuaged sense of guilt in a particular context leads him to commit acts in a very different context that eventuate in the punishment that he believes he deserves. Because he is punished for what he and some of his peers can regard as jokes, his sense of guilt is satisfied without the risks that would be involved if he were to confront its true or "serious" origins—and so a self-deception can be enforced and maintained. Again, the vandal is frequently more self-deceived than misled by others in the supposition that his social situation constitutes his fate. The image awards this motif a centrality and emphasis that are important for interpreting to himself a creature who requires more than anything else the willingness and skills to step back and see himself freshly and gain some perspective upon his own perspectives. Third, vandalism is as common as the untenanted house across the road or the playground down the street, but it also draws attention to less familiar landscapes within the self that cannot be mapped because they disclose no patterns or stability. Representations of the self as criminal or rebel or terrorist will not serve as well as the figure of the vandal, for it is not difficult to discover the motivation for what these others do. Rebellion or crime or terrorism are immoral by all conventional standards, but at least they are rational ventures in that they involve goals which are more or less clearly discerned, and these goals determine the conduct that is oriented toward their realization. The vandal, however, is a figure who stands in large measure outside a rational universe, intending damage without motive or cause. His shadow reminds us of the irrationality and vulnerability of the self, when he sometimes confesses that he does not know what compelled or possessed him to do something that he did not intend to do.

If the figure of the vandal is to serve as a master image for understanding ourselves, however, we must repudiate the way conventional wisdom employs more or less inflexible person-property and self-other distinctions in order to discriminate between vandalism and other forms of antisocial behavior. Neither distinction is satisfactory: the actions of vandals are much too complex to be described as a sort of perverse capitulation to the world of objects that others possess. First, the self-other polarity is inadequate because the destruction of someone else's property is frequently an act that is done for the sake of the vandal's own self-understanding. Perhaps we wish to be punished for a "joke" because, although we know that we are deserving of punishment, we are unable or unwilling to confront the "serious" source of our sense of unworthiness. Or perhaps the violence of our deed indicates that it was done in order to maintain a self-deception about our indifference toward conventional values and standards. Second, the person-property distinction is suspect when conventional persons measure themselves and others in terms of their possessions, thereby denying their difference from everything else in the world. Writing of the cultural importance of the display of property as a badge of status and an index of accomplishment, Cohen characterizes vandalism as "an attack on the middle class where their egos are most vulnerable. . . . It expresses contempt for a way of life by making its opposite a criterion of status."[25] If property is a representation and disclosure of the worth of the person, then the attack upon it is an attack upon the self-image of its owner and, therefore, upon the person himself—and all the more so because "money and other valuables are not, as such, despised by the delinquent."[26] The statement by the Chicago vandal that it would "make us laugh and feel good, to have so many jokes," renders the distinction between person and property even more dubious. Jokes can be played only against persons, not against things, for joking requires another center of consciousness, and frequently an "offended" consciousness, that can acknowledge and appreciate whatever has been said or done. Malice, too, can be directed only against selves, not toward objects that remain annoyingly indifferent toward our disposition, whatever it may be.

The image contributes, however, not only to our understanding of selfhood but also to recognition of the injustice of a social order in which many are deprived of the possibilities that others are awarded without regard for either potential or achievements, while still others are denied the appropriate rewards for their services. It is true that the important problem concerns not whether social conditions influence vandalism, for it is obvious that they do, but rather what must be said about the self if persons respond to a variety of conditions either internal or external in this deviant fashion. Nevertheless, the connection that Margaret Mead discerns between some vandalism and a sense of shame that is related to the disadvantaged situation of the family, for example, illuminates the relevance of the image for portraying a social order in which questions of status are decided by contingencies and not merit, or by accidents instead of justice. Vandalism can be a choice of deviant behavior under the guise of the denial of any possibility of choice: inexorable and unfair social fatality consigned us in our parents to be figures of shame, so there is nothing to express except resentment. We make our mark upon things because we go unremarked, and we go unremarked because this is a world in which persons define themselves in terms of the services they command and the property they own. The unpropertied man is the invisible man, and through him there is access to the social order for that other invisible man who is lurking within us all. The anomaly, then, is that vandalism cannot really be distinguished from other forms of deviant behavior by reference to the difference between person and property, but that in considerable measure it is a socially engendered response to a community that itself refuses to honor such distinctions.

The pervasiveness of vandalism accentuates the element of risk involved in our conventional understanding of community as bound together by the dictates of fair play. Playing fair entails an assumption of basic trust that becomes more and more difficult to sustain when we are the victims of random and motiveless violence, or when resentment against someone else or some class or ethnic group or constellation of standards and values expresses itself against us or ours despite the fact that we have incurred no blame and are in no way at all identifiable with the class or group. In crimes directed against persons, it is frequently argued that something the victim either did or failed to do contributed to the act— perhaps a deliberate courting of danger, perhaps just a failure to exercise the sort of carefulness that is appropriate in a violent neighborhood. So we have at least a minimal "explanation" for the assault, a scrap of reassurance for those who have not yet been victimized. But the random destructiveness of the vandal suggests that everyone is vulnerable and finally helpless, no matter how carefully the neighborhood has been chosen or how high and sturdy the fences may be. Precisely because playing with peers, together with the household or nuclear family, has been one of the fundamental instruments of socialization in the West, it becomes one of the most powerful threats to the maintenance of life together whenever it assumes a deviant form. Like some malign god, the anonymous individual or band can destroy in a moment the property, security, and sense of selfhood of persons who derive their assurance of identity from what they possess, and strike into the hearts of total strangers a terrible reminder of the contingency and impermanence of the world and of all who live in it.

The delinquent's description of vandalism as a joke merits further attention. When a joke consists of something *done* to excite laughter rather than something said, it is called a *practical* joke. Not all vandalism can be satisfactorily construed as joking, of course, for this suggests the presence of wit and intentionality; joking involves a degree of reflection and self-awareness that is notably absent from much vandalism, for often vandals act without any real understanding of the reasons for their behavior, and sometimes even without a clear conception of the consequences of what they are doing. The representation of the self as a vandal explicitly includes, as the notion of joking certainly does not, a reference to unconscious and subterranean dimensions of selfhood that spoil and interrupt the rational narrative of character, as in the instance of someone who says, "I don't know what made me do it." Furthermore, the ferocity that is often evident in the sort of vandalism that is intended to reinforce a project of self-deception seems far removed from our conventional understanding of jokes. Then, too, there is no reason to relate joking to one or another set of social conditions, while in cases of vandalism these can be not unimportant. Nevertheless, it would be a mistake to discount the innumerable references to vandalism as a joke by delinquents themselves, especially because this description more than anything else demonstrates that the focus of vandalism is finally upon persons and not upon the things that persons amass. Boredom is cited more often than any other condition as the antecedent of vandalism, and it is also the apparent context for many practical jokes. Bored with itself and its situation, the self plays a joke that enables it to become a *voyeur* that feeds and fattens off the confusion or disarray that its joke has caused in the life of someone else: for a time it trades its nullity of a life for the existence of someone else.

In this trade, particularly when it involves someone who is a stranger, evil emerges in the form of malice toward other persons that is entirely unmotivated and entirely intentional. The joke is unmotivated in the sense that "boredom" does not provide a sufficient explanation, even though it may be a necessary condition, for references to it tell us nothing about why release should be sought *in this fashion.* But it is intentional in the particularly bleak sense that the joker cares only and without reservation for his intention, and he is either indifferent toward or merely curious about whatever direct or indirect consequences it may have, even if they entail wounding or destroying the victim of the joke. The consequences are intended even though they cannot be foreseen with any precision, in the sense that the whole point of the joke is to create as many and as dramatic consequences as possible, without any concern for what they might be. Now there are no limits, and indeed, the vandal has become "a special monster." In acts of vandalism understood as jokes by their authors, the most common form of antisocial behavior discloses a potentiality that more often than not has been understood by the Christian tradition as entirely diabolical—motiveless malevolence. The familiar sight of vulgar language that has been sprayed in paint on a concrete wall can be a faint adumbration of something far more disturbing because it is really directed against persons and not things: the possibility of malice that is intentionally directed against strangers for no reason except to see what the consequences will be, or to discover what vulnerable and unsuspecting people are really like, or simply to salt a bland day. The only excuse is the most terrible caricature of an excuse imaginable: "I just wanted to see what would happen."

In "The Joker in the Pack," W. H. Auden describes Shakespeare's Iago as "a practical joker of a peculiarly appalling kind."[27] Auden recognizes that practical jokes are not always immoral, for sometimes they can puncture the illusions of someone who cannot relate to himself or to others until he is confronted with this sort of firm dose of reality. Nevertheless, they still involve a threat to human community because of the way they violate the distinction between serious and playful uses of language and demonstrate that "a man does not always require a serious motive for deceiving another."[28] When the deception is disclosed, Auden argues, what really provokes the astonishment on the faces of others is the news "that all the time they were convinced that they were thinking and acting on their own initiative, they were actually the puppets of another's will."[29] Consequently, there is something "slightly sinister"[30] about every practical joke, for those who perpetrate them are people whose ambition it is "to play God behind the scenes."[31] Sinister it is, certainly, to reduce another self to a puppet, to an object that we can manipulate as we wish if only we have accurately assessed its prejudices and weaknesses: "even the most harmless practical joke is an expression of the joker's contempt for those he deceives."[32]

Contempt for others, Auden continues, is matched by and has its origin in contempt for the self. When the joker discloses what he has done, the victims may learn something about themselves, but they are none the wiser about the person who has played the joke, knowing neither why he has done whatever he has done nor what sort of self it is that would relish and enjoy such a deception. The joker has become a paradigm of the *voyeur,* someone whose life becomes entirely derivative from the lives of others, someone who appears to be without independent existence apart from his exercise of the power to manipulate and embarrass and dupe another human being.

His goal, to make game of others, makes his existence absolutely dependent upon theirs; when he is alone, he is a nullity. Iago's self-description, *I am not what I am*, is correct and the negation of the Divine *I am that I am*. . . . In any practical joker to whom playing such jokes is a passion, there is always an element of malice, a projection of his self-hatred onto others, and in the ultimate case of the absolute practical joker, this is projected onto all created things.[33]

Iago is motivated neither by resentment nor by a thirst for revenge; nor does the suggestion that he fears "being nobody" provide a real clue to the motive for his behavior. He can achieve no rational understanding of himself at all; the occasional reasons that he offers for his conduct are not persuasive even to Iago himself, much less to anyone else. He intends simply to play a joke and that is the end of the matter. There is no reason for the joke except a desire to see what will happen, a certain interest in discovering what Othello is really like.

"The Joker in the Pack" concludes with some reflections concerning the Iago who dwells at least potentially within every child, and whose shadow falls all the more heavily across human affairs because of the reigning orientation of contemporary Western culture. Auden claims that "none of us can honestly say that he does not understand how such a wicked person can exist. For is not Iago, the practical joker, a parabolic figure for the autonomous pursuit of scientific knowledge through experiment which we all, whether we are scientists or not, take for granted as natural and right?"[34] When neither limits nor qualifications are placed upon the autonomous pursuit of knowledge about the self and its communities through experimentation, then Iago has become us all. It appears to Auden that the illegitimate extension of scientific method beyond its own proper realm is a process already far advanced. He warns that:

Iago's treatment of Othello conforms to Bacon's definition of scientific enquiry as putting Nature to the Question. If a member of the audience were to interrupt the play and ask him: "What are you doing?" could not Iago answer with a boyish giggle, "Nothing. I'm only trying to find out what Othello is really like."? And we must admit that his experiment is highly successful. By the end of the play he does know the scientific truth about the object to which he has reduced Othello. . . . What makes it impossible for us to condemn him self-righteously is that, in our culture, we have all accepted the notion that the right to know is absolute and unlimited. . . . To apply a categorical imperative to knowing, so that, instead of asking, "What can I know?" we ask, "What, at this moment, am I meant to know?". . . . that seems to all of us crazy and almost immoral. But, in that case, who are we to say to Iago—"No, you mustn't."[35]

Unquestionably, Auden misunderstands the scientific process, ignoring the crucial roles of humility and imagination there and the need to correlate methods with the nature of their objects if procedures are to be truly scientific. It is scarcely disputable that there are worlds of difference between the self-effacement of the scientist and the nullity that Iago becomes whenever he is alone. But, if it would be a mistake to agree with Auden and regard Iago as "a parabolic figure for the autonomous pursuit of scientific knowledge through experiment," it would be equally mistaken to ignore him and fail to recognize that the potential presence of Iago shadows each and every aspect of the human enterprise. Because the play impulse can manifest itself in practical jokes in which the motiveless malevolence sometimes revealed in vandalism is now undisguised and visible to the eyes of everyone, because there is a relish for violence and destructiveness in the self and no form of destruction is so absolute as the control of other persons that reduces them to objects and nothing more, because we so often and sometimes so unwittingly raise our hands against ourselves as well as against others, there is always a potential for deviance hidden in our play. Within all the allegedly secular projects that we baptize in the name of Prometheus there lurks something darker, the different but perhaps inseparable reality called Prometheanism, for the artificers of every human work are sometimes tempted to see themselves as titans and are sometimes capable of pleasure instead of terror at the onset of the strange creatures of the night. Precisely in our most creative and rational ventures, there is the possibility that we will pursue the most irrational and destructive ends, and technology furnishes us with apparently limitless opportunities to practice terrible jokes against ourselves. If we choose to do so, there is always the joker's counterfeit of an excuse: "I'm only trying to find out what people are really like.

The "slightly sinister" ingredient in practical jokes, the fact that there are persons who like "to play god behind the scenes," is certainly not absent from vandalism, particularly when it is explicitly represented as a joke. Insofar as motives cannot be specified, there is good reason to explore causal "explanations." Insofar as it is behavior that is out of character or compulsive or done apparently "despite oneself," with a range of consequences that were in no way intended, there is even better reason to explore them. But it is even more important to recognize that the specification of necessary conditions does not constitute a sufficient explanation, except at the price of a denial that there is any serious sense in which the conduct is "yours" or "mine." After all, we must consent to the promptings that are related to the conditions in which we find ourselves, or that we find within ourselves. There are a great many different sorts of causal explanations, of course, and they can be complementary rather than mutually exclusive, each relevant to the extent that others display a certain phenomenological inadequacy in the face of the richness of what is there to be explained. But the utility of explanations that focus upon the family or peers, social situation or sexual identity, is so extraordinarily limited that we must speak not only of different sorts but of different levels of causal explanations, and search for a level that can address the various forms of the question with which we began: What sort of creature is the self if it responds to its circumstances, whatever they may be, in these deviant ways? Why is it that the self is tempted to play god and, simply by that determination, tends to lose its life instead of gain it? Why is it that the self finds its pleasure where it does?

A new level of causal explanation is offered, for example, in the biblical story of the fall, where the serpent urges what is no more than a minor act of thievery not unrelated to vandalism—stealing and eating the fruit of a tree that belongs to someone else. But there are some mysterious and finally opaque dimensions to this not uncommon act, and St. Augustine is reminded of them when, in the *Confessions,* he describes some deviant behavior of his own at the age of sixteen. Close to the vineyard of his family there was a pear tree that belonged to a neighbor, a poor tree whose fruit had little appeal to either eye or palate. One night Augustine and a pack of friends stole whole armloads of the pears and threw them to a herd of swine. The boys had no interest in the pears themselves; they were "compelled neither by hunger, nor poverty, but through a distaste for well-doing."[36] He recalls that there was "no inducement to evil but the evil itself. . . . I pilfered that of which I already had sufficient, and much better. Nor did I desire to enjoy what I pilfered, but the theft and sin itself."[37] Memory can isolate the intention, but everything else is hidden. So his reminiscences conclude with a series of questions:

> What, then, was it that I loved in that theft? And wherein did I, even corruptedly and pervertedly, imitate my Lord? Did I wish if only by artifice, to act contrary to Thy Law, because by power I could not, so that, being a captive, I might imitate an imperfect liberty by doing with impunity things which I was not allowed to do, in obscured likeness of Thy omnipotency? Behold this servant of Thine, fleeing from his Lord, and following a shadow! . . . Could I like that which was unlawful only because it was unlawful? . . . Who can unravel that twisted and tangled knottiness?[38]

Augustine is unwilling to claim that he can untangle the intricate knottiness of intentions and motives or the absence of motives and isolate either his own reason or, should it be different, the real reason for the act. On the other hand, he does claim to know some necessary conditions for the jokes of the thieves and vandals who like to play god behind the scenes, although he also knows that the conditions do not constitute a sufficient explanation because the robbery of the pears was an expression of his own freedom of choice. In his eyes, there is a warping and a conflict within the self, an estrangement of the self from itself that no human medicine will ever cure because it is rooted in the self's estrangement from God. Persons can neither remedy their own disorder nor isolate the virus so that it will be restricted to a particular age or caste or clan. In everyone there is the potential vandal; in everyone there is vulnerability to the whisperings of the invisible man who lives somewhere inside the self, and so there is always the need for vigilance.

The representation of the self as vandal cannot, and is not intended to, provide a comprehensive phenomenology of the creature's alienation from God, for the Christian tradition has insisted that sinfulness infects the individual's highest aspirations and greatest creativeness as much as his deviations from reigning standards and values, that it is evident in his thoughts as well as in his deeds and in what he fails to do as often as it is in what he does. But the image does incorporate a considerable range of the evils persons commit and the sinfulness they express, including acts of motiveless malevolence that at first seem diabolic instead of recognizably human possibilities. So familiar and so foreign, the image reminds us of what we all have seen, and it confronts us with what we have all tried not to see: malice that is intentional but without motivation; evil that is done compulsively by people who do not know what possessed them and that involves a freight of consequences no one ever intended; the interruption of the rational narrative of character by a strange "despite oneself"; the pervasiveness of self-deception not only in strategies to deny our lapses of integrity but equally in our attempts to persuade ourselves that integrity is not important; the projection upon others of our self-hatred and of all that we do not want to confront in ourselves, so that they become daimons that obsess and torment us. Something still worse can happen, too: as Auden says, we can project our self-hatred "onto all created things," so that we vandalize not only our cities but the earth that supports them, spoiling the world as well as its citizenry, using our technological power in order to practice, all unsuspecting, terrible jokes not only upon ourselves but upon our children's children.

Now the project of selfhood discloses even greater hazards for those persons who seek to understand themselves as players and sufferers. The voices that compete for our attention not only counsel us to define ourselves wholly in the terms they offer, not only lie to us so that we will serve ends that we would repudiate if we could see them clearly, not only contain an inordinate element of self-interest that conflicts with our own possibilities of self-affirmation. Now there is motiveless malevolence. Now there is the boy who says there is a wolf abroad when there is none. Now there are all the children who dance in front of the stake on which the bloody head of the Lord of the Flies is impaled. Now there are the invisible men in the streets of the city. Now there is Iago. The distinction between serious and unserious usage of language is violated by jokers who practice deceptions for no reason except the fun that deception affords. So the assumptions that ordinarily invest suffering with significance become suspect. Then, too, our own thirst and talent for self-deception render it even more difficult to discriminate between the serious and the unserious, truth and illusion, reality and its thousand shifting reflections on the surface of a stream.

The real problem, of course, is not that the assumption of basic trust and the dictates of fair play are overturned by the actions of jokers and vandals: it is not "the others" but the self. Everything is jeopardized because something within the self, not chosen yet still there and still its own, does not love walls and limits and order. Have we deceived ourselves in believing that we are dealing fairly with others, or are we fair in the way that we are asking others to deal with us? In the intensity of our commitments to fairness have we, so readily vandals and jokers, managed to be more than self-deceived?

At the same time, however, the phenomena of vandalism and practical jokes illuminate the significance of the representation of the self as a player and sufferer. Responses to the appeals of others are all the more urgent when those who ask for our aid are victims of a social world where crime and punishment or achievement and reward are so frequently and so greatly incommensurate, and where accident and contingency and random violence strike the ones who are least able to shoulder new burdens, the weak and the innocent and the poor.

In Christian perspective, the figure of the vandal-joker can express in a negative and twisted fashion everyone's imperious desire for something more than confinement to the factual order, for definition in different and better terms than those which are provided by conventional images of selfhood that represent persons as little more than the worth of the objects they possess and the services they can command. The rebellion against the factual order is sterile, of course, for the vandal is made all the more its prisoner because of the seriousness that he awards it, but for Christian persons the revolt is still an adumbration of their conviction that the self is intended for more than its environment—for communion with God. Vandalism manifests the disordering of a natural impulse that we share with all other animals but that we have corrupted in a way uniquely our own. In the claim that we do these things "for fun," there is a covert acknowledgment that we are sometimes helpless in the face of ourselves. As the disclosure of a disordering of nature that is bound up with the rejection of limits and that can eventuate in evils that are done deliberately but for no reason at all, as a preference for the unlawful simply because it is unlawful, vandalism is a category that brings some measure of concreteness and specificity to Christian claims about the sinfulness of all persons although, of course, it does not begin to exhaust their meaning.

As a joker, the vandal like Iago seeks to play god, treating as objects and puppets those subjects whom God has called to communion with others and with himself. Choosing the moment when he will reveal himself as author of the situation, the joker fabricates a false *kairos* that is a parody of the *kairos* created by the disclosure of the holy. As a vandal, the joker is a rebel, expressing the negativity of rebellion just as the figure of the player who adheres to rules represents its affirmative aspects,[39] and differing from the player because he has been trapped by the factual order into awarding it a greater seriousness than it merits. As a joker, the vandal plays the greatest joke against himself insofar as his actions are dictated by the exigencies of the maintenance of a self-deception. As a vandal, the joker warns us all that much of ourselves and of the careers of our communities will elude all our essays at comprehension and efforts at manipulation, for there are elements in the unconscious that subvert our understandings of ourselves. As a joker, the vandal is a *voyeur,* feeding off others, living only to watch their lives until the disclosure of the joke, self-exiled from a life of his own. So he is the final corruption of the man of sight, last victim of the illusion that he is the master of all he surveys, choosing to play as though he were god while, in fact, he is the negation and antithesis of divine self-sufficiency.

Jokes, humor, comedy—these are among our best defenses against a world that counsels us to regard it with unqualified seriousness and treat it as though it were ultimate. But there is something within us that rots our defenses: so we rebel against the constraints and limits that are indispensable to finite creativeness. Jokes turn sour and play becomes a bunch of dirty tricks. The promise of fulfillment that other imagery of the self affords is always accompanied by the shadow of the invisible man, the vandal, Iago, the children who hunt for wild pigs, "a beastie, a snake-thing," and so the darkness of the heart becomes the heart of the darkness that waits to surprise the unwary and seize the day.

The self as player, as sufferer, as vandal: these will suffice for self-recognition and for the appropriate exercise of our freedom and agency. Always together, never separately, they provide us with the necessary resources to dominate, qualify and clarify, unite and reconcile the welter of more particular and often conflicting images of ourselves that emerge inevitably in the course of our ordinary experience. As player, the self is called to offer unqualified devotion and unqualified seriousness to nothing except the holy, while at the same time offering no less than fairness or justice toward everything else. As sufferer, the self discovers both a measure of fulfillment through its relationships with others and its reduction to the plaything of other selves, communities, and institutions. As vandal, the self is constrained to recognize that not only circumstances but also some disordering within itself warp and spoil its play so that it becomes a joker impatient with fairness, intent upon acts of foul play simply in order to see what the consequences will be.

Play remains throughout the dominant motif, but now a dark and insistent counterpoint has added its complexity to the original melody, and the melody itself refuses to conclude. How can we reassure ourselves that, with our penchant for self-deception, the images of player and sufferer will not be held in unrighteousness? Second, how can we hold together the master images that are intended to reconcile and unify subordinate imagery, when the representation of the self as vandal conflicts with the dialectic of liberty and limitation that the figures of the player and sufferer express and that is the core of their complementarity? How is it possible to unite the figure of the vandal with the images of player and sufferer? Third, how can we represent the last word to the self as forgiveness and futurity, rather than simply judgment and the foreclosure of possibilities, when our last image is the portrayal of the self as vandal? These are questions yet to be resolved, and resolution depends upon recognition that images beg for more than images if their own significance is to be fully understood. The meaning of images is bound up with the stories that engender them and, much as a stonecutter brings life to the uncut stones that lie so dully upon his bench, display their many facets.

Chapter Five

IMAGERY AND STORIES

In *Christ and Prometheus,* William Lynch contends that "there is no freedom without the transformation of our images." He means that everything depends upon a new angle of vision, a new perspective that captures different dimensions of what has become all too familiar, and thereby confers new possibilities upon the self. Lynch continues:

> Freedom is not a thing we add to a man; it is a state of everything in man, but especially a state of his images. We can perform a thousand heroic feats of the will; this will be only a substitute and an imitation of that substantive freedom which can only come by changing our images from old to new. . . . Any fact is contained within a way of looking at things, within a context, within a pattern, within an image. . . . All the day long I form and reform the world, moving from image to image, trying never to submit to endlessness or senselessness.[1]

It is true that nothing is as important as the angle of our vision, for the possibilities that actually confront us will scarcely exceed our imaginative grasp of what they might be. Yet Lynch claims too much for images, because images of the self, at least, are slippery, ambiguous, and obscure until they are named. Does the image of the player, for example, mean that one ought not to devote particular seriousness to one's different roles because the world of appearances is inconsequential or illusory? Or is it intended primarily to show what moral conduct means in our diverse roles and to emphasize the importance of fairness as a regulative principle in human affairs? The image itself is amenable to either interpretation; it derives its specificity from the particular way that it is named. If we do not choose to name it in one way, we shall find that circumstances eventually conspire to name it in another.

How important the choice of names becomes for the determination of what images of the self signify can be illustrated by baptizing the player, the sufferer, and the vandal in a fashion that renders the imagery rigid and inflexible, doing violence to the texture of experience, so that it excludes possibilities instead of providing new options and stifles debate rather than provoking it. As one who seeks to create his own inviolable world, ordered exclusively by the dictates of human imagination, signifying nothing beyond itself, responsible to no values or principles beyond its own, the player could be named Prometheus. The patron of human culture, Prometheus was the titan who brought people the gift of fire, then became their tutor in all the arts, and who finally was punished by Zeus for divulging the secrets of the gods. Chained to a lonely Caucasian mountain, he suffered daily torment by a vulture. As cosmetic man, the creature of a thousand masks who is given his form and functions by the voices of others and who will be as others desire him to be, the sufferer could be called Proteus. This lesser god of the sea could change his shape whenever he chose, from lion to fire to dragon to flood, in order to avoid capture by the gods and mortals who pursued him. Only if he were captured would he halt his endless transformations, assume his own proper form, and carry out his function of prophecy. As one who is not so much a player as a plaything of greater powers than his own, trapped within a world of objects where things crowd and clutter all the space that consciousness provides, the vandal might be identified with Sisyphus. He was a criminal, although the precise nature of his crime is obscure. Consequently, we can imagine that his crime might have begun as a practical joke or an instance of vandalism. In any event, Sisyphus is certainly trapped within the realm of objects, for the gods condemned him to roll a huge stone up a hill, only to see it constantly fall to the bottom again, and the punishment is to endure forever.

Each of these names is cogent for the interpretation of some of our experience. Robert Jay Lifton, for example, has argued that "the image of personal identity, insofar as it suggests inner stability and sameness, is derived from a vision of traditional culture in which man's relationship to his institutions and symbols is still relatively intact. And this, of course, is hardly the case today."[2] Therefore, he continues, our contemporary experience of selfhood can best be understood from the perspective of the myth of Proteus. Nevertheless, these names severely distort the meanings of the images of player, sufferer, and vandal as they have been presented in this essay. It will be sufficient to confine attention to a single deficiency: the way in which they address the theme of limits and guilt. In the myth of Prometheus, limits are interpreted from two perspectives. On the one hand, they are indices of a failure of human creativity and power. Limits exist only to be surpassed in the pursuit of limitless dominion. They play no role in the creative process; they are merely left behind, broken, ignored. On the other, the limits have been ordained by the gods; so human creativeness is always and everywhere a tainted affair, a source of guilt. The self is guilty because every attempt to realize its possibilities is a venture that brings it ineluctably into collision with divinely ordained limits that diminish and fetter its potential. For Proteus, too, there shines the lure of the limitless. Like Prometheus, he need acknowledge no internal limitations; there is no shape he cannot assume, no form he cannot call his own. The measure of his cunning is his success at evading capture; unless he is trapped by someone more cunning still, there are no limits to which he must submit. Consequently, for Proteus there is no need ever to accept the burden of guilt, for always there exists the possibility of a new and untarnished beginning. Inventiveness consists in the evasion of every limit: sometimes it means an attempt to elude external constraints, and sometimes it is expressed in the flight from any identity that we must claim as our own and for which we must acknowledge that we are accountable.

Prometheus is eventually freed from his mountain and the daily torment of the vulture, for his punishment is remitted when an immortal agrees to die in his behalf. But Sisyphus will pay forever: he is declared unforgivable by the imposition of a penalty that can never be remitted. Guilt is unfading and eternal. From the limits that constitute his fate Sisyphus learns nothing, except that they preclude human creativity absolutely and forever. Of this most unhappy of men, who perhaps once scorned with fine equality the conventions of the world and the will of the gods and who now pays for that levity by returning forever to the bottom of the forbidding hill on which his torment occurs, Albert Camus writes:

> I see that man going back down with a heavy yet measured step toward the torment of which he will never know the end. That hour like a breathing-space which returns as surely as his suffering, that is the hour of consciousness. At each of those moments when he leaves the heights and gradually sinks toward the lairs of the gods, he is superior to his fate. He is stronger than his rock. If this myth is tragic, that is because its hero is conscious. Where would his torture be, indeed, if at every step the hope of succeeding upheld him? . . . The lucidity that was to constitute his torture at the same time crowns his victory.[3]

Sisyphus is without illusions, and his lucidity can be construed as a sort of triumph over his rock. But if consciousness involves a victory, the content of consciousness is the certainty of irremediable defeat: the limit is inexorable, ineluctable, pitiless; forgiveness and release from guilt are beyond imagining. The limit as fate in the instance of Sisyphus, as illusory in the case of Proteus, and as an index of human failure in the myth of Prometheus—none of these rigid and undialectical equations are consonant either with the actualities of experience or with the dialectic of liberty and limitation that the images of player and sufferer affirm.

What is absent from the three myths is some recognition of the creative role that limits perform in conferring orientation and specificity upon freedom. The sufferer, for example, meets his limit in another self, but the meeting can occur in such a fashion that the sufferer's own possibilities are expanded and his selfhood enriched. Limits are integral to the player's expression of his inventiveness and strength; the cruciality of limits for the exercise of finite freedom is one of the first lessons taught by such forms of playing as literature and the arts. Furthermore, none of the three myths provide a world in which forgiveness can be offered and guilt expunged. Proteus is not familiar with the taste of guilt, Sisyphus is eternally unforgivable, and in the story of Prometheus guilt is merely the inevitable correlate of all human creativity. These names and the stories to which they introduce us warp and distort what the images of the self as player, sufferer, and vandal are intended to mean. The imagery needs greater density and specificity so that it will not be vulnerable to misinterpretation, but already it is sufficiently concrete to resist being named in these particular ways.

We begin, therefore, with the recognition that we cannot content ourselves with images because, until they are named, they are liable to misinterpretation. To name an image is to furnish it with a context—in other words, to place it within a story. When images lose their anchorage in stories, they are divested of much of their significance and begin to drift aimlessly, growing enigmatic and increasingly indeterminate. Our goal is the exploration of a story that is sufficiently expansive to include all the dimensions of the representation of the self as player, sufferer, and vandal, while bringing to the im-

ages themselves a new enrichment and concreteness.[4] The
pursuit of the story must be postponed, however, until some
preliminary questions are addressed. First, we must show how
the elaboration of a story can compensate for some of the
inherent limitations of imagery that we have already encountered. Second, it is also necessary to show what the form of
a story, quite independently of its particular content, contributes to self-understanding. Finally, we must ask why the self's
search for intelligibility in its ordinary experience cannot
finally be satisfied except by stories that tell us about beginnings and suggest how things might end.

First, then, in addition to the ambiguity of images apart
from the stories that interpret them, there is also the problem
of their externality to one another. The figure of the vandal
certainly illuminates the extent of the risk involved in understanding the self as a player, while the latter image expresses
the standard of fairness by which the sufferer can appraise the
appeals levied against himself. In this way, the images are
incremental, together building a larger picture of the possibilities and perils of humanness than each can offer alone.
But the three images do not constitute a rational composite;
their relationship is not one of simple increment but of tension and conflict. A story can provide comfortable lodging for
all of them, however; in it they can interpenetrate and interpret one another until they are not merely juxtaposed or
incremental but so thoroughly unified that they convey a single mosaic of the self. Only the art of narrative can disclose
how different images are intended to be weighed in relation
to one another, or which of various subordinate images the
crucial ones are meant to include and which they are fashioned to deny.

Furthermore, not only do stories bring specificity and unity
to diverse images, they also suggest from among several possibilities the particular type of interpretation that is most appropriate. The significance of an image, for example, will
appear very different if it is approached from an historical
perspective than it will if it is viewed in the context of myth.
But there is nothing in the image itself that precludes either

approach. Imagery will assume still a different set of connotations if it is interpreted in an ontocratic context, in terms of
a divine universe the patterns of which are reflected in the
patterns of human affairs, which, therefore, are as unalterable
as their cosmic ground. Arend van Leeuwen has commented
that "the major theme running right through the Old Testament is that which proclaims the kingship of the Lord and the
unremitting struggle against the challenge of the ontocratic
state."[5] But the problem is that when it is uprooted from its
context in the story much of the political imagery of the Bible
lends itself readily to an ontocratic interpretation. This is
certainly one way in which images allow themselves to be held
in unrighteousness when they have lost their stories. The way
that stories mandate one type of interpretation of their imagery rather than another is particularly important, for example,
because the phenomena of play and suffering and vandalism
are not unambiguously religious until they are located in an
appropriate narrative. Only a story can show that the understanding of the self as player is more than merely congruent
with faith in God, but has in fact been adopted in response to
what is believed to be the initiative of the holy, or that the
sufferer believes himself in actuality marching to a different
cadence than the one enforced by social conventions and
needs. It is possible, of course, for an image to express the
fact that the self remains forever *homo religiosus,* but this immanent religiosity does not become seriously theological apart
from an appropriate story. Camus, for example, presents us
with images of the self hungering for infinite meaning and
transformed life while the world steadfastly refuses to honor
the claims placed upon it by the creatures it has spawned. But
the self remains an ineffectual passion: the disparity between
its hopes and the world's answer is best described as absurd
and theology as mere folly. Stories can accomplish what images cannot do—the representation of time as process, development, and change, replete with intimations and
anticipations of *kairos*—and because of this they can disclose
the theological dimensions of the images they contain.

Finally, images are proposed as instruments for self-recognition, but we have seen that they can be employed to maintain a self-deception. Of what use are these instruments to a creature who does not will to know himself? The figure of the vandal incorporates the theme of self-deception, but the other images do not confront us with the possibility that they can be held in unrighteousness. Yet it is the person whose sense of integrity is greatest, the person perhaps most readily persuaded to understand himself as player and sufferer, who is most easily tempted to ignore whatever is not consonant with accustomed behavior. We need perspective upon the untruth our idealism breeds and a way to acknowledge the limits of our claims to righteousness. Sometimes we feel there is good reason not to explicate too carefully the nature of some transactions with other selves, and not only do we evade the explication but we also manage to evade consciousness of our evasion of the explication. These occasions represent not only strange interludes in our lives but also a more or less consistent policy that is necessary if we are to save from jeopardy the essential pattern that we intend our life to display. Hauerwas remarks: "the less integrity, the less motive there is to enter into self-deception. . . . It is because the movement into self-deception is rooted in a concern for integrity of spirit that we temper our condemnation of the self-deceiver. . . . Our urge to be good, to have a coherent and unified self, our need to have a sense of worth, is strong."[6]

The problem cannot be resolved by the creation of another image that will capture the ways in which moral idealism can inaugurate a process of self-deception, for there is no reason why such an image should bite deeply and therapeutically into the conscience of the deceived self. Images have little power to enforce a sense of their relevance upon persons who are best pleased if they can maintain their flight from self-recognition, for images do not have the requisite structural complexity. The form of a narrative, however, is far more complex, so that it can serve as a medium of disclosure in ways that images cannot match. It can conclude in a fashion that falsifies the expectations of the reader, for example, expectations that inevitably reflect his understanding of himself and of his relationships with other selves. The disclosure not only offers us new knowledge, it testifies that our previous schemes of interpretation have been deficient and, therefore, our understanding of selfhood inadequate. Perhaps only because our vision was not as expansive as it might have been, or perhaps for more complex reasons, we have been deceived about the nature of things. From a Christian point of view, then, one criterion of the adequacy of a religious story is that it must relate the self's proclivities for self-deception not only to the figure of the vandal but also to moral passion and integrity, and then by the power of its incongruities, by its success in the overthrow of expectations, invite the self to a new perspective upon and a new appraisal of itself. In a later examination of the structure of narrative, we shall return to reasons why stories can bring to light self-deceptions that images themselves can always be utilized to maintain.

These comments on some of the ways that stories can compensate for the inherent limitations of images resolve one of the questions with which the last chapter concluded: How can diverse images be reconciled and united with one another? They also begin to answer a further question: How can we prevent imagery for self-recognition from being held in unrighteousness? In addressing our second topic, the contribution of the form of stories, without regard to their particular content, to the venture of self-understanding, we confront the last of the questions: How can the final word to the self offer the hope of forgiveness when the final image remains the figure of the vandal in the daimonic guise of a practical joker named Iago? Stories, particularly in the complex form that we describe as a novel, are an important affirmation of personal life. The existence of a novel testifies that experience is amenable to humanization, in the sense that the environment of the self can be represented as a world and that some patterns of intelligibility can be found in what persons do and suffer. It testifies that communication among selves is possible and worth whatever effort it involves. Communication is worthwhile, however, only if selves are worthwhile, only if there is reason to affirm the others with whom this work creates a relationship, only if the careers memorialized in the story and those affected by it are worthy of attention and care. As a public event, then, the novel says not only "I" but "You and I together." It is written in order to be shared and it states that human life is intended to be a relational affair.

But not only is the existence of the novel a vindication of human agency and creativeness; in the necessary symmetry between the beginning and the end of the narrative, in the congruence shaped by human actions and decisions, there is a further vindication of the self as an agent and not merely as a victim of its world. The form of the novel affirms unconditionally that life is worthwhile. No matter how many and vicious are the crimes that it charges against mankind, no matter how bleak are its prophecies concerning the future, the art of narrative remains *formally* an unconditional affirmation of personal life. Therefore, it provides a structure that is appropriate to express the unconditional affirmation that is *materially* implied in an offer of forgiveness. If forgiveness is imaginable, then it is the last and most important word of all: consequently, the possibility of it must find expression in an appropriate structure, and this occurs in narrative where the form affirms unconditionally the existence, though scarcely the acts, of the elusive first person singular who is a player and a sufferer and the source of instances of deviant behavior too many and various ever fully to chronicle. The form of the novel affirms that the last word to the self, even as vandal, remains the possibility of forgiveness. Yet, because this is no more than a formal statement, it does not represent forgiveness as necessary; it does not portray affairs as though the forgiver were deprived of his initiative and freedom or the act of its unforeseeable and undeserved character.

There is a complementary aspect of the form of narrative that also deserves examination. In his study of evil from the perspective of Christian faith, John Hick writes:

> Sometimes we see good being created out of evil: we see
> sin ending in repentance and obstacles breeding
> strength of character, dangers evoking courage and un-

selfishness, or calamities producing patience and moral steadfastness. But too often we see the opposite of this in wickedness multiplying and in the disintegration of personalities under the impact of suffering: we see good turned to evil, kindness to bitterness, hope to despair. And from our own observations, even when supple-mented by the entire scroll of recorded history . . . we have to say simply that the incomprehensible mingling in human experience of good and evil, virtue and vice, pain and pleasure, grief and laughter, continues in all its char-acteristic and baffling ambiguity throughout life and ends only with death. . . . Any revision of the verdict must depend upon lengthening the perspective out until it reaches a new and better conclusion. If there is any even-tual resolution of the interplay between good and evil, any decisive bringing of good out of evil, it must lie beyond this world and beyond the enigma of death.[7]

"Lengthening the perspective out" until it reaches beyond the interruptions and terminations and failed beginnings that infect the present is a necessary venture if the self is to func-tion as an agent at all. The strategy of evil, as we have said, is to deny us any perspective upon itself or context in which to appraise it, so that we are unmanned because it occupies the whole horizon of our vision. Images of evil seem to remain nothing more than an agglomeration of nominalist particu-lars that we can never incorporate into some greater and more humanizing complex of experience. So they can obsess and terrify people, bringing them to despair and thereby com-pounding their tyranny, unless stories lengthen perspective until people are no longer paralyzed by whatever they have seen. This is not to express a preference for illusion rather than reality: a lengthened perspective may begin as a fiction devised by hope when there were no persuasive reasons for hope, but it becomes the real determinant of our actions. Consequently, we are empowered to deal differently with the evils that we confront, to act more resolutely and creatively than it would ever be possible to do if we were deprived of our sustaining stories. Even in the most bleak and unrelieved of tragedies, the form of the narrative suggests that perspective can be lengthened still further, and the events of the story set in a new and more expansive context where their significance will be invested with additional and somehow different dimensions. Narrative form involves lengthening the perspective, then, and this is to imply anew the possibility of forgiveness, just as one aspect of the offer of forgiveness is a lengthened perspective that can see beyond insensitivity or insult or an instance of betrayal.

More often than not, however, we fail to keep events in perspective, despite all the possibilities that a lengthened perspective affords for the transformation of the time between the times. The present does not seem amenable to transformation, for the narratives in which we are engaged are constantly broken off, interrupted by guilt and remorse and sudden impotence, allowed to lapse because of indifference or enervation, denied sometimes because their exigencies are simply too much for us. The disconnections in our lives are so obtrusive, our blame for them so obvious, or else our relief at them so vast, that we have neither relish nor strength to search for a beginning, for wherever the blame or fault, the entanglement or captivity, began. And yet, does not a lengthened perspective mean that we must discover the beginning of everything? And, if there is consonance between the beginning and the end, will we not find our end prefigured when we arrive at the point where we began? Must we not turn toward the origins of affairs, for how can their end otherwise be foreseen?

In another fine novel by William Golding, *Free Fall*, Sammy Mountjoy tries to revisit the beginning in order to comprehend the reasons why he has become what he is, in order to find where the first link was forged in the chain that binds and fetters his spoiled nature, what might be "the connection between the little boy, clear as spring water, and the man like a stagnant pool."[8] In a camp for prisoners of war, Mountjoy —"You know of me, Samuel Mountjoy, I hang in the Tate"[9] —sets out to discover how he became his own prisoner before he became a prisoner of others: "When did I lose my freedom? For once, I was free. I had power to choose."[10] No longer are the choices his, however, not because of con-

straints externally imposed but rather because the molten
metal of the beginning has cooled into obdurate forms that
are unalterable now, so that everything has become predictable, stale, fated, resistant even to the alchemy of penitence.
Beyond comprehension yet demanding comprehension if the
beginning is ever to be found, the cooled metal

> is the unnameable, unfathomable and invisible darkness
> that sits at the centre of him, always awake, always differ-
> ent from what you believe it to be, always thinking and
> feeling what you can never know it thinks and feels, that
> hopes hopelessly to understand and to be understood.
> Our loneliness is the loneliness not of the cell or the
> castaway; it is the loneliness of that dark thing that sees
> as at the atom furnace by reflection, feels by remote
> control and hears only words phoned to it in a foreign
> tongue.[11]

In his remembrances of the little boy, who never was half
so clear as spring water, there is no answer to Sammy's question, even though there is a sort of consonance between what
he has become and its youthful precursor who floated
"through life like a bubble, empty of guilt, empty of anything
but immediate and conscienceless emotions, generous,
greedy, cruel, innocent."[12] There is a haunting certainty of
responsibility, the sharp taste of darkness, but the origin of
everything continues to elude him; at every juncture, the answer is: "No, not here." Earlier, then? Or not yet?

> The smell of today, the grey faces that look over my
> shoulder have nothing to do with the infant Samuel. I
> acquit him. He is some other person in some other coun-
> try to whom I have this objective and ghostly access. Why
> does his violence and wickedness stop there, islanded in
> pictures? Why should his lies and sensualities, his cruelty
> and selfishness have been forgiven him? For forgiven
> him they are. The scar is gone. The smell either inevita-
> ble or chosen came later. I am not he. I am a man who
> goes at will to that show of shadows, sits in judgment as
> over a strange being. I look for the point where this
> monstrous world of my present consciousness began and
> I acquit him.[13]

Somewhere near the heart of the matter is his relationship with Beatrice, the mistress whom he had pursued with
passion but without freedom, bereft of choice, for even
then "in all that lamentable story of seduction I could not
remember one moment when being what I was I could do
other than I did. . . ."[14] Their affair has a taste of ashes:
moments of pleasure are never linked to one another by
disclosures of the person who pleases, for in Beatrice there
is a dark emptiness and vulnerability that eventuates in in-
curable schizophrenia. But Sammy cannot see far enough
to envision her imminent illness when he tells her: "I said
I loved you. Oh God, don't you know what that means? I
want you, I want all of you, not just cold kisses and walks
—I want to be with you and in you and on you and round
you—I want fusion and identity—I want to understand and
be understood—oh God, Beatrice, Beatrice, I love you—I
want to be you!"[15]

Even if Sammy was no longer free, however, long before he
cried out for "fusion and identity," those words carry us as
close as possible to the mystery: what account can be offered
for this rupture in the rational universe of Sammy Mountjoy,
this burning desire to leave himself? What source can be
found for this passion beyond taming to have nothing, not
even pleasure; to be nothing, not even one's own self; to lose
everything, the other and the self together, as well as the
whole world that the other has now blocked from the self's
view? For certainly there is no less than all of this at stake
when he says, "I want to be you!" There is another occasion,
weeks earlier, when Sammy converses with himself after an
evening swim:

> What is important to you?
> "Beatrice Ifor."
> She thinks you depraved already. She dislikes you.
> "If I want something enough I can always get it provided
> I am willing to make the appropriate sacrifice."
> What will you sacrifice?
> "Everything."
> Here?[16]

Was it here, the beginning and the loss? There is no certainty. Even if the roots of the loss of freedom can be traced to the evening of the swim, still the mystery remains: the flaw in nature that nourished the roots, fed and fattened them so that in retrospect "I could not remember one moment when being what I was I could do other than I did." What is there hidden somewhere in a Sammy Mountjoy that drives him to offer everything, even identity, and so deprive himself of the possibility of any relationships at all and deny himself the possibility of any satisfaction ever, for nothing could return the totality that he is prepared to sacrifice? In the end he has only the certainty with which he began: "Somewhere, some time, I made a choice in freedom and lost my freedom."[17] That scrap of knowledge accompanies and enforces the twisted desire that was voiced in his ambition to be Beatrice and that is expressed again in a darker and more defeated vein when he cries: "Oh, the continent of a man, the peninsulas, capes, deep bays, jungles and grasslands, the deserts, the lakes, the mountains and high hills. How shall I be rid of this kingdom, how shall I give it away?"[18]

Sammy feels the taste of guilt on his tongue, its bitterness all the greater because of his conviction that "nothing can be repaired or changed. The innocent cannot forgive."[19] He seems as unforgivable to himself as she is manifestly innocent now, for whether or not Sammy was the instrument of her disaster, Beatrice has stepped irrevocably across the border that separates sanity from madness. But if forgiveness seems impossible to Sammy, comprehension is no less so, for the roots of the flaw or fault, or whatever it is, strike too deep. Comprehension would at least enable Sammy to claim as his own what he already knows is his, but even this small triumph is denied him. The beginning remains dark, elusive, beyond recall, and so there can be found no prefiguring of the end of things. In a middle that is illuminated by neither, there is nothing except endlessness, the tyranny of habits, the hegemony of compulsions, the reality of bondage, the painful knowledge that, being what he is, there is little reason for surprise that he has done what he has done. There is the suspicion of a consonance between the middle and its beginning, but that affords no grounds for hope. In the endless world of the middle there can be no hopes, only expectations; there are no more first nights, just a succession of rehearsals of last season's fare.

The problem is not so much that Sammy cannot find with any certainty the crucial anecdote in the story of his life; it is, instead, that he can never bring quite into focus the cruciality of them all. But at least it is clear that in the beginning there was not simply an unknown father, a perpetually drunken mother, abject deprivation, persons who excused him too freely, others who beat him too quickly, the conventions and injustices of the social order—there was also something more. If it cannot be recovered by revisiting where everything began, perhaps the incandescence of a sense of an ending can shed its light even as far as the origins of things and render the middle, the time between the times, an occasion for hope, healing, and renewal. Perhaps in some way the end is immanent in the beginning, but perhaps it is only through the illumination cast by a sense of an ending that the proportions of the beginning can be revealed. If we cannot foresee where everything will end, at least hope and anticipation can introduce us to tomorrow or next month, or to another season or a new year—or to a different generation. Then we can imagine differences from the present that have at least some modest capacity to make the present different than it is. Sammy's quest concludes in defeat because, in his search for a lengthened perspective, he turned in the wrong direction. It is the end that tells us the significance of origins, the future that discloses the full meaning of the present and past.

Before turning in a different direction than the one that Mountjoy chose, however, it must be acknowledged that the frustration of his ambitions raises in a very urgent way the question of whether narrative form is an appropriate instrument for the organization of experience or whether "lengthening the perspective out" simply traps us in new folly and illusion. Perhaps it would be better to content ourselves with the moment and seize the day. But this is finally impossible because, as Stephen Crites reminds us, experience has *inherently* a narrative quality. Consequently, stories are not arbitrary devices that have been invented for the organization of what is intrinsically featureless and inchoate; they are responses to and more complex representations of a structure that experience itself possesses. "Stories give qualitative substance to the form of experience," he writes, "because it is itself an incipient story."[20] In the before and after of memory and the now and not yet of anticipation, we confront the sequential character of life, even if not the distinctions between past and present and future. But remembering and anticipation are acts that occur in the present; from this perspective we can speak of future and past and, because we thus encounter our coherence and persistence through time, we can claim that future and past as our own. Crites writes:

> Precisely as modalities of the present of experience, the past remembered is determinate, the future anticipated is indeterminate, and the distinction between them is intuitively clear and absolute. But how can the present contain such tension, on the one hand unifying, on the other hand absolutely distinguishing its tensed modalities? It can do so because the whole experience, as it is concentrated in a conscious present, has a narrative form. Narrative alone can contain the full temporality of experience in a unity of form. But this incipient story, implicit in the very possibility of experience, must be such that it can absorb both the chronicle of memory and the scenario of anticipation, absorb them within a richer narrative form without effacing the difference between the determinacy of the one and the indeterminacy of the other.[21]

This rudimentary narrative quality of all experience does not dictate one interpretation of temporality rather than another, nor does it counsel that the connections between discrete moments are "either magical, causal, logical, or teleological."[22] Different understandings of time are derived from diverse cultural forms, from the structure of a particular language and from the particular stories with which the self most intimately identifies itself. Therefore, "in principle, we can distinguish between the inner drama of experience and the stories through which it achieves coherence. But in any actual case the two so interpenetrate that they form a virtual identity, which, if we may pun a little, is in fact a man's very sense of his own personal identity."[23]

Our purpose is not to argue anew the case that Crites has presented for the narrative quality of experience, but only to emphasize that stories are necessary complements to images of selfhood not only because of the inherent limitations of the latter but also because nothing else can do justice to the form of our experiencing and the texture of our experiences. Without narrative, we would be unable to grasp the actuality of our experience. Existence does not consist of a series of "now" and "now" and "now." It involves remembering and anticipation as present activities that at once distinguish past and future from the present and relate them to it so that experience is always characterized by a rudimentary narrative form that can be expressed only by stories. On the other hand, like Sammy Mountjoy we have encountered many reasons why it is difficult to discern this inherent narrative element. Evils spread like cancer across the field of vision until we can see nothing else. Motiveless and compulsive instances of behavior appear to relate to nothing beyond themselves. Indifference and cruelty, shame and guilt, repression and essays in self-deception eventuate in still more disconnections and dislocations in the fabric of life. So we become suspicious of narrative form: it seems nothing more than fiction, even more fictional than the fictions that the form was devised to convey. The skepticism is reflected in and reinforced by much of the conventional wisdom of our society: that the moment is all, that life begins at forty, that ours is a world without consequences, that this is the first day of the rest of one's life. Precisely because it is not easy to see the threads of a narrative amid all of the interstices that divide the episodes of common experience, however, stories become even more critical for the health of the human enterprise. When the narrative quality of experience is ignored or can no longer be discerned, the consequences are many and considerable. In its apparent divorce from past and future, the present is reduced to a vanishing point: the self is disoriented; the significance of its freedom and the proportions of its agency grow obscure.

Anticipations concern today as much as they do tomorrow; while the anticipation cannot be realized until tomorrow, the entertainment of it both enriches the present and awards to it the particular orientation that it has. Because of our anticipations, we can savor the present and the future together in the present and we find motivation now to exercise our freedom and agency, not only in relation to the present but also with reference to goals that can barely be glimpsed against the horizon. Therefore, when a sense of the narrative quality of life is lost, not only does the future become increasingly indeterminate and forbidding, but the present is impoverished as well. If we cannot relate it to anything else, it soon grows senseless—and, if we cannot relate it to anything else, there is reason to suspect that the senselessness is endless. "It's a wearying business, being plague-stricken," confesses Tarrou in *The Plague,* wearying to be trapped always in the time between the times, in the middle, caught in the midst of the ceaseless round of suffering and evil, of the emergence of new possibilities and their spoilage or cancellation because, no matter what modest transformation of itself the self achieves, it still remains very much as it has always been, not so much renewed by forgiveness past as yet in need of forgiveness future and frequent.

So the self yearns for a sense of an ending, for the disclosure of a conclusion and consummation that can invest the time between the times with greater significance, provide new reasons for the daily battle of the self against itself, banish the suspicion of endlessness that renders life a wearying business, and sort into sense the apparent senselessness of things because endings that remain stubbornly future still have their own mode of immanence and transformative power in the present. The self is an eschatological passion, living the present in relation to a future filled with things hoped for, able to devise new hopes even beyond the hopes that now sustain it, capable of imagining a future beyond the farthest shores of the future that it has yet envisioned, restless with every consummation because it is always possible to entertain new anticipations, reaching always for a "something more" in the future that can never be fully or finally specified. So the story is the most characteristic of all the self's creations and nothing else will satisfy its deepest passions, for stories afford the sense of an ending that can provide a context for the interpretation of the present, which now discloses more and richer dimensions than hitherto it seemed to possess. In the form of narrative, in the movement from "once upon a time" to "happily ever after," we find the answer to our final question: because *the self is an eschatological passion*, its quest for intelligibility can be satisfied by nothing less than a sense of an ending that invests the present with its essential orientation and meaning. The self is the only creature that not only has a future but knows that it has a future. Only when the anticipations and apprehensions that inevitably arise from that knowledge are consolidated in a story orienting the self toward whatever is "not yet" can the freedom and agency of the individual be satisfactorily expressed. As Frank Kermode has commented in his fine essay, *The Sense of an Ending:*

> It makes little difference—though it makes some— whether you believe the age of the world to be six thousand years or five thousand million years, whether you think time will have a stop or that the world is eternal; there is still a need to speak humanly of a life's importance in relation to it—a need in the moment of existence to belong, to be related to a beginning and to an end. The physician Alkmeon observed, with Aristotle's approval, that men die because they cannot join the beginning and the end. What they, the dying men, can do is to imagine a significance for themselves in these unremembered but imaginable events.[24]

We have seen that a sense of an ending affects the present as well as refers to the future: expectations for tomorrow award present patience a new significance, endow present planning with new urgency, invest present leisure with greater preciousness because there will be none tomorrow. A sense of an ending means the transfiguration of the events that lead toward it and not merely their termination, for it is immanent in the present as well as imminent in the future— immanent not only in the sense that the "not yet" will display some continuity with the "now," but in the more important sense that the "not yet" provides us with motivation to act in order to transform the present until the "now" is brought into some conformity with the imagined future. So the ending not only provides us with more complex schemes of interpretation than the present alone affords, it also counsels us to act differently, to conduct ourselves in some sense against the present and as though the future were already realized. It persuades selves that they may and ought to live "as if" and "as if not," as if the future were already present and as if the elements in the present that resist the future were not, as if they were consistent players in a world that elicited and supported basic trust, and as if they were not in the world as it is. So the present may begin to achieve a scrap of congruence with a future that does not yet exist but that is sometimes more powerful than everything that does; what is first encountered as a fiction can, by its capacity to persuade and challenge, function as a reality empowering the self to struggle against all the realities by which it was hitherto oppressed.

In the light of this emphasis upon the cruciality of a sense of an ending, however, perhaps it would be well to distinguish between stories and narratives. The latter tell of the past and present and future, but they can be undertaken at any point one chooses, suddenly broken off or interrupted, perhaps resumed later or perhaps never finished. A story that is useful for purposes of human definition is different, however, for in it everything is related to a beginning and an end. The ending is not merely a cessation of events; it is a consummation that persuades us that it is "appropriate" in relation to what was

immanent in the beginning, "appropriate" to the character of
the persons whom we met there, to the nature of the particular world they inhabit, to the exigencies of its temporality and
to the perils of its contingency.

Between the beginning and the ending, then, there must be
congruence, but as Frank Kermode reminds us in *The Sense of
an Ending* there must also be an element of incongruity, the
appearance of what was unexpected and imprevisible, for otherwise the story will scarcely serve as the instrument of a
disclosure that is humanly interesting. On the one hand,
therefore, there must be the concordance between beginning
and end, else we shall not only have displayed the merely
contingent and accidental character of our existence but re-
signed ourselves to it. On the other, the concordance must
occur against our expectations, it must surprise us and overthrow our assumptions, for otherwise we learn nothing that
we have not always known and in the predictability of the
march toward the ending there is little to grasp our attention
and no trace of human freedom and inventiveness.

One example of this relationship of congruence and incongruence can be found in the sense of an ending that the
Christian tradition has derived from faith that the universe
has declared itself personal, that God has come among selves
in the person of Jesus Christ. The congruence exists because
the end is envisioned as the fulfillment of what selves were
originally created to become. The incongruence arises from
the fact that persons could not achieve fulfillment for themselves, because they had become the victims of a self-deception that obscured its meaning as well as the path toward its
realization. Consequently, the story can serve as a medium of
disclosure for everyone who misunderstood fulfillment and
sought it where it could not be found. Now, in the time between the times of beginning and end, the characters in the
story and all others who identify themselves with it may and
ought to live in accordance with a gift that they could never
have gained for themselves. In this gracious appeal to live "as
if" and "as if not" there is a renewed affirmation of human
freedom and creativeness.

Kermode contends that if a story is to express congruence between the ending and the beginnings of a creature endowed with its own finite freedom and agency, the ending must be envisioned as a consummation that occurs within the historical process and not as a "timeless" affair above or beyond history. He phrases his argument in the context of a sharp distinction between myth and fiction:

> Myth operates within the diagrams of ritual, which presupposes total and adequate explanations of things as they are and were; it is a sequence of radically unchangeable gestures. Fictions are for finding things out, and they change as the needs of sense-making change. Myths are the agents of stability, fictions the agents of change. Myths call for absolute, fictions for conditional assent. Myths make sense in terms of a lost order of time, *illud tempus* as Eliade calls it; fictions, if successful, make sense of the here and now, *hoc tempus*. [25]

He illustrates the difference by reference to the contrast that Erich Auerbach develops in *Mimesis* between the story of the scar of Odysseus and the story of the sacrifice of Isaac, which "is perpetually open to history, to reinterpretation— one remembers how central the story was to Kierkegaard—in terms of changed human ways of speaking about the single form of the world. The Odyssey is not, in this way, open."[26] It is Kermode's judgment that myths present the self and its world and their mutual end as antecedently determined, while fictions are useful devices for discoveries and the exercise of inventiveness within a world that is seen as amenable to transformation by human agency. The story of Isaac is an invitation to new discernment, not a declaration of what is fixed, unalterable, exhausted of its possibilities of disclosure; it does not "represent the world of potency as a world of act."[27] In his terminology, then, any sense of an ending that is consonant with our beginnings as creatures endowed with finite freedom is a fiction.[28] To live as if the future were present and as though the present in some sense were not is an imperative or invitation that testifies to the importance of human agency, freedom, and creativity in the realization of the end, even though, at least in the instance of the biblical narrative, the achievement is guaranteed by powers more than human. It is not yet clear what we shall be: the biblical ending is definite and yet partly indeterminate, revealed and yet still partly hidden, because ingredient in it will be the variegated and unforeseeable experiences and actions of persons who may and must struggle to live "as if" and "as if not."

From the perspective of the Bible, if we are to speak of fulfillment, it is also necessary to focus upon judgment, because of all there is within persons that causes them to savage others and themselves. Fulfillment without judgment is impossible, and so the incongruity between beginning and end must be stressed as much as the consonance. The representation of the incongruence must be accomplished in a way that renders the story an instrument for heightened self-recognition on the part of those to whom it is told, a medium of disclosure that upsets their perspectives and counsels them to repent. They have been deceived by conventional expectations or else they have deceived themselves, but now the story counsels them to lay the deception aside. To cite Kermode again:

> The story that proceeded very simply to its obviously predestined end would be nearer myth than novel or drama. Peripeteia, which has been called the equivalent, in narrative, of irony in rhetoric, is present in every story of the least structural sophistication. Now peripeteia depends upon our confidence of the end; it is a disconfirmation followed by a consonance; the interest of having our expectations falsified is obviously related to our wish to reach the discovery or recognition by an unexpected and instructive route. . . . The more daring the peripeteia, the more we may feel that the work respects our sense of reality . . . finding something out for us, something *real.* The falsification of an expectation can be terrible, as in the death of Cordelia; it is a way of finding something out that we should, on our more conventional way to the end, have closed our eyes to. Obviously it could not work if there were not a certain rigidity in the set of our expectations.[29]

The story, then, sets us at some remove from our conventional world and the rigidities of our expectations there and presents us with something to which we would have shut our eyes and about which we would have preferred to remain deceived. Our interest in having our expectations falsified did not comprehend or desire the prospect that they would be falsified in this fashion. The rigidities of our expectations have their origins in the way we understand ourselves, as we have said, for our perspectives are enshrined in our self-images. So the incongruity that derives its revelatory power from this inflexibility in ourselves implies criticism of and offers some remedy for an understanding of the self that is partial or shallow or inflated. In other words, the structure of the story depends for its effect upon the extent to which persons deceive themselves and are deceived about themselves, as this is disclosed in the rigidity of their expectations.

In summary, the questions with which the previous chapter concluded led us to explore some of the ways that stories, by their form as well as by their content, prove indispensable to the venture of self-understanding. Stories capture, as images do not, the ironies of human history and the temporality of the self. They provide an anchorage that confers new and crucial specificity upon images, and they can unify images that initially seem unrelated. The novel testifies that human life is memorable and is worthy of whatever craft and passion memorialization requires; it is an appropriate form for the expression of the unconditional affirmation of the self, even the self of the vandal, that forgiveness involves. It is a formal witness that forgiveness is forever possible, though never assured.

At the same time, the effectiveness of the story constrains its reader or hearer to confront the rigidity or superficiality or viciousness, sometimes self-induced, of his own vision. Because stories afford a sense of an ending, they lengthen perspectives so that evil is no longer a nominalist particular against which there is no defense. Because there is a narrative quality written into our experience and because the self is incorrigibly an eschatological passion, nothing less will satisfy the appetite of the individual for intelligibility than a sense of an ending that will add new richness to the present and orient our agency and freedom. Perhaps our endings are immanent in our beginnings, but the travail of Sammy Mountjoy is sufficient warning that it is not toward the origins of things but toward their eventual destiny that we must turn. Indeed, were it possible to discover a beginning that could explain all that followed after it, the tale of origins would be closer to myth than fiction, to return to Kermode's terminology, for it would have displayed the world of potency as though it were a world of act. If the quest for self-understanding can be fulfilled only in relation to a story, however, it is still to be determined how we can discriminate among better and worse. Furthermore, if the search can be satisfied only by a story that is religious, what standards can we employ to distinguish the religious story from others that are merely mundane?

The world abounds with shards and fragments of images of the self, and these have their lodgings in many different stories or in bits and pieces of narrative. Sometimes intentionally, more often without quite recognizing what they have done, persons identify themselves with some stories and discard others that seem trivial or frightening or perhaps too exigent. The choices seem to represent little more than individual preference; there are always conflicting assessments of the "expressive adequacy" of a particular narrative, its capacity to exhibit the self as it is and as it desires to be. But there are criteria for distinguishing between better and worse that have nothing to do with idiosyncratic judgments concerning expressive adequacy. It has been implicit in the course of the argument that the figures of the player, the sufferer, and the vandal afford norms for evaluation of a religious or crypto-religious story, even though their full significance remains opaque apart from the story that they are intended to crystallize and the particular sense of an ending that is expressed in it. Although we have insisted that images grow enigmatic and slippery when they are separated from their stories, it is equally true that they retain a certain concreteness and specificity even in isolation, as we discovered from the way that the figures of the player and sufferer resisted the names of

Prometheus and Proteus. If we must interpret images in the light of the narrative they inhabit, we also find in them adumbrations of, clues to, and canons of interpretation for the story itself, so that we are enabled to discriminate between better and worse rehearsals of it; the relationship between them is necessarily circular.[30] Images afford a critical perspective upon particular renditions of a story; the story provides critical perspective upon different interpretations of the imagery.

But there is another critical role that images can also perform. Many of the implications of the images of player, sufferer, and vandal can be justified only by faith in God. There is certainly no more than modest verification in experience of some of the assumptions that playing involves, for there is little reason to qualify our seriousness toward what we love most if there are no hands except our own to sustain and cherish it. On the other hand, these images also have an empirical dimension, roots in common experience and a large measure of justification in the nature of the self's sensory commerce with its natural and social worlds. It is appropriate, therefore, to criticize the stories we are told in the light of the possible or actual experience that these three images include. Is the narrative sufficiently complex and expansive to accommodate all the experience that they suggest and to offer a model of the self that includes the cellarage of the mind as well as the commitment to truth and justice? There are many stories of God, and there are many others that declare there are no gods at all. Which we choose is, finally, a question of faith; the only option closed to us is that we might choose none at all. But one thing is certain: there is no rectitude to the storytelling of either theist or atheist if the partner in dialogue with either God or endless night is represented as though persons were without the potential to live as players and sufferers, and as vandals, too. When an allegedly religious story conveys less than this, story means no more than illusion and persons would be well advised to forget it.

The claim that fidelity to these images is a significant gauge of the truthfulness of a religious story requires some clarification. Despite their legitimation in common experience, the images have been chosen not because of their familiarity but through dialogue with the biblical tradition and in response to it. From the perspective of Christian faith, the determination of whether or not they are adequate instruments for self-recognition depends upon whether or not they are able to express the rudiments of the biblical understanding of selfhood. It is the Bible, not the imagery, that is authoritative. It is important to emphasize this derivation because it reflects a particular understanding of natural theology as a discipline entirely subordinated to the self-disclosure of God, not an independent inquiry but a response to divine initiative. Like its predecessors, this essay employs the resources of the Christian tradition to explore the texture of our ordinary experience for its witness to the holy and its disclosures of the human, without any pretense of neutrality or "objectivity," in order that Christian language about God and his creatures might not lose touch with the immediacies and ambiguities of our condition.

So the use of this imagery to gauge the truth of a certain type of narrative does not mean that religious stories can be assessed from some external perspective that is innocent of theological commitment. In this context, then, the question of truth becomes a question of function: Does a story, and do these images themselves, communicate powerfully and expansively the core of the biblical message concerning the world, the self, and God? Truth is measured in terms of functionality in relation to the biblical universe, and this functionality must be appraised in two ways if, indeed, this essay is to be represented as an essay in natural theology. On the one hand, there is the question of fidelity to the biblical sources, which is addressed in the following chapter. Certain motifs, for example, can scarcely be absent: judgment and liberation, the need for expiation and forgiveness, awe and loyalty, the possibility of reconciliation, and triumph over evil. On the other hand, there is also the question of the "empirical fit" of a religious story and of these particular images, our ability to display their power to organize experience in a way that points to the truth of Christian claims.[31]

There are several reasons why empirical fit is a more complex affair than at first it seems. The ways of God surpass our powers of discernment except as God wills to make himself known, and so natural theology is impossible except as ancillary to revelation; only if we begin with God shall we end with him. Consequently, we can entertain only the most modest expectations for our imagery and stories, for whether or not a story is religious depends at least in part upon whether or not it actually functions as such in the life of a particular individual, and this is finally determined by powers greater than our own. As I. T. Ramsey writes:

> Whether the light breaks or not is something that we ourselves cannot entirely control. We can certainly choose what seem to us the most appropriate models, we can operate what seem to us the most suitable qualifiers; we can develop what seem to us the best stories, but we can never guarantee that for a particular person the light will dawn at a particular point, or for that matter at any point in any story. Need this trouble us? Is not this only what has been meant by religious people when they have claimed that the "initiative" in any "disclosure" or "revelation" must come from God? It would certainly not accord with what religious people have claimed if we could take some particular model, develop it with some particular qualifier, and produce God. That would be semantic magic. Nor if we could develop some particular story could we guarantee God's emergence. For we should then have a technique which gave us power over God.[32]

"God" is an indispensable term to describe the substance of Christian commitment, the orientation of Christian discernment, the motive for the intentionality and consistency that we term Christian character. Consequently, the question of empirical fit concerns the extent to which religious stories provision us to recognize and respond to the presence of the holy in and among the other agents abroad in the world. But the problem is that we are in principle committed to the thesis that some persons are not able to see that a religious story is in fact religious and more than a bit of mystification. The remedy for their disability lies neither in the devising of a better story nor in all our powers of persuasion. Perhaps the incapacity of many people to recognize the religious dimensions of certain stories is not a significant issue, for narratives of great complexity never lose their power to evoke different and conflicting interpretations.

There is, however, a more serious complication that is suggested by the notion of empirical fit. It arises from the classical Protestant insistence that not only can God be known only where and as he wills, but also that there can be no knowledge of God without acknowledgment of him, no knowledge apart from commitment. Therefore, empirical fit cannot involve less than persuasive evidence that the story actually shapes persons in a way that is congruent with the perception of reality that it offers. In other words, the story must function to develop Christian character; the question of whether it communicates "powerfully and expansively the core of the biblical message" cannot be reduced to less than this. "Character" is a word that indicates we have managed to tell one principal story in our life, a story full of digressions and aborted minor plots and inexplicable inconsistencies, certainly, but still a more or less rational and disciplined narrative. Our ability to accomplish this depends not so much upon our own initiative and creativity as it does upon the stories that we have heard. Stanley Hauerwas properly emphasizes the integral relation between the two:

> Our moral lives are not simply made up of the addition of our separate responses to particular situations. Rather we exhibit an orientation that gives our life a theme through which the variety of what we do and do not do can be scored. To be agents at all requires a directionality that involves the development of character and virtue. Our character is the result of our sustained attention to the world that gives a coherence to our intentionality. Such attention is formed and given content by the stories through which we have learned to form the story of our lives. To be moral persons is to allow stories to be told

through us so that our manifold activities gain a coherence that allows us to claim them for our own.[33]

The primary reference of empirical fit, then, is not to the
relevance of the story for the organization of experience but
to its capacity to transform the one who experiences. "Experience" is not a cognitive object but simply a term to describe
our constant engagements with ourselves, other selves, a multitude of things, and in and through some of these, sometimes, also with the presence and power of God. The quality
of this ceaseless commerce depends upon our receptivity to
the overtures of these entities and upon the resources that we
possess for grasping their different identities, significations,
and possibilities. These resources consist of the whole gamut
of images that constitute the symbolic universe in terms of
which we see and evaluate everything we meet. It is true, of
course, that reality can lash out to confound and overwhelm
imagination; such happenings are not frequent, however, and
we have many defenses against them. If our store of imagery,
then, is not hospitable to theological engagements, we shall
not recognize intimations of the holy for what they are. On
the other hand, it is equally possible for us to be indiscrimi-
nate in our claims to see the presence of God, deceiving
ourselves by the confidence that the hand of the Lord is here,
there, and everywhere.

In any event, the ambiguity of experience is so great that
it will often afford a measure of verification to all sorts of
patterns of interpretation. It is amenable to organization in
ways that are not only different but in conflict, and so a certain
amount of empirical fit is predictable for any serious attempt
at interpretation, whether religious or not. But this is not a
sort of verification that is of particular importance for Christian faith, because unless it eventuates in the transformation
of personal character it collides with the principle that there
can be no true knowledge of God without acknowledgment of
him. Consequently, the focus of the question of empirical fit
must remain upon the renewal of the self, even though the
capacity of stories to accomplish this is difficult to assess be-

cause so much of the future is hid ¹en from us. Because the self is in process, is becoming, is oriented toward its future— because the self must live "as if" the future were present and in some measure "as if not" in relation to the presentness of the present if it is to realize its present projects, empirical fit can be satisfactorily verified only when the "not yet" has become "now." Because it refers to the character of the one creature who not only possesses a future but knows that he possesses a future, it cannot be divested of its stubbornly eschatological cast.[34] Empirical fit, then, directs us primarily forward rather than toward the present and to the one who experiences more than to the nature of the experience that one undergoes.

The self and its world are correlative, however. The subjective cannot be divorced from the objective because if the self loses its world, it loses itself. Stories could scarcely function to transform character, therefore, if they launched no claims about the world and its history as well as about the persons who live in it. In conclusion, then, we must address the question of what it is about the world that a religious story is intended to convey. How do religious narratives differ from the commonplace stories that are our ordinary fare? In *Religious Language*, I. T. Ramsey discusses the "nature miracles" of the New Testament, which seem to furnish us with a paradigm of the religious story at its most naïve, and he comments: "What a miracle claims about the universe is, then, that on some occasion the universe 'comes alive' in a personal sort of way." Then Ramsey proceeds to tell us a story:

> It is as though, day after day for years, a ticket examiner at the station has impressed us by his machine-like efficiency, reversing our ticket, clipping it at the appropriate point. . . . Then, one day, we book a ticket to a certain remote village which proves to be the very spot where he was born, and which he has not seen since a child. In naming our destination today, there is still the routine answer with machine-like precision, but there is maybe an oddity of pronunciation, maybe a quiver in the voice; but in any event our "eyes meet" and we think to our-

selves: "By jove, he is human after all." An impersonal
situation comes alive in a characteristically personal sort
of way, there is "more" to it than on earlier occasions,
and we have a situation reminiscent of a miracle. . . . A
miracle-story in general tells of a "disclosure"; of a characteristically theological situation; of a situation which
has "depth" and "mystery"; a situation which is more
than "what is seen." About such a situation, a miracle-
story makes a special and particular claim, *viz.* that in it
is exhibited a "personal intervention" . . . a "power"
which is "personal concern." So we may say summarily
that miracle-stories are endeavors in terms of public language to express the fact that certain situations possess
observable factors of a nonpersonal kind which by their
odd pattern are nevertheless expressive of characteristically personal activity. In a miracle the Universe declares itself personal at a point where persons are not;
and the miracle-story must be odd enough to make this
remarkable claim.[35]

A religious narrative, then, at least one that is compatible
with the Christian tradition, is a story wherein "the Universe
declares itself personal at a point where persons are not." To
be more precise, since our concern is not strictly with "nature
miracles," *a religious story is one in which the universe declares itself
personal at a point where persons are not adequate to account for the
magnitude of the declaration.* Sometimes the transformation of
the impersonal into the personal can occur in our transactions
with nature; more often, as Ramsey's analogy suggests, it
happens in a social world that hitherto was marked only by
convention and routine. Most frequently, perhaps, its context
is our most intimate and cherished relationships. Sometimes,
too, it occurs in relation to some symptom of the self such as
Rubashov's toothache in *Darkness at Noon.* If the requisite
imagery is at hand, many events can intimate the presence of
a personal power that is more than human.

What does it mean, however, to claim that the universe
declares itself personal in this way? It is to affirm, first of all,
that there is a power that can grasp and challenge the self at
its core, constraining it and enabling it to respond in a total
fashion of which it was not previously capable, upsetting its

postures and routinized ways, bringing to it an enrichment that it had never known in such great measure, and that it had never known at all except in the context of personal relationships. But now, even though the enrichment comes "in and with and under" personal relationships, they are not sufficient to account for it; in their midst there is a "beyond" that is personal, not *a* person but personal in the sense that this "beyond" enables the self to become more completely realized as a person than it has ever been able to do in the course of its human relationships. Second, in consequence of this experience, the self is constrained to commit itself to the service of personal values before all else; now it lives in faith that persons and personal values will not be consigned to an end that is incommensurate with their irreducible worth, for they are significant to a "beyond" that is personal but that does not share the vulnerability of persons to corruption and decay. The encounter with power that touches the self more intimately than the self can relate to itself furnishes reason to believe that an end appropriate for persons, but which they cannot achieve for themselves, will be realized nonetheless, for they have not been left alone in an alien and indifferent land.

The meaning of the claim that the universe declares itself personal, then, is that selves will be granted an end that is appropriate to their nature and enduring value. What a religious story offers, in other words, is simply a sense of an ending. The ending belongs to the self and is appropriate for it; so there is congruence between beginning and end. But there is also an element of the unexpected, an incongruity, for the self cannot find fulfillment for itself but must depend upon a greater power. Because it is a vandal and a joker, there is no way to its fulfillment except through radical judgment upon all there is within itself that vitiates and wars against the personal. *A religious story, therefore, is like all other stories, providing in much the same fashion as its secular counterparts a sense of an ending that can irradiate the present with new significance and orient human agency and liberty.* There are many and various ways to adumbrate or intimate an ending that expresses the faith that the universe has declared itself personal.

Religious stories differ from other narratives only because of the intensity of the illumination that they cast upon the present, offering not an ending that is also a new beginning, or else a foreclosure of new beginnings, but an ending beyond all possible beginnings and beyond all apparent foreclosures of them, an ending that can slake the insatiable eschatological passion of persons who are at once condemned and privileged to dream beyond all the ends and beginnings that they have ever seen. A religious story affirms that the farthest and most remote "not yet" is "now"—not only immanent in human hopes and therefore in some human ways, but present because the power that shapes it is present and has disclosed something of its design. It is only when selves live "as if" and "as if not" that they grow toward reality and truth, or so the story says, for the future has come and the present is passing away. Whatever else must be said of religious stories can best be stated in the context of exploring the particular narrative from which the representations of the self as player, sufferer, and vandal have been derived, and by which the worth of these images must finally be judged.

Chapter Six

THE STORY OF ADAM

In a work titled *The American Adam*, R. W. B. Lewis explores "the first tentative outlines of a native American mythology"[1] that portrayed the new world as Eden and unfallen Adam as a type of its citizens. Lewis is certainly not unaware that the story was employed in ways that were "crowded with illusion, and the moral posture it seemed to endorse was vulnerable in the extreme. But however vulnerable or illusory. . . . Its very openness to challenge, its susceptibility to controversy, made possible a series of original inquiries and discoveries about human nature, art, and history."[2] In its historical account of the way that a particular narrative shaped not only individuals but the character of a whole people, *The American Adam* documents the intimacy of the relationship between character, stories, and imagery for self-recognition. Precisely when America sought to liberate itself not only from political domination by Europe but from its cultural legacies as well, it fell back upon a particularly old and important part of that heritage in order to understand its trials and potentialities in a new land and in a revolutionary situation. The biblical figure of Adam proved itself crucial for the appraisal of the new beginning and for the discovery of paths toward the fulfillment of what had only been begun. Because of all the ambiguities that the narrative contains, it seemed to disclose more of its richness to each new generation, shaping character and self-understanding in more subtle and complex ways; rather than stifling debate, it continued to provoke impassioned discussion concerning the nature of selfhood and the possibilities and perils of life together. Among all the diverse lessons that it could teach, however, none was more important than the truth that without an old story there could be no new world; indeed, there could be no world that selves could inhabit at all.

Nineteenth-century accounts of experience in America, then, were immensely varied, and yet they also displayed a certain unity; although different in other ways, they still shared a specific form that was derived from the biblical tale of Adam. The earliest of them seemed to express little more than an exuberant and unqualified optimism, the conviction that persons were now freed from the taints of their ancestors and from the constraints of outworn conventions. The narratives were animated by

> the image of a radically new personality, the hero of the new adventure: an individual emancipated from history, happily bereft of ancestry, untouched and undefiled by the usual inheritances of family and race; an individual standing alone, self-reliant and self-propelling, ready to confront whatever awaited him with the aid of his own unique and inherent resources . . . the new hero (in praise or disapproval) was most easily identified with Adam before the Fall. Adam was the first, the archetypal man. His moral position was prior to experience, and in his very newness he was fundamentally innocent. The world and history lay all before him. And he was the type of creator, the poet par excellence, creating language itself by naming the elements of the scene about him. All this and more were contained in the image of the American as Adam.[3]

But if Thoreau and Emerson, and especially Whitman in *Leaves of Grass,* employed the story to represent innocence

166 IMAGES FOR SELF-RECOGNITION

rather than sinfulness as the first attribute of the American character, others utilized it to scout the territories within the self far more carefully. Horace Bushnell and the elder Henry James sought to correct their more optimistic contemporaries, insisting that "innocence is inadequate for the full reach of human personality; that life, in James's words, 'flowers and fructifies . . . out of the profoundest tragic depths.' "[4] So in their hands the Adamic narrative becomes an instrument that is used to uncover the illusions of others who had relied upon it; more discerning interpretations of the story expose ways in which it had been held in untruth.

In one area after another, the story of Adam functioned much as it did in philosophical discussions, rendering debate concrete, establishing the perimeters of the conversation, suggesting new avenues when familiar paths seemed to lead to barren ground. In the realm of imaginative literature, the tale provided "the essential and recurring anecdote of American fiction."[5] As the biblical figure of Adam before the fall points toward fallen Adam, so in fiction there is a development from Natty Bumppo, the innocent of James Fenimore Cooper's *The Deerslayer,* to the more fully realized and sometimes tragic Adamic figures of Hawthorne and Melville, about whom Lewis comments: "The significant fact is that the literal use of the story of Adam and the Fall of Man—as a model for narrative—occurred in the final works of American novelists, the works in which they sought to summarize the whole of their experience of America."[6] *The Marble Faun* and *Billy Budd* are the last novels that Hawthorne and Melville created, and in them, where the Adamic imagery "is altogether central," we verge "perhaps as close as American culture ever came to the full and conscious realization of the myth it had so long secreted."[7] Finally, the innocent has become a tragic presence in whom the light and the darkness meet. With these novels, the native American mythology is richly and securely established and, as Lewis understands the matter, it endures still. He concludes:

> *The Marble Faun* completed a cycle of adventures carrying
> a representative American fictional hero from his ritual

birth (in Cooper) through a "fall" which can be claimed as fortunate because of the growth in perception and moral intelligence granted the hero as a result of it. If we abstract an anecdote, in this hazardous way, from a series of novels taken in sequence, we find something dealt with so often and so variously by American writers after Hawthorne that it may be regarded as the major (if not the only) "matter" by which they have sought to advance their craft. We can call it "the matter of Adam," since for those who have recognized it—Hawthorne, Melville, James, and Faulkner at the least—it was as usable as "the matter of France" or "the matter of Troy" once was for poets in the medieval world. It has been the primary stuff by which the American novelist has managed to articulate his sense of the form and pressure of experience and by which he has extended the possibilities of the art of fiction.[8]

The richest and most complex stories are also the most vulnerable to misinterpretation; so the biblical tale can be reduced to Emerson's "plain old Adam, the simple genuine self against the whole world."[9] Yet the amplitude of the narrative is so great that partial interpretations of it elicit complementary responses; rigid explications suggest despite themselves a host of different possibilities. Consequently, the story has not dictated answers that are beyond debate; instead, it has served to enrich and focus the discussion of different answers, suggesting the provisionality and partiality of each one, posing further questions, motivating new investigations of the nature of the self. If the dangers of the Adamic ideal have been acknowledged in many ways and at many times, it has been the Adamic story itself that afforded the most incisive perspective from which to undertake the task of criticism. In "The Bear," for example, Isaac McCaslin can speak of "the new land which He had vouchsafed them out of pity and sufferance, on condition of pity and humility and sufferance and endurance, from that old world's corrupt and worthless twilight." But Faulkner's young protagonist has also been sufficiently instructed by the tale of Adam to recognize the virus, the perhaps irremediable disease, the pollution that is carried, if not in the blood, then "in the sailfuls of the old world's tainted wind which drove the ships"[10] across the seas to a new land. He warns: "This whole land, the whole South, is cursed, and all of us who derive from it, whom it ever suckled, white and black both, lie under the curse. Granted that my people brought the curse onto the land: maybe for that reason their descendants alone can—not resist it, not combat it—maybe just endure and outlast it until the curse is lifted. Then your peoples' turn will come because we have forfeited ours. But not now. Not yet. Don't you see?"[11]

The Adamic promise remains, though muted and qualified, but now Adam has been scarred by suffering and evil and by that experience has become more fully realized as Adam than ever he was before. In similar fashion, the finest nineteenth-century rehearsal of Adam, *Billy Budd*, presents not only an innocent savaged by a world that he cannot comprehend but also the need for a greater Adam who can rescue persons from their betrayals of hope and their betrayals by hope that fail to measure the remorseless actualities of fallen life. Lewis comments that "Melville salvaged the legend of hope both for life and for literature: by repudiating it in order to restore it in an apotheosis of its hero. There will be salvation yet, the story hints, from that treacherous dream."[12] Only when the curse and the suffering and the tragedy and the evil have entered the story does it become more than simply a "treacherous dream," but it is the story itself that enforces this recognition upon us.

In the argument of *The American Adam* there is much to suggest the empirical fit of the biblical tale of Adam: in the American context, at least, it did in fact prove formative of individual and communal consciousness and character. It served to organize and develop a cultural inheritance for those who had believed themselves to be unburdened of cultural legacies, providing a necessary thread of continuity with the past as well as a challenge to surpass it, and thereby redeeming a young nation from the condition in which persons "are conscious, no longer of tradition, but simply and coldly of the burden of history."[13] It became an instrument for self-recognition on the part of those who, endeavoring to slip their moorings in history, still hungered for a relation to something else than the time between the times in order to invest the present with more than negative significance, and who, pitting their strength against the unknown, still needed tokens and reminiscences that would arm them against the endless repetition of their fathers' mistakes.

At least at the time he wrote *The American Adam,* Lewis appeared unwilling to separate the future of the American imagination from the question of the endurance and vitality of "the matter of Adam," and he expressed his confidence that the story could, "after all, continue to present us with the means of grasping the special complexities, the buoyant assurance, and the encircling doubt" of our age.[14] While his record of the debates among philosophers and historians, journalists and theologians, and many other persons has certainly demonstrated the cogency of the narrative, it is also true that from its beginning their discussion would have been less profitable, less enduring, and less profound if it had not found its focus in a story, for "the narrative art inevitably and by nature invests its inherited intellectual content with a quickening duplicity; it stains ideas with a restless ambiguity. For the *experience* of the aims and values of an epoch is apt to be more complex and even more painful than the simple statement of them; and narrative deals with experiences, not with propositions."[15] Insofar as the experience of earlier generations is not unrelated to our own, insofar as it is not peculiarly American but more generally human, and insofar as character involves the intentional identification of selves and communities with stories that enable them to knit together their future and past, the biblical narrative of Adam that has shaped our corporate history seems as consequential for personal identity today as it was important in many and different ways for those of whom Lewis writes.

"The matter of Adam" has derived much of its formative power in society, as Lewis observes, from the malleable and indeterminate element that it has seemed to enshrine within its concreteness, from the multitude of ambiguities that are always inherent in the form of narrative art. Because it has seemed amenable to divergent and often conflicting interpretations, it has served as a recurrent invitation to dialogue rather than as ideology or myth for, in Kermode's terms, at least it need not represent the world of potency as though it were a world of act. The price of its social functionality, of course, is that not only can it still be mined for new and richer veins of meaning, it can also be understood in ways that truncate and distort it and obscure its significance for a Christian vision of selfhood. In the end, there is no certain remedy for this. The possibilities of misinterpretation are lessened, however, when the narrative is read in the light of the master images that are intended to convey the core of its anthropology, and when the utility of the images is constantly appraised anew in the light of the story.

On the one hand, Adam is player, sufferer, and vandal—much more as well as somewhat less than Emerson's "simple genuine self." On the other, the player, the sufferer, and the vandal are Adam, and it is only in the context of his story that their nature is clarified and something of their opacity dissolved. The circularity of the process of interpretation is essential, partly because of the inescapable limitations of images, and partly because of the irreducible ambiguities of narrative. We come, then, to the last and most important questions that must be addressed. First, what are the themes in the original Adamic narrative that are particularly significant for the conclusion of this attempt at self-understanding? Second, what sort of sense of an ending does the story provide and how does the ending serve as a principle of interpretation for all that has preceded it? Third, how does the story function as an instrument of religious disclosure? Fourth, do the figures of player, sufferer, and vandal actually find such lodging in the narrative that they function as master images that can crystallize and powerfully express its significance for self-understanding? Do they guard its integrity and richness so well that it is persuasive to claim that they have indeed been derived from it, not projected upon it from some alien or partial perspective?

Thorough explication of the story of creation and fall in the first chapters of Genesis lies beyond the scope of this book, of course, but certain motifs that are present there must be cited in order to explain and clarify some of the emphases that have marked the treatment of the self as player, sufferer, and vandal. First, the fall is itself a religious event and not a flight toward the secular. The woman eats the forbidden fruit neither because she is hungry nor because of its intrinsic allure, but simply for the reason that she is beguiled by the voice of the serpent when he counsels: "Ye shall not surely die: For God doth know that in the day ye eat thereof, then your eyes shall be opened, and ye shall be as gods, knowing good and evil."[16] In *Creation and Fall,* Dietrich Bonhoeffer emphasizes the completely and incorrigibly religious character of the fall; in it there is perfect congruence between the religious nature of the woman and the religiosity of the serpent's words:

> The serpent claims to know more about God than man, who depends on God's Word alone. The serpent knows of a greater, nobler God who does not need such a prohibition. . . . It knows that it only has power where it claims to come from God, to be pleading his cause. It is evil only as the religious serpent . . . with the first religious question in the world evil has come upon the scene. Where evil appears in its godlessness it is powerless . . . we do not need to fear it. In this form it does not concentrate its power . . . here it is wrapped in the garment of religiousness. The wolf in sheep's clothing, Satan in an angel's form of light: this is the shape appropriate to evil. "Did God say?"; that plainly is the godless question.[17]

Second, the fall involves a project of self-deception. The attention that Eve gives to the serpent indicates that she has already suffered the disruption of her orientation toward God: the world that was once a unity has become pluralized, and this pluralization is at the same time the beginning and the consequence of the fall. She now hears conflicting voices, but her own nature still begs to yield all of itself to a single ultimate goal. So she can succumb to the serpent's wiles only because the tempter deceives her by pretending to speak in the name of God. She could not be a victim, however, were she not also an accomplice. In the presence of the holy, there is no way to avoid recognition of the abyss between God and the creature, of the impossibility of bridging it by creaturely initiative, and least of all of bridging it by means of the magic or manna imputed to a forbidden tree. If the project were ever brought into focus by the full light of consciousness, there could be no evasion of the terrible discrepancy between the serpent's promise and the boundaries and limits that are essential for creaturely life. So the scope of consciousness is restricted until it need not admit the discrepancy. Eve is deceived not only by another but also by herself, just as her fallenness expresses itself not only through the act that another creature suggests but also in her own admission of the possibility of such an act. You shall be as gods: the deception can be entertained only by those who have managed to deceive themselves.

Third, the violation of limits carries its own inherent punishment. Adam is called to exercise dominion over the world and all its creatures, but the lordship granted to him is possible for him only so long as he acknowledges his creaturely limits. Adam is *homo religiosus;* in other words, he has been created in order to orient himself toward and live in communion with God. If he fails to honor the one who has granted him his dominion over the earth, then the exigencies of his nature consign him to a search for some surrogate for the Lord whom he has rejected. The only possible substitutes are the creatures about him, but to regard them as though they were divine means that the earthly has now become disordered in such a fashion that it rules its appointed ruler. The master is himself responsible for the revolt that costs him his position. The acknowledgment of limits, then, is not simply a condition of Adam's dominion that was externally imposed by God. Instead, it has an indispensable role to play in the maintenance of the dominion because of the nature of Adam himself. When the limits are ignored, the self becomes the victim of its world.

Fourth, the punishment that is always inherent in the abrogation of limits is also apparent in the consequences of Eve's choice. The fall is religious not only because it is occasioned by a religious question, but even more because it expresses a religious appetite and discloses the irremediably religious nature of the creature. It is very important that, while the serpent speaks only to Eve, he tells her that the impossible promise is offered to the man as well as to herself. Adam will also be like God, not only Eve. At the heart of the story there is the crucial statement that the promise is given to both, must be granted to both. It has power to snare the woman only because it applies equally to the man. Nothing could be more important than the inclusion of Adam, too, as the serpent is sufficiently wise to know.

Why? Eve is intended to live with Adam, and so the promise gains its power because it is also directed to him. Although Adam and Eve are created for one another, what is most important is that they can exist for one another only and precisely because both have been created to live in relation to God. Like the man, the woman is endowed with a nature that can find fulfillment only in relation to the divine. Consequently, the possibility that the serpent offers can be understood as possible for her only if Adam becomes a god, and for him only if he can believe that he will find in her what he was intended to find in her creator. So the question of the divinity of the self is actually subordinate to the necessity for the divinity of the other. The nature of the self is such that it cannot turn away from God without projecting elsewhere its dreams of what divinity is like: there is no flight from God that does not lead to idols. Fallenness does not quench religious passion but inflames it, for selves are *homines religiosi* still. Now the self is fated to regard others with unqualified seriousness and fated, too, to regard itself with absolute seriousness in relation to others and everything that they possess. Because they will to see one another as gods, however, they no longer are able to see one another as persons. We cannot have it both ways: only once does God become man. The choice is made and it enshrines its punishment within itself: the human is obscured and distorted. The fallen pair have achieved a terrible likeness to God, for there is a sense in which they, too, have become creators: they have loosed the daimonic and consigned themselves to live always in its shadow. The daimonic is not an independent power; the word simply describes the transformed appearances of the human and its endless power of oppression after the fall, as persons begin to obsess and terrify one another. The daimonic is born when persons seek to locate the divine in the human, for then both the human and the holy are lost, not the holy alone.[18]

Fifth, now humanness is inseparable from posture and no longer an instrument of disclosure. It is inevitable that with the intrusion of the daimonic:

> The eyes of both were opened, and they knew that they were naked and they sewed fig leaves together and made themselves aprons. And they heard the sound of the Lord God walking in the garden in the cool of the day, and the man and his wife hid themselves from the presence of the Lord God among the trees of the garden. But the Lord God called to the man, and said to him, "Where are you?" And he said, "I heard the sound of thee in the garden, and I was afraid, because I was naked; and I hid myself."[19]

How can the self play god for others if others see it in its nakedness, shorn of its defenses, deprived of all its postures, bereft of all its possessions? If ever they saw it as it is, how could the self be for others what it is not? Certainly these verses address the mystery of sexuality, but that does not exhaust their meaning. They also raise the different question, which is not finally answerable apart from a self-deception, of how we shall manage to appear like gods to one another as we flee from the true God and yet find that none of us are able to live without any gods at all. How shall we posture as though we were gods not first of all because it pleases us but, instead, because the burden is imposed upon us by religious appetites that we share with all other selves? The appearance of the daimonic divides the individual against himself, for now he is the victim of his own inhuman and impossible expectations of others and of himself, while they are equally inhumane and misled in their anticipations and appeals to him.

The shame that Adam knows not only serves to remind him of the lost character of his relationship to God; it also intimates a falsity in all other present relationships, and so it poisons and corrodes them still more. Because the self is ashamed, it is not free; because it wills to be free, it projects the source of its shame upon others: "The woman whom thou gavest to be with me, she gave me fruit of the tree, and I ate."[20] Or else, because there can no longer be clear lines of demarcation and boundaries between selves that are fated to the terrible intimacy of playing god for one another, the self's sense of shame enrages it against the others with whom it has become entangled and against their daimonic expectations. The shame and rage are exacerbated because the self also can no longer see itself in sufficiently clear perspective to weigh the expectations of others against its own human gain. Bonhoeffer comments:

> Man without a limit, hating, avidly passionate, does not show himself in his nakedness. Nakedness is the essence of unity and unbrokenness, of being for the other, of objectivity, of the recognition of the other in his right, in his limiting me and his creatureliness. Nakedness is the essence of the ignorance of the possibility of robbing the other of this right. Nakedness is revelation. . . . But the greatest contradiction here is that man, who has come to be without a limit, is bound to point to his limit without intending to do so. He covers himself because he feels shame.[21]

Humanness is no longer an instrument of disclosure because we cannot afford disclosure any more; therefore we conceal it. This evokes an act of concealment on the part of the other self, so that it is no longer a mirror in which we can discern something of our own nature. As the human is obscured, it becomes ever more vulnerable because persons have become uncertain of its worth—and so Abel will soon be destroyed by Cain.

Sixth, evil is simply a deflection of creaturely will. There is no reason to identify the serpent with Satan; it is one among God's many creatures, although perhaps it is more subtle than the others. The story insists that when evil is introduced into the world its means of access is a creature; it is not a mythic power that possesses some measure of independence in relation to God. We learn nothing more of its provenance: why the woman succumbs to temptation or why the serpent poses as the authoritative spokesman for God are questions that have no answers. Certainly the actions of the serpent, however, can be described as a practical joke as satisfactorily as they can be interpreted in any other terms. What "reason" has the tempter, except to see what the consequences will be when the woman discovers the appalling magnitude of the deception that has been practiced upon her and in which she has conspired? The act of disobedience itself is no splendid Promethean gesture, but merely something that a child might do. It is true that a commandment is disobeyed and a boundary is transgressed, but only in the course of stealing and eating what is in itself an inconsequential fraction of the fruit of a tree that belonged to someone else. Everything is played in a minor key; the mysteries that the story contains stubbornly refuse to dissolve.

Like Augustine after her, Eve was "compelled neither by hunger, nor poverty." It would be an error to apply Augustine's confession that there was "no inducement to evil but the evil itself" to the disobedience in the garden, for Adam and Eve are represented as originally innocent of knowledge of the distinction between good and evil. But the story of the events in Eden prefigures the ways in which persons who are condemned to posture as gods in consequence of their fallenness would thereafter "imitate an imperfect liberty by doing with impunity things which [they were] . . . not allowed to do, in obscured likeness of Thy omnipotency."[22] The narrative of the fall establishes the possibility of crimes without reason after the loss of innocence, when the unlawful would be chosen for no reason except that it was unlawful, when malice would find expression simply because of the pleasure that maliciousness affords, and when selves as well as property would become fair game for the motiveless malevolence of Iago and his friends. As a paradigm of the criminal without motivation, whose "distaste for well-doing" involves a love of destruction for its own sake, the figure of the vandal lurks close by the precincts of the garden of Eden.

Seventh, evil also becomes more than a deflection of creaturely will. The temptation is addressed to the woman by another creature and, when she yields to it, evil has become a reality within human affairs. The emergence of moral evil, however, is accompanied by the appearance of natural evil when God himself ratifies the choice of Adam and Eve and affirms a world congruent with the deflected will of the creature. The pair have relinquished their dominion because they have confused the creaturely with the divine by regarding the serpent as though it could speak for God better than God could speak for himself. Consequently, the creation that Adam was intended to rule now rules him and grows unruly because it has lost its steward. Persons are now vulnerable to contingencies and accidents; they become the victims of this new unruliness of the structures of finite life, the *stoicheia tou cosmou.* God affirms the cosmic consequences that must follow ineluctably from human choice, for self and world are correlative. He utters the curse: "I will greatly multiply your pain. . . . cursed is the ground because of you."²³ There could not be a more intimate relationship between the idolatry that the story of the fall suggests and the subordination of Adam and Eve to the new oppressiveness of the *stoicheia tou cosmou* that they have themselves rendered possible, although the possibility is realized only when God exercises his justice by ratifying their own choice. So evil becomes an element in the cosmos apart from mankind and it is no longer only a deflection of creaturely will. As C. K. Barrett persuasively contends:

> Idolatry, it is true, is not specifically mentioned in Gen. i–iii, but it may justly be said that it is from confusion of creation and Creator that idolatry springs. "In listening to the voice of the serpent, Adam has not only failed to

exercise his rightful dominion over creation, but, by placing himself in subservience to a creature, has opened the
way to idolatry". . . . Man upset the balance of God's
creation by reaching for that which was above him, for
which he had not been made and was not fitted. Out of
this unbalance arise both the anthropological and the
cosmical *malaise* of the universe: man attempts to live
independently of his Creator, treating himself as his own
god, and thereby not only ceases to be truly himself but
also loses control of what should have been under his
dominion.[24]

The account of evil that the story provides, then, affirms
that persons are responsible for its genesis. Although it is
located in the world of nature as well as in the warped will,
its presence within the *stoicheia tou cosmou* can be traced at least
indirectly to human initiative and its power there is contingent upon a divine decision. The evil that now is wrought by
the structures of finite life is the external correlate of what the
self has become; therefore, it is one expression of the victimi-
zation of the self by the idols that it has crafted with its own
hands. Persons are the artificers of what torments them, but
now it is stronger than they because it has found a lodging
outside their communities. "Through the fall, each man finds
himself in an inimical universe, under the dominion of usurp-
ing powers, of which sin itself is one; and, apart from the fact
that these powers exercise dominion over him for their own
ends, the inevitable and normal reaction of man in a dangerous situation is—self-defense. And this is sin, because its concern is with self, and not with God."[25]

Evil does not become an independent power, however,
standing against God and able to maintain itself by its own
resources in contradiction of his will. In its subordination to
God there is an intimation that its power will eventually come
to an end, for the divine curse is still accompanied by a rem-
nant of the original promise implicit in the statement that
"the Lord God made for Adam and for his wife garments of
skins, and clothed them."[26] So there is reason for hope,
though not in what the self can achieve for itself. The fact that

the origins of evil are related to a corruption of creaturely will is in no way intended to suggest that a particular individual deserves whatever random violence he suffers. On the contrary, Genesis offers no sketch of a theodicy but simply contents itself with the affirmation that the world is entirely good as it originally comes from the hands of God. It is an appropriate arena for the fulfillment of the divine promise and a fitting context in every way for creaturely life. There would be no reason whatsoever not to trust the world, were it not that the corruption of the human will has cosmic consequences. Now, however, the disordered world reinforces the corruption of the will, counseling us, as Barrett observes, to defend ourselves. The vulnerability of everyone to the ravages of accident and contingency inspires the maintenance of all sorts of policies of deception and self-deception: selves posture as though they were gods in order to foster in those who depend upon them a sense of trust and security that is an indispensable requisite for a child's progress toward maturity. The deceptions are practiced not against selves but in order that they might one day be able to defend themselves against a world that is profoundly different from what they first were told of it. So the good world counsels and appeals for basic trust while at the same time basic trust is never justified by the appearances of the world and their dreadful power, for when selves surrendered to what had been placed in their custody, they exposed themselves to whatever potential for randomness and capriciousness it contained.

While these comments scarcely begin to disclose the proportions of the story of Adam, they stress the presence there of refrains that have become more insistent in the course of the search for adequate images of selfhood. If the refrains were not to prove particularly important in the story, of course, it would certainly not be possible to defend the claim that the images of player, sufferer, and vandal were themselves derived from it. Genesis portrays the fall as a religious event; it is a movement toward gods rather than away from them when the woman treats the serpent as though he could speak authoritatively for God, granting his words an unqualified seriousness they do not deserve. She is the victim of a lie of motiveless malevolence, and yet she could not become a victim unless she conspired in her own deception. If Adam and Eve lie to themselves, thrusting responsibility for their acts upon one another or upon the serpent, they lie then only because they have lied to themselves antecedently. Belief in the promise that they could be like gods reflects self-deception as well as ignorance, for ignorance of such proportions is unimaginable for those who live in the presence of the one who alone is God. While evil appears in the mundane guise of the temptation to eat a bit of fruit belonging to someone else, their disobedience eventuates in a disordering not only of human community but of the entire world.

The magnitude of the disparity between act and consequences constitutes a disclosure that invites the hearer of the story to assess in new perspective the significance of his own instances of disobedience and transgressions of boundaries. The prohibition that Adam and Eve choose not to obey constitutes a warning that creaturely freedom gains its significance and concreteness only in relation to limits: the attempt to divest existence of limits and boundaries is equivalent to the rejection of what it means to be human. The sense of shame that torments Adam and Eve after the fall has its source in the nature of persons who can live only toward one god or another; in their flight from the holy they must regard one another as gods and attempt to find the entire meaning of their lives in this relationship. But there is no way to do this without posture and pretense, and so they must hide the nakedness that is now cause for shame. Nevertheless, the self cannot fulfill expectations that are so much at odds with its potential: from inhumane expectations and the creation of idols there emerges the daimonic. The human becomes daimonic whenever it must bear the imputation of divinity. If the daimonic is no more than implicit in the first chapters of Genesis, it becomes more apparent in later representations of a fall, such as Augustine's account of his theft of pears, when he did what he was "not allowed to do, in obscured likeness of Thy omnipotency." In the act of the serpent there is a disclosure of motiveless malevolence, a prototype of all the practical jokes undertaken for no purpose except to see what the consequences might be and of all the crimes that are committed for no reason whatsoever.

Among the different crimes that recur in the course of our common life, perhaps it is the senselessness, purposelessness, and irrationality of vandalism that affords the most adequate image of such behavior. Although the fall unleashes evil outside human community as well as within it, the world itself is still intended to evoke as much as to disappoint basic trust, for its evil originates in creaturely decisions rather than in God or powers independent of God. Finally, there is an irreducibly religious dimension to the human enterprise, for the exercise of finite creativity is now entangled with pursuit of the realization of the serpent's promise that persons can be like gods. So there will be at least latent antagonism between human culture and the holy as selves seek to secure themselves against the contingencies of their environment.

Adam is a concrete universal: his is the name of an individual and yet the name of mankind, a fully individuated image but also a narrative of everyone. Adam is a coincidence of image and story: an image so expansive that the master imagery of the self as player, sufferer, and vandal can find lodging in it, and a story that the images interpret and by which they must be interpreted. Within the whole narrative of the Bible, the story of Adam does not end with expulsion from the garden and entry into a new and forbidding land; it tells of other times and places, too, and even of the end of time. It appears in the teachings of Jesus, through whose words and deeds new canons for its interpretation emerge. In *The Glass of Vision*, Austin Farrer argues that the message of Jesus was typically expressed in the great images of the Hebrew tradition which, certainly including the image of Adam, gained new significance in the light of the events of his ministry and passion and then were enriched and transformed in even greater measure by the apostolic writers to become the core of the New Testament. The Bible is not a congeries of propositions, either cosmological or anthropological, but more or less a unity of complex and variegated imaginative acts that build upon and in new ways illuminate one another. Farrer writes:

> The thought of Christ Himself was expressed in certain dominant images. He spoke of the Kingdom of God, which is the image of God's enthroned majesty. . . . Again, He spoke of the Son of Man, thereby proposing the image of the dominion of a true Adam, begotten in the similitude of God, and made God's regent over all the works of his hands. Such a dominion Christ claimed to exercise in some manner there and then: yet in another sense it was to be looked for thereafter, when the Son of Man should come with the clouds of heaven, seated at the right hand of Almightiness. He set forth the image of Israel, the human family of God, somehow mystically contained in the person of Jacob, its patriarch. He was himself Israel, and appointed twelve men to be his typical "sons." He applied to himself the prophecies of a redemptive suffering for mankind attributed to Israel by Isaiah and Jewish tradition. He displayed, in the action of the supper, the infinitely complex and fertile image of sacrifice and communion, of expiation and covenant. These tremendous images, and others like them, are not the whole of Christ's teaching, but they set forth the supernatural mystery which is the heart of the teaching. Without them, the teaching would not be supernatural revelation, but instruction in piety and morals. It is because the spiritual instruction is related to the great images, that it becomes revealed truth.[27]

While Farrer's interpretation of the teaching of Jesus is open to dispute, there is no reason to question his understanding of the apostolic writers and especially of Paul, in whose letters the offer of reconciliation with God is continually expressed through the use of the imagery of the Old Testament. Paul understands the history of the relationship between humanity and God in terms of figures such as Abraham and Moses, who are significant not only as individuals but also as representatives and images of everyone. No other name, however, has the crucial significance of the name of Adam, for Paul sees Jesus as a new Adam. The story of the two Adams, then, provides the beginning and the end for the whole narrative within which Abraham and Israel and Moses have their respective places and roles. The Adamic imagery is central not only in the letters of Paul but for the interpretation of the New Testament in its entirety: no other figure encompasses the full dimensions of the self as fallen and as restored, including the redeemer as well as the ones who are redeemed, and capturing the cosmological as well as the anthropological aspects of the history of salvation. The search for an ending and the quest for beginnings coincide in the narrative of Adam cursed and Adam blessed, the first Adam and the last.[28]

We must, however, proceed from the New Testament to the Old in order to understand the matter of Adam. Neither the full significance of the story in Genesis nor the importance of the image of the player for grasping the anthropology of the Bible can be satisfactorily explored apart from the sense of an ending that is provided by the last chapters of the narrative as they occur in the letters of Paul. The disclosure of the end acts reflexively upon everything that occurs on the way toward it, affording a perspective upon the beginning and the time between the times that they could not provide for themselves. Unless there is an ending that overturns every rational expectation and yet persuades us of its profound symmetry with the tale of origins in Eden, we shall find excellent reasons to deny that our own search for beginnings can conclude there and we shall echo the words of Sammy Mountjoy, "No, not here." Karl Barth is correct to claim, as he does in *Christ and Adam*, that:

> The meaning of the famous parallel (so called) between "Adam and Christ" . . . is not that the relationship between Adam and us is the expression of our true and original nature, so that we would have to recognize in Adam the fundamental truth of anthropology to which the subsequent relationship between Christ and us would have to fit and adapt itself. The relationship between Adam and us reveals not the primary but only the secondary anthropological truth and ordering principle.

The primary anthropological truth and ordering principle, which only mirrors itself in that relationship, is made
clear only through the relationship between Christ and
us. Adam is . . . *typos tou mellontos,* the type of Him who
was to come. Man's essential and original nature is to be
found, therefore, not in Adam but in Christ. In Adam we
can only find it prefigured. Adam can therefore be interpreted only in the light of Christ and not the other way
round.[29]

Barth's insistence that the first Adam must be approached
through the figure of the second is a distinctive theological
claim, but it is also an acknowledgment of what is necessary
for any literary criticism that intends to rehearse the whole
matter of Adam as the writers of the New Testament present
it. In some sense the end must be immanent in the beginning,
but its realization must also be so different from its initial
prefiguration that it upsets our anticipations, discloses something that previously we had not known or had not known so
well, and causes us to examine our own assumptions more
carefully than hitherto. Otherwise, the story offers no real
testimony to human freedom and inventiveness and spontaneity, and certainly it provides no lodging for what is not
only one of the most common and ordinary elements of life
in community but also the real subject of the Adamic narrative
—the reality of grace, the appearance of gifts that are unexpected and undeserved and beyond all our powers to repay.
So the matter of Adam is not apparent until we speak of Adam
twice.

Formally, the story is a paradigm of what stories are intended to be. As it is expressed in the fifth chapter of Romans,
there is complete consonance or parallelism between the beginning and the end:

> Therefore, *as by* the offense of one judgment came upon
> all men to condemnation; even *so by* the righteousness of
> one the free gift came upon all men unto justification of
> life. For *as by* one man's disobedience many were made
> sinners, *so by* the obedience of one shall many be made
> righteous.   . That *as* sin hath reigned unto death, *even*

so might grace reign through righteousness unto eternal
life by Jesus Christ our Lord.[30]

Just as the disobedience of one brings condemnation upon
all, so does the obedience of the other render possible forgiveness for all. Even though this formal parallelism is under-
scored by the assertion that the first Adam "is the figure of
him that was to come,"[31] the consonance embraces such a
variety of discontinuities and apparent incongruities that the
story can shatter the rigidities of the expectations on which it
depends for its effect, and it can disclose truths to which we
would otherwise have no access at all. Formally, the discontinuities are suggested by the recurrence of "much more" in
Romans 5, verses 9, 10, 15, 17, and finally in the preface to
the conclusion in verse 21: "But where sin abounded, grace
did *much more* abound." At the center of the apparent incongruities, contradicting the ways of human affairs, lies the as-
tonishing claim that:

> Christ died for the ungodly. For scarcely for a righteous
> man will one die: yet peradventure for a good man some
> would even dare to die. But God commendeth his love
> toward us, in that, while we were yet sinners, Christ died
> for us. . . . For if, when we were enemies, we were recon-
> ciled to God by the death of his Son, much more, being
> reconciled, we shall be saved by his life.[32]

The incongruence is not simply that the sacrifice was offered for those who were "helpless" and "sinners," but that
they could not even recognize themselves as "ungodly" and
"enemies" except in the light of the event. Only when the
debt is paid is it possible to understand the indebtedness on
the part of those who had become "vain in their imaginations,
and their foolish heart was darkened. Professing themselves
to be wise, they became fools, . . . who changed the truth of
God into a lie, and worshipped and served the creature more
than the Creator."[33] Identification with the second Adam is
not something that the self can achieve for itself; everything
occurs *kata charin,* by grace alone. The gift is not only wholly

undeserved but necessarily unexpected, because the need for it was not acknowledged. Expectations are correlates of self-understanding, and the self cannot recognize that it has been deceived about itself and by itself until its illusions have been stripped away by the offer of the gift. When the fulfillment that persons sought is granted, not only is it given by powers other than their own but they are constrained to acknowledge that nothing impeded its realization as much as their own greatest efforts and their most noble aspirations.

Again, the incongruence is not simply that the judge decides to acquit the guilty, but that he pronounces the verdict of acquittal without compromising his own integrity as judge or subverting the dictates of justice. The incongruence is not simply that the judge submits to judgment in the place of the accused so that their guilt can be expunged, but that the sacrifice is fitting because in fact he is "made a curse for us"[34] and made "to be sin for us, who knew no sin."[35] The apparent incongruities have many dimensions and can be stated in many ways, but they never dwindle to absurdity or contradiction because the figures of Adam are not only individual but representative. All persons are incorporated in them, so that their careers are our own: we have been where they have been and we have done what they have done. The consonance between beginning and end is preserved despite the incongruences because the Christ is a concrete universal: an individual and the race, he is even Adam his predecessor for the sake of the children of Adam, and they share "the righteousness of God in him."[36]

The consequence of Adam's fall is that persons are tyrannized by sin; the effect of Christ's triumph is that persons reign with him as sin and death begin to lose their power. The end transcends the beginning; the beginning displayed no evidence that it could end in this fashion, and yet the bonds between beginning and end have their own logic and strength. Finally, among the most important of the incongruences, there is the original loss of freedom where it is sought and the eventual attainment of it where it is relinquished. The ambition to expand human potentiality through the rejection of limits leads to bondage instead of liberty in the instance of the first Adam, for creaturely freedom is progressively divested of its possibilities as it loses its limits. The way of the second Adam drives ever more deeply into the density and limits and constraints of what is finite and definite, and this is the single path that leads to the Father. It is the movement downward that generates the movement upward: the *kenosis,* the *plerosis;* the limitations, the liberty; the exploration of the detail of the finite, the unity with God. Were it not for the descent, the ascent would be impossible. The classic statement of the way of the second Adam appears in the second chapter of Philippians:

> Let this mind be in you, which was also in Christ Jesus: Who, being in the form of God, thought it not robbery to be equal with God: But made himself of no reputation, and took upon him the form of a servant, and was made in the likeness of men: And being found in fashion as a man, he humbled himself, and became obedient unto death, even the death of the cross. *Wherefore,* God also hath highly exalted him, and given him a name which is above every name.[37]

When Adam seeks to emulate God and gain unlimited freedom, he loses his freedom. When the Christ subjects himself to all the constraints of the finite and creaturely, he comes to the Father, renders perfect his freedom, and fulfills the quest of the first Adam in a way that could never be foreseen. The lost Adamic lordship is restored in the obedience of the second Adam: against all expectations, lordship belongs only to the perfectly obedient. The lost Adamic liberty is recovered in the acceptance of limits: freedom is sterile until they award it specific possibilities. Against all anticipations, the passion for the increase of liberty must someday defeat itself.

The sense of an ending that is conveyed by the Adamic narrative constitutes a thoroughly distinctive vision of the fulfillment of creaturely life, for it is entirely concrete and yet in large measure indeterminate at the same time. It is concrete because the end has already been disclosed to mankind in the passion and resurrection of Jesus Christ. The end is past as well as future. Jesus is "the first fruits of them that slept"[38] and, for those who have been incorporated by grace into the second Adam, his end is theirs as well. So Paul counsels:

> Know ye not, that so many of us as were baptized into Jesus Christ were baptized into his death? Therefore we are buried with him by baptism into death: that like as Christ was raised up from the dead by the glory of the Father, even so we also should walk in newness of life. For if we have been planted together in the likeness of his death, *we shall be also in the likeness of his resurrection.* [39]

To be "in the likeness of his resurrection," however, still involves an indeterminate element, for the second Adam who has come among us at a particular time and place is the lord who is yet to come, and the form of his future advent is veiled from us. So the first letter of John states that although "now are we the sons of God . . . *it doth not yet appear what we shall be:* but we know that, when he shall appear, we shall be like him; for we shall see him as he is."[40] There are signs and tokens of what persons shall be, certainly, for "ye know that he was manifested to take away our sins; and in him is no sin. Whosoever abideth in him sinneth not: whosoever sinneth hath not seen him, neither known him."[41] Nevertheless, what persons shall be is not yet entirely apparent.

The element of indeterminacy is all the greater because of the way that life "in the likeness of his resurrection" refers to the present as well as to the future. In relation to the future it is a description and a promise; in relation to the present it is a prescription and a challenge. The sense of an ending that is communicated by the news of the resurrection could scarcely leave the present untouched: "like as Christ was raised up from the dead by the glory of the Father, *even so we also should walk in newness of life.*" Only by grace, only by incorporation into the second Adam, is newness of life possible for the progeny of the first Adam. It is equally true, however, that by grace this changed mode of existence becomes a genuinely *human* possibility. The work of Christ means the restoration to persons of a measure of freedom of which they have deprived themselves as a consequence of their fallenness. Its achievements cannot be foreseen, for they are the expressions of individual spontaneity and inventiveness. Those who are "in Christ" have yet to learn much more about living in a way that corresponds to what they are. Those who have been liberated have yet to learn much more about the dimensions of their liberty. Even so, the newness of their lives has begun. Therefore, the end that has been disclosed has not been entirely disclosed: not only because in the time between the times it can be completely envisioned by God alone, but also because it is not imposed upon the creature in some external fashion. It involves the exercise of the self's own imprevisible liberty and creativeness, the actualization by the self of possibilities that not even God himself could realize in the mode that is appropriate to creaturely life. Human history has its own irreducible and unpredictable contribution to offer to the ending, even though the ending is not only in the future but also concretely disclosed in the past.

Therefore, although the story of Adam has often been interpreted as though it were simply a myth, in the sense in which Kermode uses the word, in fact it is an appeal to human resourcefulness rather than the declaration of a conclusion that renders human resources gratuitous. For those who are persuaded by it, the narrative offers a sense of an ending that is certain and unalterable, and yet it does so in a way that does not represent the world of potency as though it were a world of act. Precisely because the end is act as well as potency, and neither one alone, persons gain new motivation and strength to pursue in this world moral possibilities that have been hitherto unrealized. The mixture of concretion and indeterminacy that characterizes the end of the story of Adam can be expressed by the statement that the end is already real but not yet realized. In part, its realization depends upon the human agency of those who are in Christ. The sinfulness for which selves have been forgiven must still be combated if they are ever to be freed of its dominion. "Newness of life" has yet to be displayed where suspicion and indifference or enmity still reign. C. K. Barrett writes with fine balance that:

> The basic terms in which Christian existence must be understood are eschatological. It rests upon Christ's own resurrection and victory over the powers brought forward from the time of the End, and upon the verdict of acquittal brought forward from the last judgement. It is thus a unique eschatology, since it asserts that, notwithstanding appearances, the End has already come, and further that, notwithstanding this confident assertion, the End is not yet. Out of this formula, "Already—Not yet," which is the fundamental pattern of the Christian life, we see evolving in Paul the more developed maxim of "As if not" *(hos me)*. . . . The Roman Christians are manifestly not living the resurrection life of freedom from sin; they are, however, commanded to live as if they were already free from sin, since in truth it no longer has any claim upon them; to live as if they were not, in this age, under the bondage of sin and death.[42]

The assurance that the dominion of darkness, suffering, evil, and death has been broken in the garden where the second Adam was raised from the tomb is coupled with a consistent focus upon the power that they still exert. So persons are challenged to struggle against them in the confidence of the final realization of the victory that has already been achieved. There is no justification for flight from the combat, and there is too much evidence to the contrary for the self to ignore the remnants of their former tyranny that continue to despoil and violate the present. Human responsibility is all the greater because these cosmological conditions "are so far anthropological that their existence is due to the fact that man has abandoned his appointed standing in creation."[43] According to the Adamic narrative, not only the origin but also the continuation of the hegemony of darkness is related to the self's own fabrication of idols from among its works, its communities, its peers, and its loves.

On the one hand, then, insofar as the self is incorporated into the new Adam, the cosmological conditions that engender suffering and death have been decisively defeated, and the power that they now exert is a reflection of the agony of their own dying. On the other, the end that is already a reality is not yet realized, the self has not yet conquered the sinfulness within itself, and many persons have not yet acknowledged their election in Jesus Christ. Consequently, the dying life of the *stoicheia tou cosmou* is prolonged. Because the end has already occurred, a lost liberty has been restored to people by the grace of God; because this ending also lies in the future, selves are called to employ their freedom in the present to combat conditions whose oppressiveness is a consequence of the misuse of their freedom. In the perspective of the Pauline letters:

> It must never be forgotten that in the present age this heavenly life is anticipated truly, but only anticipated. The evil powers, though their decisive defeat has already taken place, retain their capacity for inflicting pain and harm, and for leading astray. Death still reigns, and will continue to do so until the *parousia* and the End. Christians, including not least the apostles (I Cor. iv. 9–13), are constantly in peril from demonic forces.[44]

The concrete sense of a real ending that remains partly indeterminate because it is not yet realized—this is an indispensable complement to the master images of the self as player, sufferer, and vandal, because it can solicit human agency and freedom, as the bare images themselves can never do in equivalent measure, in order to combat the cosmological circumstances that contribute their own evils to human affairs and that persons have themselves unleashed. As we have seen, images will not prove sufficient for an understanding of selfhood until they find their anchorage in a story. Only a narrative can acquaint us with the actual character of our experience. But self and world are correlative; the self that has misunderstood its world will necessarily err in measuring its own possibilities and powers. Therefore, the only narrative that can provide satisfactory lodging for these master images is a story that, like the matter of Adam, can illuminate not only the ways of the heart but also the *stoicheia tou cosmou,* all the various circumstances that are external to the self but never unrelated to it and that still retain their power to deepen and prolong the darkness of the heart. Whether or not the Adamic narrative and the sense of an ending it affords actually function as an instrument of religious disclosure and an invitation to the achievement of new moral possibilities, however, must depend upon the extent to which the story can liberate us from the deceptions practiced upon us and from the deceptions we practice upon ourselves.

For several reasons, the tale of the two Adams possesses an inexhaustible capacity to expose our self-deceptions and bring us to a new encounter with ourselves. First, the story insists that the gifts and promises of the second Adam are intended exclusively for those who come to recognize themselves as "enemies" of God who are "ungodly" and "helpless." The gifts are offered only to those who know that they do not deserve them; the promises are free, but they can be heard only by those who see that the judgment and condemnation endured by the Christ are properly their own. Everything occurs by grace alone, and yet there is a single condition that is itself an effect of grace rather than a human attainment: the acknowledgment of the truth of the portrayal of the self as ungodly and helpless and an enemy of God. When everything depends upon a certain sense of the unworthiness of the self, not in relation to other persons but strictly in relation to the mercy and love of God, there is no longer room for self-deceptions that are rooted in moral idealism or religious passion.

Second, it is not as though the self could confess its original unworthiness and ungodliness but claim a subsequent righteousness and superiority to other people. Because the end not only has come but also has not yet come, the renewal and transformation of the forgiven self are present more in anticipation than in actuality. It is true that persons can grow toward greater conformity with Christ, but this occurs only by grace and provides, instead of reasons for boasting, further grounds for acknowledging that in relation to God the self depends wholly upon powers other than its own. In the time between the times, there is no way to stand in the light of the promise except to continue to confess that the self is helpless and ungodly. Third, there is the importance not only of the content of the narrative but also of its form, the incongruence that accompanies the consonance between beginning and end. Adam is brought to a fulfillment appropriate to his nature but he comes to it in a way that shatters our expectations and exposes their rigidity. The desired is found only by way of the confession that it is not deserved. The vindication of the worth of the self by God presupposes the admission of its unworthiness by the self itself. The human that is lost in a quest for divinity is restored only when divinity becomes human. It is religious passion itself that otherwise blocks fulfillment in God. Our expectations, of course, reflect a certain understanding of the nature and possibilities of selfhood. Insofar as the incongruence in the story and the anomalies that it enshrines upset all reasonable anticipations and canons of probability, the narrative counsels that we have always been deceived concerning ourselves and, in our understanding of the self in relation to God, radically deceived.

Finally, and this brings us to the heart of the matter, there is the "as if... as if not" that lies at the center of Pauline ethics and that is demanded by the eschatological character of the Christian message. Because the end has been secured and partly disclosed in the career of Jesus Christ, persons are admonished to live toward it and from it, as though it were now, in this world as if they were in the new world. Paul warns the Corinthians that "the time is short: it remaineth that both they that have wives be as though they had none; And they that weep, as though they wept not; and they that rejoice, as though they rejoiced not; and they that buy, as though they possessed not; and they that use this world, as not abusing it: for the fashion of this world passeth away."[45] In other words, they are to live in this world as though it were not. So the Colossians are asked, "Wherefore if ye be dead with Christ from the rudiments of the world, why, as though living in the world, are ye subject to ordinances, (Touch not; taste not;

handle not; Which all are to perish with the using;) after the commandments and doctrines of men?"[46] The end still lies in the future, however; it is yet to come. The injunction to live "as if . . . as if not" is intended for a fallen world that has yet to pass away.

In the eyes of this world, the Pauline maxim can appear either conservative or revolutionary, but it is not necessarily one rather than the other, for it is a religious imperative and not a political dogma. It simply exhorts those who are alive in this world to live as if they were dead to it, and it urges the progeny of the first Adam to conduct themselves as if they were not the children of their father. On the one hand, therefore, the maxim can function conservatively, persuading individuals to content themselves with their roles and perform their functions faithfully. They have no reason to protest their station in life because they have no reason to identify themselves with it if, in fact, they are living in this world as if they were in the new world, and if they know that "the fashion of this world passeth away."[47] On the other hand, the imperative can also arouse people to struggle against the appearances of a world that is destined to pass away and to work for the transformation of things in the light of the new world which is now so close at hand that "the time is short." What is important, however, is that in either instance the persons who are admonished to live as if the old were not and as if the new had come must adopt a radically different perspective upon themselves. They cannot yield to conventional self-understandings, and they must not measure their worth in terms of their functions and roles; on the contrary, "if ye then be risen with Christ, seek those things which are above, where Christ sitteth on the right hand of God. Set your affection on things above, not on things on the earth. *For ye are dead, and your life is hid with Christ in God.*"[48]

But this life that "is hid with Christ in God" remains future; the complete transformation and renewal of the fallen self are bound up with the realization of the end that has not yet come. So the self must recognize itself as still a sinner, though forgiven for its sins. There can be no undialectical representation of the self at all, then; neither its old understanding of itself nor the interpretation of itself as a new creation is satisfactory without qualification. It is impossible to encounter the "as if . . . as if not" without a renewed awareness that the self is not as it would like itself to be or as it would like to perceive itself. While the imperative is concerned with conduct, it is phrased in such a way that it also directs attention to the nature of the person who acts and insistently challenges his self-understanding and questions his fidelity to the self-imagery that he has chosen to espouse. So the story of the two Adams affords inexhaustible opportunities for stepping back, for a perspective upon our perspectives, for a new and more discriminating sense of the differences between appearance and reality. The apparently anomalous injunctions that we who have died with him should become what we are and that we who have been raised with him should be what we yet are not, neither of which persons can achieve for themselves, constitute our best remedies for self-deception. The matter of Adam, therefore, provides a distinctive sense of an ending that satisfies the demand for concretion and yet retains the indeterminacy that can solicit human agency and inventiveness. It can fulfill both requisites because the ending that includes all possible beginnings and ends within itself is an event in our history as well as resident in the future. The story functions as an instrument of religious disclosure, not only because it tells of an end that lies beyond all others imaginable but also because of its singular capacity for liberating the self from its deceptions of itself, and especially from the illusions that the self entertains concerning its situation before God.

There is a final question, however, that has yet to be addressed: what is the relation of the master images of the self as player, sufferer, and vandal to the whole fabric of the Adamic narrative? The tale of the fall, particularly when it is viewed in the light of Augustine's reflections upon his own experience, can support the representation of the self as vandal and profit by interpretation from this perspective. In its mixture of ordinariness and senselessness and irrationality, in

its random and purposeless destructiveness and adumbrations of motiveless malevolence, and in the ways that it can
support and reinforce a project of self-deception, vandalism
seems frequently to differ from all the other crimes that persons have invented in order to achieve one aim or another. So
it can capture something of the completely gratuitous nature
of what the serpent does, and something, too, of the mystery
that is hidden in the woman's acquiescence to the tempter.
The figure of the sufferer can represent the way of the second
Adam far more satisfactorily than any other image. Jesus is the
paradigm of the suffering servant and the Christian tradition
has found few texts as cogent for understanding him as the
prophecy in the Book of Isaiah of one of whom it would be
said:

> Surely he hath borne our griefs, and carried our sorrows:
> yet we did esteem him stricken, smitten of God and
> afflicted. But he was wounded for our transgressions, he
> was bruised for our iniquities: the chastisement of our
> peace was upon him; and with his stripes we are healed.
> All we like sheep have gone astray; we have turned every
> one to his own way; and the Lord hath laid on him the
> iniquity of us all. He was oppressed, and he was afflicted,
> yet he opened not his mouth; he is brought as a lamb to
> the slaughter, and as a sheep before her shearers is
> dumb, so he openeth not his mouth.[49]

As the second chapter of Philippians affirms, it is only by
way of his suffering that he comes to fulfillment and lordship.
His freedom is found through obedience and made perfect
through the exploration of all the detail of creaturely life. In
relation to God, no portrayal of the self can be more appropriate than the command and obedience model of selfhood that
suffering suggests. Of what relevance, however, is the image
of the player now? What reasons are there still to claim that
it is demanded by the matter of Adam and illuminates his
story?

EPILOGUE:
FAITH AND PLAY

The second Adam "took upon him the form of a servant" and at Golgotha "hath borne our griefs, and carried our sorrows." Those who are in Christ begin to grow into his form and away from the image of the vandal that is a legacy of the events in the first garden, although the figure of the fallen self retains its relevance even for them until the end of time. The way of the Christian is the passage from vandal to sufferer, and in suffering there is joy and not only pain, fulfillment as well as the possibility of loss. The importance of the representation of the self as player, however, is less obvious. Certainly the man and woman who figure in the story of the first Adam could neither understand themselves as players nor trust the country of their exile after they are barred from the garden: "Cursed is the ground for thy sake; in sorrow shalt thou eat of it all the days of thy life; Thorns also and thistles shall it bring forth to thee; and thou shalt eat the herb of the field; In the sweat of thy face shalt thou eat bread, till thou return unto the ground."[1]

One cannot play freely and consistently in a land where powers of darkness roam, where vandals terrorize, where lies are told for no purpose except the pleasure of the lie, where accidents occur with brute and random violence. Yet such are the appearances of the world in which we live; only children can fail to see that playing by the rules is a taming of the world that will never long endure, for neither nature nor the vandal in themselves have agreed to honor the little orders we construct. The story of the first Adam insists that evil is related to and rooted in a deflection of creaturely will and that the world itself is entirely good as it comes from the hands of God. But the narrative also affirms that God ratifies the cosmic consequences of human disobedience; despite their origin in Adam's abandonment of his delegated authority, the powers of the *stoicheia tou cosmou* become more than a match for human ingenuity. So persons seem to have no option except to defend themselves and those they love as best they can. Their strategies of defense, of course, not only will not prevail but will actually reinforce the powers of the *stoicheia tou cosmou*, and so there is progressively all the less reason for basic trust and all the more for people to defend themselves with unyielding seriousness and by whatever means they can devise.

What is important, however, is not first of all whether the image of the player is itself at the center of the whole narrative and justified by every part of it. The crucial question, instead, concerns whether it is true that the significance of the story for self-understanding is most satisfactorily summarized when those who are acquainted with it are persuaded to see themselves in a particular way as players. There is much evidence that can be enlisted to support this claim. First, as the substance of the temptation implies, the particular disease of the sinner is irremediable self-seriousness, for the sinner stands alone and there is no one to defend him but himself. But the disclosure of God as redeemer as well as judge in the second Adam means that persons can no longer regard their own projects and purposes with unqualified seriousness nor represent themselves as though they were ultimately responsible for the world. No longer are they by themselves. The disclosure of that which alone is ultimately serious renders all else, in comparison with the holy, no more than relatively serious. The representation of the self in this world as a player acknowledges this relativization; it precludes the misdirection of the unqualified seriousness that now can be appropriately given to one reality only, God himself, and that becomes the source of the daimonic whenever it is oriented toward the creaturely.

Second, the sense of an ending that is offered by the Adamic story insists that the human enterprise is and can be sustained only by a power that is more than human, and it is to this gracious and sovereign reality alone that ultimate allegiance is due. But the narrative also constitutes an invitation to exercise human inventiveness and liberty in the confidence that creaturely effort now will not eventually prove futile and its effects will not vanish into endless night. This revelation of an end beyond all possible beginnings and endings, an end that even though unrealized is real nonetheless, instills and encourages the assumption of basic trust that is integral to understanding life in this world as play, while playing teaches and affirms this assumption in response to God's revelation. Basic trust is certainly not synonymous with thoughtless optimism: it affirms that we can learn from every battle, not that we can win them all; that we must cherish ourselves, not that we can trust ourselves; that darkness can elicit from us new strength and courage, not that it can always be dispelled; that we need not suffer alone, not that we need never suffer at all.[2]

Third, the representation of the self as player is not, of course, intended to imply that one need not or ought not be serious about roles and functions in the everyday world, for it is only in and through the everyday world and one's responsibilities there that God discloses himself. The image does mean, however, that persons cannot be wholly identified with their functions and roles, for they are also creatures whom God has willed and sustains and addresses. The qualification of seriousness has nothing to do with its absence. In many of its expressions, the play impulse is a profoundly serious affair, even though the players are not unaware that what they do is simply a game and that there is another realm beyond the boundaries they have established for themselves.[3] The image is intended, then, to confront the self with what should be involved in all its conduct in functions and roles: fidelity to the dictates of justice as fairness or fair play, without an approximation of which community must inevitably dissolve. Without the qualification of the seriousness of the sinner in worldly affairs there can be no end to the invention of idols, but this relativization will legitimate nothing less than fair play toward others and not least of all toward one's own self, for each is a creature of God. The image possesses a twofold significance, because it expresses the dialectic of the freedom from the world and the responsibility toward it that are congruent with God's self-disclosure in Jesus Christ.

So the complementarity of the two images of player and sufferer, which begins with their mutual testimony to the involution of limits and liberty that Adam ignores, displays many facets. The figure of the sufferer can represent the self's capacity for love, for the second Adam is the paradigm of the sufferer, while the figure of the player can express the self's responsibility for justice. The sufferer can represent the self in its responsiveness to other selves; the player can express the self in its affirmation of the norms without which relationships are spoiled. The sufferer can represent the self in relation to the sovereign initiative of God; the player can portray the relationship of the self to the world in consequence of the disclosure of God. When the story of the Adams is read from the second to the first and interpreted in the light of its ending, the image of the self as player seems essential as at least a partial expression of the mode of existence that is rendered possible by the disclosure of God, as a warning against and remedy for the idolatries that burden fallen life and that began when Eve regarded the serpent as an authoritative spokesman for God, and as a representation of the need for justice or fair play if persons are to live in community as God has intended them to do. It confronts the self with a conjunction of may and ought: descriptive of a way of life that is open to all, prescriptive because none attain it consistently or perfectly, for the self remains a sinner still.

Fourth and most important, insofar as the matter of Adam actually functions as a religious story, it begins to transform the character of those who believe in it from their similitude to the first Adam into the likeness of the greater who came after him. "Character" designates the developed disposition of the self to speak and act in a rational and consistent fashion, and "Christian character" describes the disposition and power to live with more or less consistency in accordance with the fundamental ethical imperative that informs all of the Pauline writings and that follows from the disclosure in the story of Adam of an ending that is real although not yet realized. Together with that of the sufferer, the figure of the player becomes a central image of Christian existence because it is perhaps the most adequate of all possible representations of those who live by the injunction to conduct themselves "as if . . . as if not."

Playing means opportunities to live against appearances and as though the world were other than it is, to realize in imagination what otherwise remains stubbornly beyond our present reach, to see others and ourselves from a perspective that nothing in the world entirely legitimates, to be as we are not yet and as other than we are, and so to be less than wholly serious about the self or the world as appearances disclose them, and to transfigure reality in the fashion of the artist and in accordance with a more discriminating vision than the ones that are currently fashionable in the everyday world. Life under the "as if . . . as if not" is best captured by the figure of the player whose restlessness with things as they are is motivated neither by romantic nostalgia nor by revolutionary zeal, but by a sense of an ending that lies on the far side of all other imaginable endings and that is as certain as the sovereignty of God. Play is simply play: the end remains in the future, even though the player lives as if it were present. Yet play is also more than the stuff of which dreams are made, although without losing its character as play, for the future has been disclosed and assured in the history of Jesus Christ and is therefore present in memory as well as in anticipation. Because the present age is passing away, it would be folly to identify its appearances with enduring reality. The Adamic narrative is irreducibly eschatological and the authority of the "as if . . . as if not" is reinforced by the knowledge that now "the time is short."

> And so it is written, The first man Adam was made a living soul; the last Adam was made a quickening spirit. Howbeit that was not first which was spiritual, but that which is natural; and afterward that which is spiritual. The first man is of the earth, earthy: the second man is the Lord from heaven. As is the earthy, such are they also that are earthy: and as is the heavenly, such are they also that are heavenly. And as we have borne the image of the earthy, we shall also bear the image of the heavenly. Now this I say, brethren, that flesh and blood cannot inherit the kingdom of God; neither doth corruption inherit incorruption. Behold I shew you a mystery; We shall not all sleep, but we shall all be changed. In a moment, in the twinkling of an eye, at the last trump: for the trumpet shall sound, and the dead shall be raised incorruptible, and we shall be changed.[4]

Nevertheless, the mode of existence that the imperative enjoins is intended for life in this world; the injunction to be not anxious must never be confused with disdain or indifference toward worldly affairs. Freedom from the anxieties and conventions of the fallen world is completely misunderstood if it is not seen to involve new and even greater responsibilities toward other selves, responsibilities all the more urgent because of the revelation of the will of God in the disclosure of the end. Paul stresses this dialectic when he writes to the church at Corinth that those who had been slaves of the world but have been made free people in Christ are now slaves in his service. Rudolf Bultmann is correct to insist:

> Failure to recognize the reality of human existence in actual history involves a non-paradoxical misunderstanding of one's possession of the Spirit and of the liberty it

brings, and this misunderstanding carries with it the surrender of the *idea of creation*. But retaining both the idea
of the world as creation and the idea of de-secularization
(Ent*welt*lichung—inward divorce from the world)
through participation in the eschatological occurrence
must establish such a dialectic (paradoxical) relation to
the world as will be expressed in Paul's "as if . . . not."[5]

Paul admonishes the Christians at Corinth: "Let every man
abide in the same calling wherein he was called. Art thou
called being a servant? care not for it: but if thou mayest be
made free, use it rather. For he that is called in the Lord,
being a servant, is the Lord's freeman: likewise also he that
is called, being free, is Christ's servant. Ye are bought with a
price; be not ye the servants of men."[6] Bultmann quite properly warns that this "negation of worldly differentiations does
not mean a sociological program within this world; rather, it
is an eschatological occurrence."[7] Theology is not politics.
Perhaps Paul's words lend themselves best to a conservative
interpretation but, at least in some measure, they can also be
read as a charter for the transformation of human affairs. On
the one hand, the "as if . . . as if not" can induce the self to
rest content with its worldly situation and roles; on the other,
it can also furnish the self with motivation to struggle to
transform the world so that its ways will display new corre-
spondence with the will of God. In either instance, however,
the conduct of the self in its functions and rules can never do
less than conform to the exigencies of playing fair, for any
deviation would mean that the self no longer obeyed the
advice to "abide in the same calling wherein he was called."
Yet this commitment to fairness, which can be surpassed but
must never be ignored, must also involve the recognition that
life in the kingdom of God means much more than fidelity to
the principle of fairness. Although the standard does not lose
its seriousness for worldly affairs, it is still relativized from the
perspective of the end. Therefore, Bultmann is again correct
when he comments that "it is not always clear what specific
attitude Paul had in mind when he spoke of fleshly attitude or
conduct. It may be an 'anxiety for things of the world,' but this

need not be immoral conduct; rather it may consist of normal human affairs whenever a man devotes himself to them without the reservation of 'as if . . . not' "—without, in other words, understanding them as a form of play.[8]

So the play motif that figured prominently in the predecessors to this book is scarcely relegated to a subordinate position because of its relation to a narrative that stresses the nature of the social self as sufferer and that concerns the paradigm of the sufferer. It remains at the center, awarded greater richness and concretion because it has finally been related to the story from which it initially was drawn, secured at the center by the injunction and the permission to live "as if . . . as if not," and endowed with its particular significance by its context there of divine judgment, liberation, and companionship. Perhaps the most appropriate description of Christian existence, then, remains the statement that the life of faith means playing by ear. The end is apprehended only by entering the world of the Bible and there is no access to it that does not involve judgment, penitence, humility, and the acceptance of the command and obedience model of selfhood that is correlated with an oral-aural universe, in response to the disclosure of the sovereignty and initiative of God. In the context of the Adamic narrative, there is no conflict between this representation of the self and the model that is implied by the image of the player, for the ought and the may, command and permission, achieve perfect conjunction: one ought to play "as if . . . as if not," and one is freed to play because natural impulse is now fortified by reason for basic trust despite all there is within the world that spoils and savages persons and their designs.

The sense of an ending that the story provides indissolubly joins suffering and play: those who are sufferers in relation to God are called to play "as if . . . as if not" in relation to the world, while those who see themselves as players must then suffer their neighbors as fairness demands. The instinct for playing that is written into every animal and not least of all into the constitution of the self is, first of all, a universal instrument of socialization; then the source of an image that expresses the importance of justice or fairness; then a disordered impulse that can manifest itself in countless forms, from the most common sorts of vandalism to the motiveless malevolence of Iago; then a way to acknowledge the one reality beside whom nothing else is entirely serious; then a remedy against the daimons that our idolatries create; and finally an expression of the fundamental ethical imperative and word of liberation that lie at the core of the Christian life where grace and challenge are bound inseparably together.

There are many games that persons play and perhaps almost as many different ways in which they can envision themselves as players, but the play that is consonant with Christian commitment differs radically from all other forms, in the sense that it begins not as an expression of the will of the individual but as a submission to the will of God. It is not intended to create a new world that satisfies the heart's desires but, instead, to acknowledge the one reality that insistently exposes the darkness of the heart. The appeal to live "as if . . . as if not" distinguishes this mode of play because it means that the self must surrender all of its own quests for security and permanence in this world; the permission is at the same time a condemnation, a judgment not only against the actions and ambitions of the first Adam and his progeny but against the selves that have formed themselves in such a way that they entertain these hopes and are swayed by motives that lead them to act in this fashion. Imagination is the origin of the phantoms and daimons that torment and deceive people, not itself the instrument of their redemption. Certainly the story of Adam displays the fallenness of the power that is the source of all human games: had imagination not lost its rectitude, it could never have portrayed the self *sicut deum,* as though it could be divine. Consequently, our images must be returned to the more than human narrative from which they were first derived. Like the images of the sufferer and the vandal, the figure of the player remains indeterminate in isolation, ambiguous and elusive when it is deprived of a context; it is only in relation to the image of Adam, a man, and to the story of Adam, everyone, that the image gains its full specificity and significance. Like imagery of the self, however, stories can also be held in unrighteousness unless, as in the instance of the Adamic narrative, their promise of an ending can be grasped only by those who acknowledge that they always remain "ungodly" and "helpless." But precisely because it insists upon the inseparability of submission to radical judgment and the reception of the grace of God, this particular story constrains us to step back to question our questions, criticize our imaginings, and recognize that we who have deceived ourselves so frequently and massively must acknowledge the perennial possibility that we will deceive ourselves again.

The question that this book must leave for others to decide, of course, concerns how well these three master images of the person can express the significance of the Adamic narrative for self-understanding, and how powerfully they can illuminate the complexities of our experience. This cannot be decided satisfactorily, however, if we ignore the centrality of the ending, and therefore of faith, for the interpretation of everything else. As Karl Barth has emphasized, the first Adam can be understood only in the light of the greater Adam, not the other way round, for the first was only a shadow and sketch of the one who was and is to come. It is nowhere except in the flesh and bone of Jesus of Nazareth that the proportions of true humanity are disclosed. Consequently, there are substantial limitations placed upon every attempt to display the empirical fit of the Christian view of selfhood. On the one hand, persons do not know what they shall be when the ending that has been disclosed is realized. On the other, in the time between the times, persons are called to live against appearances, to live in this world as though the world were not and as though they were not as they so often seem to be. Yet this does not mean that the venture is flawed; it is not the question of empirical verification, it is the development of Christian character, that is the proper focus of natural theology as it has been addressed in this book.

The end is immanent in the beginning but the significance of the beginning is disclosed only by the end: so the venture rounds back upon itself, circular, the original motifs qualified and augmented as they are brought closer to an end that directs us again to the beginning, the first Adam illuminated by the incandescence of the second, the imagery of vandal and sufferer integrated with the figure of the player in actual experience, not by human striving but by the grace of God, the end transcending the beginning by his power alone. The focus shifts from ordinary experience that renders significant our language about the holy to the development of character in response to the self-disclosure of God, and then again to the texture of ordinary experience, for it is in this world that persons are called to live in obedience to God. This book, then, becomes not only a sequel to *Faith and Virtue* but a preface to *Grace and Common Life,* for intimations of grace in ordinary affairs would scarcely be recognized as tokens of the presence of God if there had been no disclosure of the end, while we would possess no language to acknowledge or express the reality of the end were there not analogies for us to discover between the grace that informs everyday experience and the grace of God in Jesus Christ. Small graces point toward the climactic judgment where grace abounds; the judgment illuminates more small graces that sparkle in the texture of ordinary life and the regenerative possibilities of other judgments to which we are liable.

The cosmization of familial imagery that enables us to acknowledge the universe as personal, so that we can respond to the gift of a sense of an ending and worship the holy, also threatens to become a cosmization of familial roles or familial status, as in the instance of the vandal. Either form of alienation becomes greater the more that the family is loved, for then the weight of shame or responsibility, guilt or obligation, is all the greater. Despite the crucial role of the family as a context for playing and for the development of basic trust, as well as for the provision of the words and images that faith requires, it threatens to become a structure of destruction in which love is the artificer of daimons that destroy the love in which they began.

What is true of the family is equally true of the other great instrument of socialization, play. It can become merely a test of strength that discriminates against the weak. It can express indifference toward others instead of a commitment to fairness toward all. It can turn sour and exhibit a relish for destruction. Only in relation to the end, only in relation to the "as if . . . as if not" can all the daimons be held at bay and the ears of the player opened to all the anguished cries that rise from the darkness of the world. The end calls us away from the family to the whole household of God, away from our small dinners to a table laid for everyone, away from favorite games to the struggle for fair play everywhere. But that common meal, which is a foretaste of things to come and which we did not lay for ourselves, is also intended to renew and redeem familial suppers and familial games so that their imagery is luminous of the holy again. It is offered for the forgiveness by children of their parents' betrayals of childish expectations as well as for the forgiveness by parents of children's expectations that involve more than mothers and fathers can ever provide. It is meant for the renewal of trust in the midst of betrayal, for the restoration of play even in storms of disorder.

To return again to Austin Farrer's comment upon the authors of the New Testament: "Divine truth is supranaturally communicated to man in an act of inspired thinking which falls into the shape of certain images."[9] The Adamic image is one of the most crucial of these; it lies at the heart of the biblical interpretation of Jesus of Nazareth, for the claim that God became man, a New Adam, is an indispensable part of the New Testament story of the redeemer. So an essay in Christian anthropology cannot treat it as though it were not an essential resource and the appropriate place to begin as well as to end. The narrative of the two Adams provides a perspective upon our perspectives and counsels us always to question our questions, but it never robs us of all those perspectives and questions. It returns us to them, for it is an invitation to the human and not a foreclosure of it. But now they have been transformed. Just as the first Adam is judged and redeemed by the second and greater who comes after him, so their mutual story becomes an instrument for self-recognition and self-transcendence on the part of those who are incorporated into both, even though some may never acknowledge their involvement with the one nor realize their incorporation into the other. The power of the story is not only the power of all good narrative, however, but a disclosure of the power of him who has come and who is yet to come, and to whom, with the Father and the Holy Ghost, be all praise and adoration, honor and dominion, power and glory, now and forever.

NOTES

Introduction

1. Austin Farrer, *The Glass of Vision* (London: Dacre Press, 1948), p. 57.
2. See David Baily Harned, *Faith and Virtue* (Philadelphia: Pilgrim Press, 1973), pp. 9–11. In my judgment, one of the intentions of some traditional modes of natural theology, the attempt to relate faith in God to some generally available characteristics of ordinary experience, is integral to the proclamation of the Christian message. But it is a mistake to regard this task as apologetic and as an attempt at verification of the proclamation. This misunderstanding causes the believer to appear as though he were temporarily suspending his belief so that he can speak persuasively to other persons. So there emerges the completely untenable situation in which the pursuit of truth seems to require that persons abstract themselves from the truth of their actual situation.
3. For a discussion of some inadequacies of the polarity of religious and secular and of the category of "religious experience," see David Baily Harned, *Grace and Common Life* (Charlottesville: University Press of Virginia, 1971), chs. IV and V.
4. Between the first and the last of these three essays, there has

been a shift of focus from "epiphanies" or intimations of God in ordinary experience to eschatology and from experience itself to the question of the renewal of the one who experiences. This is not so much a redirection, however, as it is an inevitable development, although I must acknowledge my indebtedness to those who were responsible for the "theology of hope" and who reinforced my own convictions about Christian eschatology. But examinations of experience are empty if they do not direct attention toward the nature that entertains experiences, while traces and intimations of the presence of God ineluctably orient the self toward the future in hope and anticipation, or else in anxiety and fear.

5. Mk. 13: 21–23a.
6. I am indebted to Professor Rowan Greer of Yale University—although in no way can he be held accountable for whatever errors I commit—for strengthening my own conviction that the Adamic parallel is one of the most important elements in the New Testament understanding of humanity. Perhaps it would be too much to claim that it is *the* one dominant motif, but it could certainly be argued that many Fathers of the Church believed that it was—most obviously, Irenaeus. On the one hand, it is the "Redeemer myth" that tends to integrate the Christology of the New Testament, although I do not believe or mean to suggest that it lay ready at hand, so to speak, waiting for its historical realization. On the other hand, an essential element in the New Testament rehearsal of the Redeemer myth, an element that illuminates everything else, is the claim that the Son of God became a New Adam. The argument of this essay does not depend upon the validity of the contention that the Adamic parallel is the single key that unlocks the New Testament understanding of selfhood, however, but only upon the assertion that the story of the two Adams is *one* of the fundamental motifs in the anthropology of the apostolic writers. This more modest claim seems scarcely controversial. See, for example, Reginald H. Fuller, *The Foundations of New Testament Christology* (London: Lutterworth Press, 1965), especially chs. VIII and IX.

Chapter One

1. For a perceptive exploration of the ways that will requires domestication by the imagination, see the distinction between Prometheus and Prometheanism in William F. Lynch, S. J., *Christ and Prometheus* (Notre Dame: University of Notre Dame Press, 1972), *passim.*

2. For a similar understanding of the imagination, see William F. Lynch, S. J., *Images of Hope* (Baltimore: Helicon Press, 1965), pp. 243 and *passim.*
3. Kenneth Boulding, *The Image* (Ann Arbor: University of Michigan Press, 1961), pp. 13–14.
4. Arthur Koestler, *Darkness at Noon,* tr. by Daphne Hardy (New York: The Modern Library, 1941), p. 254.
5. *Ibid.,* p. 255.
6. *Ibid.,* p. 261.
7. *Ibid.,* p. 254.
8. Our focus lies not upon experience itself but upon how persons are persuaded to *imagine* their most critical experiences. Despite occasional invocations of chthonic deities, the adult imagines in visual or else primarily oral/aural terms and this influences self-understanding. The imagining of bodily experience is consequential in two ways, for it both furnishes new images and qualifies those that have been derived from social relationships.
9. Walter J. Ong, S. J., *The Presence of the Word* (New Haven: Yale University Press, 1967), p. 6.
10. Hans Jonas, *The Phenomenon of Life* (New York: Harper and Row, 1966), p. 156.
11. *Ibid.,* pp. 141–142.
12. Christopher Isherwood, *Goodbye to Berlin* (London: The Hogarth Press, 1966), p. 13.
13. Jonas, *op. cit.,* p. 139.
14. Ong, *op. cit.,* p. 118.
15. Maurice Merleau-Ponty, *Phenomenology of Perception,* tr. by Colin Smith (London: Routledge and Kegan Paul, 1962), pp. 215–216.
16. *Ibid.,* p. 234.
17. Jonas, *loc. cit.*
18. Maurice Merleau-Ponty, *Signs,* tr. by Richard C. McCleary (Evanston: Northwestern University Press, 1964), pp. 66–67.
19. *Ibid.,* p. 67.
20. Georges Gusdorf, *Speaking (La Parole),* tr. by Paul Brockelman (Evanston: Northwestern University Press, 1965), p. 9.
21. *Ibid.,* p. 9.
22. *Ibid.,* p. 43.
23. Martin Luther, cited by Gustaf Wingren, *The Living Word* (Philadelphia: Muhlenberg Press, 1960), p. 64.
24. Thorlief Boman, *Hebrew Thought Compared with Greek,* tr. by Jules L. Mereau (New York: Norton Publishing Co., 1960), p. 205.
25. Although he does not dispute the existence of important differ-

ences between the two cultures, in *The Semantics of Biblical Language* (London: Oxford University Press, 1961) James Barr demonstrates that some of the linguistic evidence used by Boman and others to support the contrast has been grievously misinterpreted, largely because the alleged contrast between different ways of thinking has itself been allowed to shape the examination of the linguistic evidence. The theological motive for the development of the contrast is evident: there are persuasive reasons to emphasize the distinctiveness of the biblical message, especially to guard it against conflation in the modern world with other patterns of thinking that are finally alien to it and subversive of it. But in a later book, *Old and New in Interpretation* (New York: Harper and Row, 1966) Barr warns of some of the dangers to which claims for the distinctiveness of the biblical tradition can lead. First, it is clear that the contrast has been explored in order to isolate currents in *modern* culture that are judged congruent with or inimical to the world of the Bible. Were this not true, the distinctiveness of Holy Scripture would be argued in relation to its Semitic context and scarcely with reference to classical culture. In other words, it has represented a contemporary evangelical concern and has never really been quite what it depicted itself to be, an analysis of the actual intellectual life of ancient Israel and classical Greece. Second, the contrast has been intended, therefore, to maintain the purity of Christian reflection and proclamation. Oscar Cullmann, for example, contends: "We must recognize loyally that precisely those things which distinguish the Christian teaching from the Greek belief are at the heart of primitive Christianity" (*Immortality of the Soul or Resurrection of the Dead*, 1958, p. 8, cited in Barr, *Old and New*, p. 46). But this sort of aggressive theological purism must be regarded as suspect for many reasons.

First, it was the Jewish community and not the Gentiles that reacted most violently against Jesus. Second, there are no very persuasive reasons to equate the distinctive with the revelatory. Third, this sort of theological purism can become a fine vehicle for the expression of human self-assertion and self-righteousness. Fourth, the greatest dangers that the Christian community encounters are always those that arise from within itself, and not external pressures. Finally, theological purism seems to have no basis in the New Testament itself. There, as Barr correctly comments, "the suspicion of Greek thought, endemic in modern theology, is absent or inactive. The Greeks indeed, as persons are a problem, for they are persons to whom the gospel has to be preached and whose entry into the Church will occasion all kinds of problems and disagreements. But no one, going out into the Hellenistic world, takes occasion to worry for himself or to give warning to others about the dangerous nature of the Greek thought-processes and the impossibility of setting the faith within the categories formed in the philosophical tradition and conveyed in the language which everyone spoke. Thus Paul in Romans gives an analysis of Gentile life, which follows the traditional Jewish anti-Gentile polemic. . . . But at no point does he say anything which could plausibly be construed as a criticism for philosophical tendencies, whether abstractness or staticness or failure to show interest in history." (*Old and New,* p. 55.)

The deficiencies of the contrast, at least as it has been used in recent theology, for the pursuit of images of the self are very well expressed by W. David Stacey in *The Pauline View of Man* (London: Macmillan and Co., Ltd., 1956), p. 238: "Paul made no attempt to formulate a doctrine of man or to define man from a psychological point of view. He simply referred to him as the tool of evil or the recipient of God's grace and, naturally, he used whatever terminology helped to make his point more clear, regardless of the particular source from which he borrowed it. In his own mind and in the minds of those about him, Jewish and Greek anthropological terms were mixed together in carefree confusion. There were no scientific thinkers in his own environment, and Paul himself was not one. . . . Sometimes a Hebrew word expressed his meaning most happily. At other times a Greek word conveyed the vision to his hearers . . . and the fact that his terms were confused would not have bothered him."

26. See Merleau-Ponty, *Phenomenology of Perception,* p. 234, fn. 1: "It is true that the senses should not be put on the same basis, as if they were all equally capable of objectivity and accessible to intentionality. Experience does not present them to us as equivalent: I think that visual experience is truer than tactile experience, that it garners within itself its own truth and adds to it, because its richer structure offers me modalities of being unsuspected by touch. The unity of the senses is achieved transversally, according to their own structure. But something like it is found in binocular vision, if it is true that we have a 'directing eye' which brings the other under its control. These two facts —the taking over of sensory experiences in general in visual experience, and that of the functions of one eye by the other— prove that the unity of experience is not a formal unity, but a primary organization." His comments roughly parallel the

claims that have been made for vision in this work. Vision serves as a sort of "directing eye" that determines the selectivity of sight and the attentiveness or inattention of the ear while, because of their mutual subordination to vision, the various senses in their synergic unity "interpenetrate" one another: eyes feel the texture of things and the blind person sees through his fingers.

Chapter Two

1. Igor Stravinsky, *Poetics of Music in the Form of Six Lessons*, tr. by Arthur Knodel and Ingolf Dahl (New York: Random House, Vintage Books, 1959), p. 68.
2. Jonas, *op. cit.*, p. 152.
3. Plato, *The Laws*, tr. by B. Jowett, *The Dialogues of Plato* (New York: Random House, 1937), p. 558.
4. Julian N. Hartt, *The Restless Quest* (Philadelphia: Pilgrim Press, 1975).
5. Philippians 2:5–7. It must be remembered, however, that the question of the importance of the representation of the person as sufferer for a self-understanding that is congruent with the Hebraic vision of the situation of the self before God is quite distinct from two other questions—the significance of the figure of the suffering servant for the self-understanding of Jesus himself and its centrality for the apostolic writers. A severely qualified answer to the latter questions has no necessary implications for the former. For reasons to qualify the latter, see Morna D. Hooker, *Jesus and the Servant* (London: S. P. C. K., 1959).
6. Ronald S. Wallace, *Calvin's Doctrine of the Christian Life* (Edinburgh and London: Oliver and Boyd, 1959), p. 68. (Italics added.)
7. Søren Kierkegaard, *Concluding Unscientific Postscript*, tr. by David Swenson and Walter Lowrie (Princeton: Princeton University Press, 1968), p. 400.
8. *Ibid.*, p. 440. For Kierkegaard's usage of the words, "dying away from immediacy," see *ibid.*, pp. 412, 445.
9. John Hick, *Evil and the God of Love* (New York: Harper and Row, 1966), pp. 370–371. I am indebted to much of Hick's analysis. On the other hand, although this is not an appropriate context in which to debate the issues, I want it to be clear that my own understanding of the relation between God and the world makes is impossible for me to accept without severe qualifications Hick's "Irenaean" theodicy. In fact, Hick abstracts one motif in Irenaeus from others that are equally fundamental and there is no way that this can be done without a significant

measure of distortion. A more expansive interpretation of Irenaeus would furnish important reasons for modifying the rigid polarity that Hick establishes between the great Greek father and Augustine.

10. John MacMurray, *Persons in Relation* (London: Faber and Faber Ltd., 1961), p. 48.

11. *Ibid.*, p. 48.

12. *Ibid.*, p. 48. See all of Chapter Two, "Mother and Child," pp. 44–63, for a splendid analysis of the beginnings of human life.

13. *Ibid.*, p. 61.

14. Milton Mayeroff, *On Caring* (New York: Harper and Row, Perennial Library, 1972), pp. 55, 57.

15. *Ibid.*, pp. 29–30.

16. MacMurray, *op. cit.*, pp. 211–212.

17. Jeremiah 31:33–34.

18. William Golding, *The Spire* (New York: Harcourt, Brace and World, 1964), p. 179.

Chapter Three

1. C. G. Jung, *The Undiscovered Self*, tr. by R. F. C. Hull (Boston: Atlantic Monthly Press, 1958), pp. 95–97.

2. Ralph Ellison, *Invisible Man* (New York: Signet, 1952), p. 8.

3. Martin Buber, *Good and Evil* (New York: Charles Scribner's Sons, 1953), p. 7.

4. Stanley Hauerwas, "Self-Deception and Autobiography: Theological and Ethical Reflections on Speer's *Inside the Third Reich*," pp. 7–8. With the author's permission, I am quoting from a privately circulated essay that was subsequently published in revised form in the *Journal of Religious Ethics*, Vol. 2, no. 1 (1974), pp. 99–117, under the joint authorship of Hauerwas and David Burrell.

5. *Ibid.*, p. 23.

6. Graham Greene, *Brighton Rock* (New York: Viking Press, 1968), p. 292.

7. See Søren Kierkegaard, *Fear and Trembling*, tr. by Walter Lowrie (Princeton: Princeton University Press, 1973), pp. 64ff.

8. See below, pp. 106–117, for a more detailed account of motivation for which I am largely indebted to the excellent study by R. S. Peters, *The Concept of Motivation* (London: Routledge and Kegan Paul, 1958).

9. William Golding, *Lord of the Flies* (New York: G. P. Putnam's Sons, 1958), p. 125.

10. Albert Camus, *The Fall*, tr. by Justin O'Brien (New York: Alfred A. Knopf, 1959), p. 143.

11. Hannah Arendt, *The Human Condition* (Garden City: Doubleday and Company, Inc., 1959), p. 213.
12. Albert Camus, *The Plague*, tr. by Stuart Gilbert (New York: Alfred A. Knopf, 1948), p. 224.
13. *Ibid.*, p. 226.
14. *Ibid.*, pp. 228–229.
15. Camus, *The Fall*, p. 130.
16. *Ibid.*, pp. 138–140.
17. Arendt, *op. cit.*, p. 216. Miss Arendt's very incisive comments on forgiveness and promising are, as this quotation indicates, offered from a rigorously "secular" perspective. For a distinctively Christian approach, concerned first of all with the relation between God and the creature rather than with relationships among selves, the fine old study by H. R. Mackintosh, *The Christian Experience of Forgiveness* (London: Nisbet and Company Ltd., 1927), still has much to teach.
18. Camus, *The Fall*, p. 131.
19. Arendt relates forgiveness to the willingness to *respect* other persons in a fashion quite similar to my own stress upon the difficulty and importance of recognizing that "someone else is real" and must therefore be taken into account because this someone is a *creature* like myself, willed into existence by God. Both of us deny that only love can forgive. All of us must forgive, for otherwise we remain prisoners of our own and others' pasts, deprived of freedom, condemned to an endless process of reaction in which we can never find an opportunity for action. She writes (p. 218): "what love is in its own, narrowly circumscribed sphere, respect is in the larger domain of human affairs. Respect, not unlike the Aristotelian *philia politike*, is a kind of "friendship" without intimacy and without closeness; it is a regard for the person from the distance which the space of the world puts between us, *and this regard is independent of qualities which we may admire or of achievements which we may highly esteem.* Thus, the modern loss of respect, or rather the conviction that respect is due only where we admire or esteem, constitutes a clear symptom of the increasing depersonalization of public and social life. Respect, at any rate, because it concerns only the person, is quite sufficient to prompt forgiving of what a person did, for the sake of the person." (Italics added)
20. See Harned, *Grace and Common Life*, ch. VIII, "Creating."
21. Arendt, *op. cit.*, pp. 213, 218–219.

Chapter Four

1. Golding, *Lord of the Flies*, p. 31.
2. *Ibid.*, p. 27.

3. *Ibid.*, p. 106.
4. *Ibid.*, p. 125.
5. *Ibid.*, p. 127.
6. *Ibid.*, p. 133.
7. *Ibid.*, p. 141.
8. R. G. Collingwood, *The Principles of Art* (London: Oxford University Press, 1947), pp. 243–244.
9. Golding, *Lord of the Flies*, p. 141.
10. *Ibid.*, p. 144.
11. *Ibid.*, p. 166.
12. *Ibid.*, pp. 166–167.
13. *Ibid.*, p. 167.
14. *Ibid.*, p. 185.
15. *Ibid.*, pp. 186–187.
16. Albert K. Cohen, *Delinquent Boys* (Glencoe: The Free Press of Glencoe, 1955). The following five citations can all be found in Cohen, pp. 183–184. The authors are: Frederick M. Thrasher, *The Gang* (Chicago: University of Chicago Press, 1936), p. 143; Paul Tappan, *Juvenile Delinquency* (New York: McGraw-Hill Book Co., 1949), p. 143; Henry D. McKay, "The Neighborhood and Child Conduct," *Annals of the American Academy of Political and Social Science*, CCLXI (January, 1949), p. 37; J. P. Shalloo, in *Federal Probation*, XVIII (March, 1954), p. 6; and Albert K. Cohen, *loc. cit.*
17. Thrasher, *op. cit.*, pp. 94–95, cited in Cohen, *op. cit.*, pp. 27–28.
18. Peters, *op. cit.*, pp. 28–34, 152.
19. *Ibid.*, p. 31.
20. *Op. cit.*, p. 133.
21. See, for example, Eric D'Arcy, *Human Acts* (Oxford: The Clarendon Press, 1963), especially pp. 143–156.
22. Margaret Mead, *And Keep Your Powder Dry* (New York: William Morrow and Company, 1942), p. 197. Quoted in Cohen, *op. cit.*, p. 111.
23. Peters, *op. cit.*, p. 12.
24. Robert Ardrey, *The Social Contract* (London: Collins, 1970), pp. 339–340.
25. Cohen, *op. cit.*, p. 134.
26. *Ibid.*, p. 134.
27. W. H. Auden, "The Joker in the Pack," in *The Dyer's Hand* (New York: Random House, 1962), p. 253.
28. *Ibid.*, p. 254.
29. *Ibid.*, p. 255.
30. *Ibid.*, pp. 255–256.
31. *Ibid.*, p. 256.
32. *Ibid.*, p. 256.

33. *Ibid.*, p. 257.
34. *Ibid.*, p. 270.
35. *Ibid.*, pp. 271–272.
36. St. Augustine, *Confessions*, Book II, tr. by J. G. Pilkington, in *The Confessions and Letters of St. Augustine*, vol. I of *A Select Library of the Nicene and Post-Nicene Fathers of the Christian Church, First Series*, ed. by Philip Schaff (Grand Rapids: Wm. B. Eerdmans Publishing Company, 1956), p. 57.
37. *Ibid.*, p. 57.
38. *Ibid.*, p. 58–59.
39. See Harned, *Grace and Common Life*, pp. 93ff.

Chapter Five

1. William F. Lynch, S. J., *Christ and Prometheus*, pp. 76–77.
2. Robert Jay Lifton, *Boundaries* (New York: Vintage Books, 1970), p. 38.
3. Albert Camus, *The Myth of Sisyphus*, tr. by Justin O'Brien (New York: Vintage Books, 1955), p. 89.
4. The fact that images grow enigmatic and ambiguous when they are separated from the stories they are intended to crystallize must not be confused with an entirely different question, the openness that they must retain if they are to be of service to persons endowed with real freedom and futurity. Of what use would they be if they were not invitations to creativity but foreclosures of it? Chapter VI is a concrete attempt to anchor the image of the player in a particular narrative that divests it of its ambiguities, while displaying that it does no violence to the unforeseeable historicity of the self.
5. Arend van Leeuwen, *Christianity in World History* (London: Edinburgh House Press, 1964), p. 173.
6. Stanley Hauerwas, *art. cit.*, p. 104.
7. Hick, *op. cit.*, p. 375.
8. William Golding, *Free Fall* (New York: Harcourt, Brace and World, 1962), p. 9.
9. *Ibid.*, p. 7.
10. *Ibid.*, p. 5.
11. *Ibid.*, p. 8.
12. *Ibid.*, p. 29.
13. *Ibid.*, p. 78.
14. *Ibid.*, p. 191.
15. *Ibid.*, p. 105.
16. *Ibid.*, p. 236.
17. *Ibid.*, p. 192.
18. *Ibid.*, p. 191.

19. *Ibid.*, p. 248.
20. Stephen Crites, "The Narrative Quality of Experience," *Journal of the American Academy of Religion*, Vol. XXXIX, no. 3 (September, 1971), p. 297. In a footnote to a more recent essay, Crites comments: "enduring esthetic forms and genre have their correlates and indeed their psychic sources in our most basic forms of experience. I do not share a popular assumption that they are arbitrary historical products that artists have happened to stumble upon. Experience itself is mediated and conditioned at the root by esthetic forms that lend it whatever coherence it has. There is no experience so immediate that it can occur apart from *some* of those esthetic forms that are also employed (with much more formal purity and sophistication, to be sure) in the religious and cultural expressions of traditional societies and ultimately in high art." "Angels We Have Heard," in *Religion as Story*, ed. by James B. Wiggins (New York: Harper and Row, Publishers, 1975), p. 57, fn. 4.
21. *Ibid.*, p. 303.
22. *Ibid.*, p. 305.
23. *Ibid.*, p. 305.
24. Frank Kermode, *The Sense of an Ending* (New York: Oxford University Press, 1967), pp. 3–4.
25. *Ibid.*, p. 39.
26. *Ibid.*, p. 6.
27. *Ibid.*, p. 179.
28. *Ibid.*, see especially pp. 35–54 for "fictions" and their relationships to reality.
29. *Ibid.*, p. 18.
30. See Harned, *Faith and Virtue*, pp. 159–162, for some comments on the relationship between stories, character, principles, and master images. It is neither possible nor desirable to obviate the circularity of the relationship between images and stories. They interpret one another; we can do without neither the one nor the other because each in isolation, though for different reasons, is amenable to different and conflicting interpretations.
31. "Empirical fit" is an expression that I have borrowed from Ian T. Ramsey, *Models and Mystery* (New York: Oxford University Press, 1964). My usage of it in these pages, however, differs significantly from his, partly because of my focus upon the transformation of the one who experiences rather than upon the interpretation of experience, and partly because of the eschatological orientation that it is given here.
32. Ian T. Ramsey, *Religious Language* (New York: Macmillan, 1967), p. 90.

33. Stanley Hauerwas, in a private communication to the author, June 1975.
34. This emphasis upon the futurity of the verification of empirical fit as well as upon the importance of the sense of an ending that stories provide reflects, of course, more fundamental decisions that are not argued systematically in this book: that the self is an eschatological passion and that the Christian message is thoroughly eschatological in the sense that it tells of a future which is not only proleptically present but also genuinely in the future. See Jurgen Moltmann, *Theology of Hope* (New York: Harper and Row, 1967).
35. Ramsey, *Religious Language,* pp. 170, 174.

Chapter Six

1. Richard W. B. Lewis, *The American Adam* (Chicago: University of Chicago Press, 1955), p. 1.
2. *Ibid.,* p. 1.
3. *Ibid.,* p. 5.
4. *Ibid.,* p. 61.
5. *Ibid.,* p. 89.
6. *Ibid.,* p. 6.
7. *Ibid.,* p. 6.
8. *Ibid.,* p. 127.
9. *Ibid.,* p. 198.
10. William Faulkner, *The Bear,* in *Three Famous Short Novels* (New York: Vintage Books, 1963), p. 240.
11. *Ibid.,* p. 267.
12. Lewis, *op. cit.,* p. 152.
13. *Ibid.,* p. 9.
14. *Ibid.,* p. 200. Also see p. 152.
15. *Ibid.,* p. 3.
16. Gen. 3:4b–5.
17. Dietrich Bonhoeffer, *Creation and Fall,* tr. by John Fletcher (London: SCM Press Ltd., 1959), p. 67.
18. For more extensive treatment of the category of the "daimonic," see Harned, *Faith and Virtue,* ch. IV: "Dialectics and Daimons."
19. Gen. 3:7–10.
20. Gen. 3:12.
21. Bonhoeffer, *op. cit.,* p. 80.
22. Augustine, *loc. cit.*
23. Gen. 3:16a, 17b.
24. C. K. Barrett, *From First Adam to Last* (London: A. and C. Black, 1962), pp. 17, 92–93.

25. *Ibid.,* p. 20.
26. Gen. 3:21.
27. Farrer, *op. cit.,* p. 42. Despite my great indebtedness to Farrer for the interpretation of revelation that he offers in *The Glass of Vision,* I am not persuaded by two facets of his argument. First, there is the regulative role that he reserves for natural theology, which provides canons for the interpretation of Scripture. This is radically different from and incompatible with the understanding of natural theology that informs my own work. Second, his understanding of the teachings of Jesus appears to go considerably beyond the biblical evidence. Even if his comments on the teachings of Jesus require serious modification, however, this does not necessarily vitiate the force of his greater argument concerning the way that Scripture itself presents us with the Word of God.
28. See *supra,* p. 211, n.6. It is worth emphasizing again that the only claims necessary to support the argument at this juncture are that the anthropology of the New Testament cannot be severed from Christology, that the Adamic parallel is *one* of the fundamental "clues" to its anthropology, and that this clue is more or less homogenous with whatever other but equally fundamental clues, if any, appear in the New Testament writings. Even if not in this context, however, there is reason to pursue the still open question of the validity of some larger claims: that it is "the Redeemer myth" that tends to integrate the Christology of the New Testament, and therefore its anthropology as well, and that no element in the portrait of the Redeemer is more fundamental than the contention that he became a New Adam.
29. Karl Barth, *Christ and Adam,* tr. by T. A. Smail (New York: The Macmillan Co., 1957), pp. 39–40.
30. Rom. 5:18–19, 21.
31. Rom. 5:14b.
32. Rom. 5:6–8, 10.
33. Rom. 1:21b–22, 25.
34. Gal. 3:13a.
35. II Cor. 5:21a.
36. II Cor. 5:21b.
37. Phil. 2:5–9.
38. I Cor. 15:20.
39. Rom. 6:3–5.
40. I John 3:2.
41. I John 3:5–6.
42. Barrett, *op. cit.,* p. 105.

43. *Ibid.,* p. 90.

44. *Ibid.,* p. 104.

45. I Cor. 7:29–31. Also see II Cor. 6:8ff.

46. Col. 2:20–22.

47. I Cor. 7:31b.

48. Col. 3:1–3.

49. Is. 53:4–7.

Epilogue

1. Gen. 3:17b–18.

2. See Harned, *Faith and Virtue,* pp. 33–71 and 78–79, for a more extensive analysis of the nature and development of basic trust, which is there identified with certain "natural" but potentially religious forms of faith, hope, and love that are pervasive and indeed indispensable ingredients of the existence of everyone.

3. I have long been a debtor to Johan Huizinga, whose fine book, *Homo Ludens: A Study of the Play Element in Culture* (Boston: Beacon Press, 1955), not only recognizes the diversity within the human enterprise but also emphasizes the more or less unitary character that it possesses because every aspect of it in some measure reflects the play impulse that is indelibly written into the nature of the self. In the most "serious" forms of cultural activity, no less than in the most frivolous, there is a play impulse at work and its formative power is very great.

4. I Cor. 15:45–52.

5. Rudolf Bultmann, *Theology of the New Testament,* tr. by Kendrick Grobel (London: SCM Press Ltd., 1952), p. 182.

6. I Cor. 7:20–23.

7. Bultmann, *op. cit.,* p. 309.

8. *Ibid.,* p. 240.

9. Farrer, *loc. cit.*